TIME BEFORE MORNING

Art and Myth of the Australian Aborigines

TIME BEFORE MORNING

Art and Myth of the Australian Aborigines

LOUIS A. ALLEN

THOMAS Y. CROWELL COMPANY
Established 1834   New York

All objects are from the author's collection. The following photographs are courtesy of the Field Museum of Natural History: *The Laindjung Story,* by Biragidji; *Banaidja* by Libundja; *The Yam Sticks* by Dawudi; *The Rainbow Serpent,* by Midinari; *The Didjeridu,* by Midinari; *Purukapali and His Wife, Bima,* by Aurangnamiri; *Mimi Hunter and Kangaroo,* by Nguleingulei; *Purukapali and His Dead Son,* by Mandarbarni; *The Entreaty of Tjapara,* by Maniluki; *The Grief of Bima,* by Djulabiyanna; *Gurramuringu, The Mighty Hunter,* by Malangi; *Wife of the Mighty Hunter,* by Malangi; *Death of the Great Hunter,* by Malangi; *The Barnumbir Totem,* by Gakupa; *Bark Coffin, Morning Star Ceremony,* by Djadjiwui; *Murajana, The Cheerful Spirit,* by Libundja.

Copyright © 1975 by Louis A. Allen

Designed by Abigail Moseley

Manufactured in the United States of America

Library of Congress Cataloging in Publication Data

Allen, Louis A
    Time before morning.

    Bibliography: p.
    Includes index.
    1. Legends, Australian (Aboriginal) 2. Mythology, Australian (Aboriginal) 3. Art, Australian (Aboriginal) I. Title.
GR365.A44   398.2'0994   75-12812
IBSN 0-690-00999-2

1 2 3 4 5 6 7 8 9 10

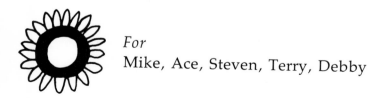

For
Mike, Ace, Steven, Terry, Debby

Acknowledgments

I HAVE DRAWN UPON a wide variety of resources in compiling the myths. First are the aboriginal people themselves; to them I express my deepest appreciation for their willingness to share their knowledge and their patience and good humor in helping me to understand their beautiful and unique art and to convert the myths to a different idiom.

A number of individuals with special knowledge of the aboriginal people have been particularly helpful. Norman B. Tindale read my book in proof and offered many valuable suggestions. An authority on the Australian aborigines, Dr. Tindale has developed a unique understanding of their culture from firsthand acquaintance and study over more than fifty years. His recent book, *Aboriginal Tribes of Australia*, is a major contribution to the literature. He has pointed out certain inconsistencies in my spelling of aboriginal names, which I have chosen to retain as being closer to conventional English and more familiar to the reader.

I wish to thank Peter Ucko, J. S. Boydell, and Shirley Andrew of the Australian Institute of Aboriginal Studies, Canberra. The Institute has been most courteous and generous. I am grateful for counsel and help from Lester R. Hiatt, University of Sydney, and chairman of the Australian Institute of Aboriginal Studies. I have also received helpful advice from J. A. Tuckson, Art Gallery of New South Wales; Graeme Pretty, South Australian Museum, Adelaide; G. W. Spence, Byron Bay; John Cawte, Sydney; Ed Ruhe, University of Kansas; Nelson Graeburn, University of California at Berkeley; Phillip Lewis, Field Museum of Natural History, Chicago; Albert Elsasser, Lowie Museum of Anthropology, Berkeley; and Thomas Seligman, de Young Museum, San Francisco.

I am particularly appreciative of the research and writings of Ronald and Catherine Berndt, A. P. Elkin, Johannes Falkenberg, Charles P. Mountford and W. E. H. Stanner, whom I could not contact in person, but whose work was especially helpful.

I wish to acknowledge the aid of the Department of Aboriginal Affairs, Northern Territory Division; Government of Australia; the United Church in North Australia; the Church Missionary Society of Australia; the Catholic Church; and the Aboriginal Community Councils at Milingimbi, Oenpelli, Port Keats, Snake Bay, Angurugu, and Yirrkala, without whose cooperation this work would not have been possible. At most of the locations I visited, mission and government officials were of the greatest help in providing transportation, lodging, and translation and interpretation assistance. I am most grateful for their friendliness and hospitality to a sometimes inconvenient visitor.

My thanks go to a number of people who have helped me to secure bark paintings and carved figures, as well as providing information for the myths. These include Dorothy and Lance Bennett, Darwin, who first introduced me to aboriginal art, and James A. Davidson, Melbourne, a past president of the Victoria Anthropological Society who has worked closely over a period of years with the northeastern and central clans and provided much background data.

Many individuals offered information and assistance at the various locations I visited. I would like to extend my thanks to the following:

Central Region, Milingimbi: Djawa, a strong and outstanding leader, who authenticated some of the data from the central region and who, with Yuwati, Marawa, Djilminy, Bawandu, and Minipirriwuy, patiently checked the reading of the Wagilag draft. At this location also, Malangi, Manuwa, and Bininjuwi were most helpful.

I am especially grateful to Ken and Judith Nowland at Milingimbi, who shared freely of their firsthand knowledge of the central region clans and who offered continuing help and support.

Alan Fidock, while at Milingimbi, taped much firsthand data for me and helped resolve some of my early problems.

Northeastern Region, Yirrkala: Biragidji, Waidjung, Lardjanga, Midinari, Naridjin, Mau, Wandjuk, and Nanjin were most helpful in both providing and checking information. Rev. W. J. Fawell, Alan Bradley, John Rudder, and James Gallarrwuy have authenticated data and aided in securing and identifying bark paintings.

Western Region, Oenpelli: Silas Maralngurra provided assistance and advice. He also checked the draft of the Ngalyod myth. Sam Manggudja saw me safely through the sites of the cave paintings on the escarpment and gave me a great deal of information. Anchor Barlbuwa and Dick Nguleingulei were also most helpful.

Peter J. Carroll, linguist of the Church Missionary Society, provided continuing advice and help, which was most valuable because of his intimate knowledge of the Gunwinggu language and culture. He has translated myths directly from the Gunwinggu tongue and has been most generous and cooperative in finding and identifying materials. Mrs. Madelon Hickin also helped with information from Oenpelli.

Melville Island: Tiwi informants who gave freely of their knowledge were Mani-luki (Harry Carpenter), Wombiaudimirra (Black Joe), Aurangnamirri (Young Brook), and Lame Toby.

I am most appreciative of the help of Grant Cole, Michael Bryanton, Doreen Wright, and Ian and Jean Rodger. John Morris, Darwin, furnished me with copies of data secured at first hand from Tiwi tribesmen.

Groote Eylandt: At Angurugu, I received help from Nandjiwarra Amagula, Kneepad Jabarrgwa, Abadjera, Old Charlie Kaliowa, and Kevin and Billie Lalara.

Judith Stokes, linguist of the Church Missionary Society at Angurugu, gave freely of her special knowledge of the Groote Eylandt tribes and provided translations from the local tongue. Lance Tremlett, Rev. James A. Taylor, William Green, and James Dunstall also furnished assistance.

Port Keats: Representatives of many tribes gather at the Port Keats settlement and I am grateful for the help of Harry Palada, Djinu Tjeemaree, and Charley Rock Ngumbe of the Murinbata tribe and Madigan and Majindi of the Maringar. Christopher Parumba, Newilli Maridjeben, Nim, Indji Tharwul, Simon Ngumbe, and Pundamunni also furnished helpful data.

At Port Keats I was helped greatly by Brother R. J. Pye of the Catholic Mission and I appreciate his continuing interest and cooperation.

Finally, I appreciate the fine help I received during the long process of typing, editing, and checking. John M. B. Edwards provided editorial counsel, while Judith Sundaram and Jenny Haskell worked with great energy and unremitting interest to bring the manuscript through its many stages to completion.

Contents

 Introduction

THE READING OF Louis Allen's book has given me much pleasure, particularly because of the skilled manner in which he has brought to focus links between the beliefs, mythology, history and art of the aboriginals of Arnhem Land. In doing this, he has filled an important place between technical works that are of greatest interest to the scholar and popularized versions that often fail to give a real understanding of the aboriginal people.

I know how difficult it is to make the lifestyle and religious beliefs of the tribal people comprehensible to the outside reader, having learned this initially in 1921 and 1922 when I spent twelve months doing the first fieldwork among the Ingura of Groote Eylandt, and had the opportunity to collect their bark paintings and to publish the earliest work on their art.

Louis Allen has skillfully surmounted the problems involved in communicating the beliefs and customs of another culture. His retelling of the myths, illustrated by his remarkable collection of bark paintings and carved figures, provides an authoritative and interesting account that should have great appeal.

The author's treatment of the mythical themes is very illuminating, for it identifies elements which also have entered deeply into aboriginal life in regions far to the south; hence may belong to early phases of their development. For this reason alone, his independent observations will be of priceless interest and help to all who attempt to understand the whole culture of the Australian aborigines.

Norman B. Tindale

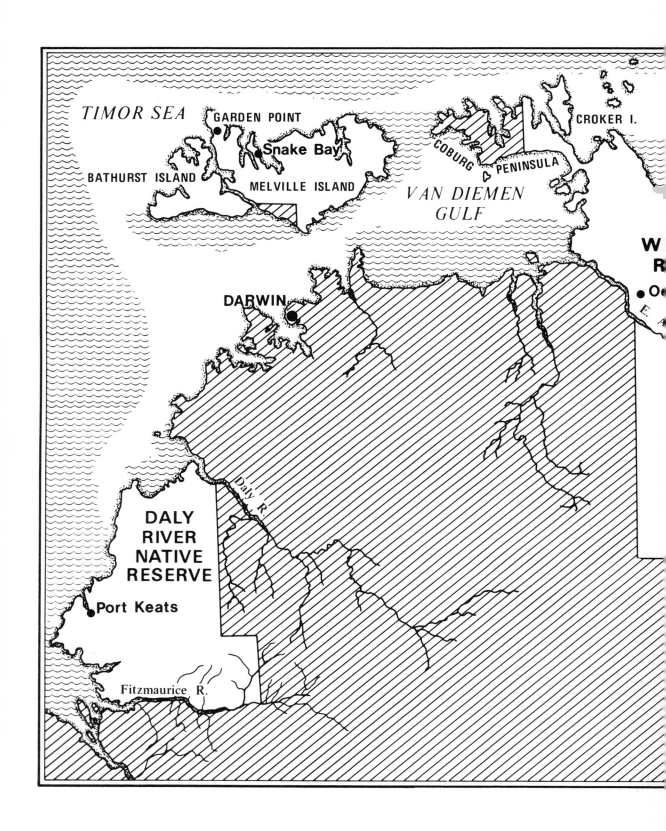

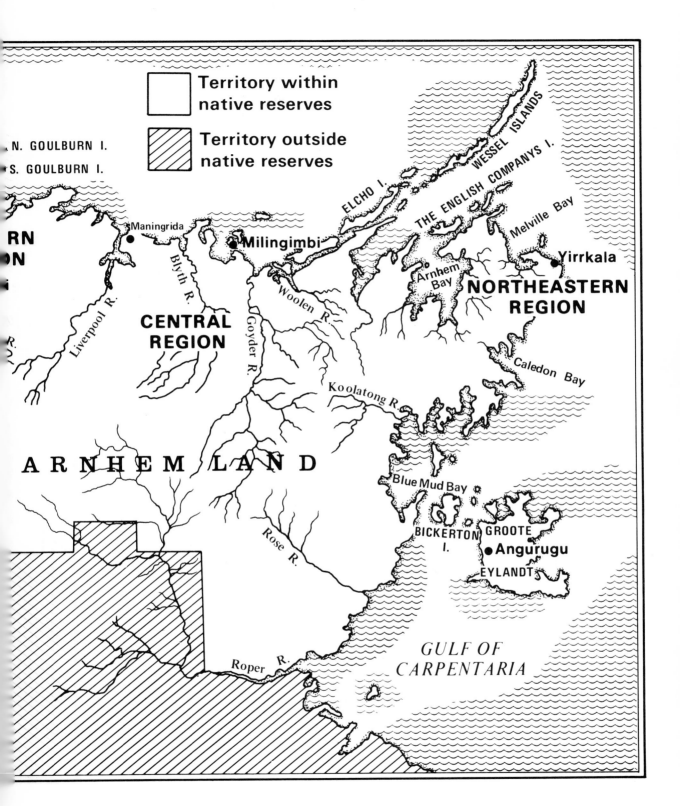

N. GOULBURN I.

S. GOULBURN I.

Territory within
native reserves

Territory outside
native reserves

Maningrida

Milingimbi

ELCHO I.

WESSEL ISLANDS

THE ENGLISH COMPANYS I.

Melville Bay

Yirrkala

Arnhem
Bay

NORTHEASTERN
REGION

Blyth R.

Liverpool R.

CENTRAL
REGION

Woolen R.

Goyder R.

Koolatong R.

Caledon Bay

A R N H E M   L A N D

Blue Mud Bay

Rose R.

BICKERTON
I.

GROOTE

Angurugu

EYLANDT

Roper R.

GULF OF
CARPENTARIA

 Foreword

THE TERM *Australian aboriginal* usually calls to mind a primitive savage: naked, barbarous, uncouth. But I have discovered that this is not the case. After fifteen years of learning to know and understand these people so recently from a Stone Age culture, I find they embody much to admire and even to emulate. Their religious beliefs are meaningful and they have preserved and transmitted a rich oral tradition for thousands of years. Steeped in tradition also are the bark paintings—graphic representations of aboriginal beliefs. Picasso, upon seeing these beautiful and unusual works, remarked, "I admire your art."

This book is an attempt to describe how the aborigines lived and to explain their beliefs through the medium of their art and mythology. There is much we can learn from the old men of this vanishing culture. As they chant their stories of the Dreamtime—the time before people, when spirits lived on earth—the strange yet familiar themes trace the beginnings of good and evil, the rebellion of youth, the dramas of forbidden love, of adultery and incest, of compassion and sharing. If we will but listen, they can speak to us with power and wisdom.

People almost invariably ask how I happened to become interested in the art and myths of such a remote and little known part of the world. The spark was kindled in 1959, when during one of my regular visits to Australia I first viewed the bark paintings that are the unique creation of the tribespeople of Arnhem Land, on the north coast of the continent.

At this time I happened to visit an exhibit in Sydney, where the craft of the aboriginal artists was being shown. The style and the designs were strange to me and I examined them with interest. I was much taken by one bark painting and wondered at the prominence given to a line of bird tracks that crossed the bark.

"What is that?" I asked the artist as I pointed to the tracks.

An interpreter translated the question then conveyed the answer to me. "He says it is an emu."

Being a rationalist, I had to ask, "An emu or the *tracks* of an emu?"

A quick exchange followed between the interpreter and the artist. "He says it is an emu, and that the emu is his father," replied the interpreter firmly.

I came to understand the artist's real meaning only after a dozen years of patient investigation and study and the synthesis of a bewildering jumble of information gathered from many sources. And so it was that I embarked upon a personal encounter with a different and therefore strange culture.

At the time I first discovered the bark paintings, there was little local interest in them; many of the earliest examples I secured had been carelessly stored in sheds or garages. A number were covered with fungus, which had to be painstakingly removed.

In my quest I sought the help of anthropologists, missionaries, traders, and government officials who had worked with the aborigines. I visited museums and libraries. Frustrated at the fragmentary nature and the apparent contradictions in the information I was able to secure, I made several trips to Arnhem Land to check directly with the old men of the aboriginal clans.

Gradually I began to assemble and index a store of information about the people, their art, and their culture. Here my firsthand acquaintance with the aboriginal peoples themselves was most helpful. To an outsider, I found, the people are at first reserved and noncommittal. Confidence and cordiality, however, came with time and repeated contacts. Each renewal of an established acquaintance brought a more friendly greeting and the imparting of additional information to supplement that offered earlier. Usually the people to whom I talked, either directly or through an interpreter, did not volunteer information. But they responded well to questions.

Several facts early became apparent. First, the bare words offered to narrate the myths or explain the paintings, no matter how accurately translated, convey to the outsider little of what the aborigines really understand and feel. To these people, an emu's print is truly more than a bird's track; it is the bird itself and also its spirit and their totemic ancestor, and this is not all. The three-toed footprint conveys to them a sense of song, dance, and ceremony.

I found that there were as many explanations of the meaning of the designs on the bark paintings and almost as many versions of the myths as there were narrators. Interpretations differed not only according to tribal beliefs, but also with the personal views of the narrator. Noteworthy events, both historical and current, had their impact. For example, when I asked old Kaliowa of the Ingura tribe of Groote Eylandt what his totems were, he solemnly enumerated not only the original spider and boat of his cultural heritage, but also the latter-day airplane.

A further complicating factor is the difference in tongues. The aboriginal peoples of Arnhem Land speak more than fifty dialects or languages, some as different from each other as English is from German. As a result, the same myths communicated by different linguistic groups bear the special nuances of their varying tongues.

Because of these considerable barriers, it early became clear that even the most skilled and knowledgeable linguist could communicate only a hint of the richness of the myths; and for this reason it probably will always remain impossible for an outsider to bridge the cultural gap. Interpreting the myths, bark paintings, and carved figures in the light of such difficulties has been both a fascinating and frustrating experience. I do not claim the version I present is accurate for the simple reason that there probably can never be a truly accurate statement in any one rendition.

To give you some indication of the difficulties I encountered, here is the verbatim account of the Mimi myth, which begins on page 140, as it was told to me by Sam Manggudja, an old man of the Gunwinggu tribe:

> Plenty Mimi live in rocks. Mimi won't go out in wind. Stops in cave. Will break neck. He got thin neck. He hunts kangaroo when got no wind. Use spear. Got big family, wife, children. He sing, make coroboree [native ceremony]. Old people sing Mimi songs. Eat wild potatoes in rocks, porcupine, wallaby. Old man tells long time story. A married man hunts in rocks. Mimi calls him. "Come on, we go home where my grandmother living and give you beef [meat]." Man went with him and saw where he was living. Saw lots of people. He gave kangaroo beef. Man didn't want to eat beef. Man said, "I'm too faint, I can't eat." Arright. It get a little bit dark. There are two women. They sleep each side this man. Everybody sleep. This man he get up and go away. The two women get up and see this man gone. Husband throw spear where he been sleeping. This man he go home and tell everybody, "I saw Mimi and he gave me beef. I didn't eat beef. He want me to marry [have intercourse with] women but I didn't marry." He tell wife. He tell everybody in camp.

This leads to the objective of this book, which is to share what I have learned about the aboriginal people of Arnhem Land, their myths and culture, and their strange and beautiful bark paintings. I have tried to convey a fuller idea of what the myths and art express by integrating in my retelling something of the landscape, the birds and animals, and the customs and habits of the people. This social and cultural material, of course, does not appear in the aborigines' narrations.

This book, then, is not an anthropological study. Neither is it simply a collection of tales but, rather, an attempt to convey to the reader an understanding of the aboriginals and their beliefs and feelings. The viewpoint is that of an interested and sympathetic but by no means omniscient observer. I have tried to recount the myths in terms I think the reader will most fully understand and not in those of the aboriginal informants. In other words, I have retold their tales, not just collected them. Most anthropologists I have consulted agree with the late Robert L. Lowie that there is a legitimate place for such "synthetic" treatment if properly identified as such. Some, however, strongly disapprove of this personalization of cultural material. Their viewpoint has much to be said for it. They should know, however, that I have attempted to check my information to ensure its accuracy or fidelity, not only by discussing it firsthand with old men from the aboriginal clans, but also by submitting it to the scrutiny of anthropologists and other knowledgeable persons who are familiar with the aborigines, their life-styles and thought patterns.

I have confined my study to the art and mythology of the northern coastal strip of the Australian continent, an area that stretches approximately from Port Keats on the west, the Roper River on the south, and the Gulf of Carpentaria on the east. This country lies in the Arnhem Land and Daly River Aboriginal Reserves. It is a large territory, extending over some thirty thousand square miles, yet it contains no more than four to five thousand aboriginal inhabitants. In this harsh and exacting land the culture changed little for more than five hundred generations, and, until recently, was probably closer to the Stone Age than any other we now know. One of my reasons for focusing on Arnhem Land was the ability to make direct communication with old men who had been part of this culture; another was that I was able to gather and refer to a comprehensive collection of bark paintings and carved figures and totems that, to a degree, serve as history books in that they confirm in graphic form what the myths tell us in words. These paintings and figures, with very few exceptions, are the work of clans who inhabit the northern coastal strip. The reason is probably that little suitable bark or wood is found in the deserts to the south.

Spelling and Pronunciation

Spelling can be a problem because of the wide variations in common use. The most authoritative body in the field, the Australian Institute of Aboriginal Affairs, has been a leader in standardization. I have, in part, followed the orthographic and phonetic conventions they have set forth, and, with certain exceptions, the Geographic II version of the International Phonetic System for spelling because this latter avoids the use of special symbols.

These conventions are based on a phonemic representation in which the three vowel phonemes commonly found in Australian languages are written as the English *i, u,* and *a.* When vowel length is significant, as in *mareiin,* the vowel letter is doubled.

In pronouncing aboriginal words, consonants are sounded at the point of articulation. Bilabial sounds, that is, those in which the lips are brought together, are indicated by the appropriate letters, as *p, b.* Velar sounds, which are made with the back of the tongue close to or touching the soft palate, are also shown by letters, as *k, g.* The velar *ng* is common and is best pronounced as in *singer.* Voiced stops that are made by vibrating the vocal cords are shown by the letters *b, d,* and *g,* but not *p, t,* and *k;* for example, *Guwarg* and not the more common *Guwark.*

Many disagreements exist among phonetists even on some of the basic rules, so I have chosen not to follow any one school but to use spellings that, I feel, will help the reader most easily approximate the proper sounds. Thus I have used Ngalyod, Yirrawadbad, Murayana, Yolngura, Bralgu and several other spellings which can be faulted on technical grounds. Although the aborigines do not use the possessive, I have used it, thus saying, for example, "Balada's mother" instead of the awkward "the mother of Balada."

The Illustrations

The myths and text are illustrated by photos of the bark paintings and carved figures I have collected. I have tried to select objects that are in good condition and photograph well; a few, however, bear the inevitable marks of time and usage. The subject, artist's name, and a brief explanatory note are included with the illustrations; detailed notes will be found at the back of the book.

There is concern on the part of the old men of the tribes about showing sacred material that should not be viewed by women or un-initiated men; therefore, I have tried to avoid knowingly using this material. The degree of sacredness, or *mareiin,* varies with the object, the individual, and the situation. Since it has proven impractical to have each item approved by the original owners, many of whom are dead, I have made several assumptions. If paintings of the same subjects or designs have already been published by anthropologists thoroughly familiar with the region and people (C. P. Mountford, A. P. Elkin, and R. M. and C. H. Berndt, for example), I have included similar material. In general, I have taken it for granted that if the painters who "own" the designs have freely sold them without restrictions, publication is permissible. And, finally, I have assumed that since prohibitions apply only to aboriginal women and children, if sacred material has been included inadvertently, sale or viewing of this book can be withheld from the very small number of persons actually concerned, rather than keeping it from the much larger number of readers who have a friendly and sympathetic interest and are not included in the ban by the aboriginal old men themselves.

Notes

Notes on the text, on the artists and their affiliations, and on the photographs appear in separate sections following the myths. Notes for the text are given sequentially by page number. Roman type is used. The book page number precedes the topic heading. I have been able to give the name of the painter or carver, his location, and his affiliation for almost all the items shown in the photographs. In developing the affiliations of the artists, I have used Tindale's classification (67a) for the northeastern and central groups.

Bibliography

References are generally used separately from the notes, so I have listed them apart, but also sequentially. In general, I have tried to provide the sources upon which I have drawn in developing the material so that the reader can look up the original material, if it has been published, or seek out my informants. I have used few direct quotations because the viewpoint I am attempting to express differs from that of most writers I have consulted; however, I have tried to cite in each case the author I have drawn upon directly even though I did not feel it desirable to quote him in his own words. I have also cited general works which have provided me with background material and which the reader will probably also find helpful.

PART I

ART AND MYTHS
OF THE ABORIGINES

The People and Their Myths

WE KNOW little about the prehistoric inhabitants of Australia. The best physical evidence comes from a scattering of skull fragments, flaked stone spear points, and stone axes. Radiocarbon dating suggests that, probably as much as forty thousand years ago, nomadic hunters first appeared on the northern coast.

To understand the nomads' appearance on these shores, we need to remember that during the last Ice Age, solid land stretched most of the way from South China to Australia. Trickles of Australoid people, probably of the same stock as the Veddas of South India and Ceylon, drifted along this sea-bordered route, presumably to find more food and better hunting. Over millennia these waves of hunters and food-gatherers slowly wandered south on the land bridge from what is now Malaya and Borneo to the coastlines and lush interior valleys. Equipped with spears and fire drills, and at times accompanied by a domesticated dog, the dingo, these people probably found dry land between Sumba, Timor, and New Guinea. They crossed the intervening straits by means of dugouts or rafts.

Small bands finally reached the coast of northern Australia, from which they spread inland along the rivers and so penetrated the interior of the continent. Much of Australia was infiltrated by these early hunters. By around 10,000 B.C., primitive artists were painting fish and animals in Australian caves. Then, with relative suddenness, around 9000 B.C. the climate changed. Great ice sheets that had covered much of Europe and northern Asia began to melt, and the level of the oceans rose by over 300 feet, gradually submerging stretches of the land bridge and isolating the continent.

These first settlers in northern Australia found a land that was largely flat, with occasional hills and scattered outcroppings of eroded sandstone. Creeks and rivers forming dense mangrove swamps threaded the tidal regions. Broad savannas, dotted by eucalyptus, acacia, and palm trees, stretched to the interior.

Then as now the aborigines were nomadic hunters and food-gatherers. The men felled kangaroos, wallabies, emus, lizards, and alligators with spears, clubs, and throwing sticks. Fish were abundant, wild fowl were plentiful in the swamps, and snakes could be found among the rocks. Great piles of middens, or shell remains, tell us that the coastal aborigines found the sea generous. The women were the most consistent providers; their daily foraging yielded a subsistence diet of bulbs and roots, seeds, fruits, and berries, yams, wild honey, snails, and grubs.

The Rediscovery of Australia

We do not know whether this first infiltration was repeated by a later influx of nomads. However, there is conjecture that five or six hundred years ago Chinese junks reached the Australian coast in their wide-ranging voyages from the harbors of South China.

The first record of a landing by European vessels is mentioned in the log of the Dutch ship *Duyfken*, which moored at Cape York Peninsula in 1606. During this early period, the Dutch presence is well marked: Arnhem Land was named after a ship of the Dutch East India Company that explored its waters in 1623; and *Balanda*, the aboriginal word for "white man," originally meant "Dutchman." Although a Terra Australis or "southern land" had been the subject of legend and conjecture since the time of Marco Polo, it was not until the seventeenth century that Spanish, Portuguese, and English navigators found their way to Australia. Among them was the Spaniard, Luis de Torres, who explored the strait that now bears his name, and the Englishman, William Dampier, who visited the northwest coast in 1688.

These first European visitors left no record of contact with the natives. However, sometime before the 1700s, the Bajini, a people from the islands of the East Indian archipelago, did establish relationships with the aborigines. Their presence is recorded in aboriginal myths, which identify the Bajini as a light-skinned people who traded for trepang (sea cucumbers), and for pearl and tortoise shell. Aboriginal songs tell of the strangers' women, their small houses of bamboo and stone, their distinctive pipes and clothing, and their tripod iron pots.

The Bajini were supplanted by a wave of visiting traders from Makasar in the Celebes islands. For a hundred years or more, the Makasans sailed south in their great square-rigged ships, or *praus*, driven by the steady winds of the monsoons. Arriving in October or November, they followed a well-defined route, moving from camp to

Makasan Ship Captain
by Mani-luki

camp along the northern coast of Australia and the Gulf of Carpentaria.

The Makasans traded tobacco, cloth, knives, axes, and food for trepang, a delicacy they boiled, smoked, and later sold to Chinese traders; they also traded for tortoise shell, pearl and pearl shell, and aromatic sandalwood. Usually they returned to their homeland months later on the southeast trade winds. Makasan camp sites can be seen today, marked by the tamarind trees these people planted and by the trepang kettles and other artifacts they left behind. A few of the older aboriginal men can still give firsthand accounts of these visits.

Because the Bajini and Makasan traders were seasonal visitors rather than permanent settlers, their presence, though enduring, did not produce the far-reaching consequences of the European contacts. European influence began in 1770, when Captain James Cook charted the east coast of Australia and took possession of the land in the name of Britain. In his wake, the continent opened up to exploration and settlement. Following the American Revolution, when Britain could no longer export its prison population to North America, remote Australia was chosen as an alternative site. Thus, in 1788, Captain Arthur Phillip landed the first party of convicts, soldiers, and sailors where Sydney stands today. Commemorated each January 26 as Australia Day, that event marked the beginning of British expansion into Australia.

Throughout the nineteenth century, a series of Englishmen explored the rivers and probed the interior. Their discoveries encouraged the establishment of settlements, soon to become self-governing colonies and eventually states. The influx of free settlers increased, prompted by the discovery of gold in New South Wales in 1851. The subsequent installation of a telegraph line from Darwin to Sydney, the completion of the first railroad, and the development of agriculture and cattle and sheep raising encouraged slow but continual growth through the turn of the century. In 1900 the British Parliament passed the Commonwealth of Australia Constitution Act, announcing the birth of a new nation. The following year Australia became an independent federation of six states (New South Wales, Victoria, Queensland, Tasmania, Western Australia, and South Australia) and two territories: the Australian Capital Territory and the Northern Territory, where Arnhem Land lies.

The Aborigines in Transition

Throughout this developmental period, ships of many nations moored at points along the northern coast, and Europeans, Malaysians, and later, Japanese, made repeated contacts with the natives. However, contempt for the aborigines and their social customs led to increasing friction. Visiting sailors made free with the women, arousing the active hostility of the aboriginal men. In 1907, following a

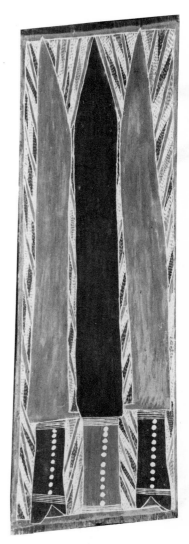

Malay Parang
by Mawulan. The long knives of the Malays introduced the aborigines to steel.

Vengeance at Buckingham Bay *by Djawa. The aborigines took revenge on trepangers who gave them bread made with flour mixed with arsenic.*

series of spearings and killings, the Australian government intervened, prohibiting the Makasans and other itinerants from further trade. In 1931 the Arnhem Land Aboriginal Reserve was created, a definitive step that excluded thereafter all but authorized persons from this aboriginal domain.

Prior to the establishment of the reserve, Arnhem Land included the northern tip of the continent, from the Daly River on the west to the Roper River on the east. Since 1931 the term *Arnhem Land* has applied only to the Aboriginal Reserve that begins at the East Alligator River and extends to the Roper River, but does not include Darwin. The reserve is part of the federally controlled and administered Northern Territory.

Missions of Protestant and Catholic churches have had a strong, positive influence on aboriginal development. Although visits by missionaries were recorded as early as 1850, the Church Missionary Society founded the first mission station in 1908, on the Roper River. The United Church in North Australia, the Anglican church, and the Catholic church have maintained mission stations, where the natives were encouraged to settle and where they tended to stay in order to secure processed food and medical aid and to receive educational and religious training. The Australian government also established stations that became centers for aboriginal settlement.

For Australians the period after World War II was one of unprecedented social and technological change. Since then the Australian government has adopted increasingly enlightened policies in administering the aboriginal settlements and in providing for the welfare of the people. The opening of bauxite, manganese, and uranium mines and the development of agriculture and fishing have brought the Northern Territory to the early stages of industrialization, with its attendant problems.

Today the aborigines are still very much in transition. The Austra-

The Angel of the Lord
by Mahkarolla. Missionaries had a strong, positive impact on the aborigines.

lian government has adopted a policy of giving them home rule as soon as possible. Local government is exercised through community councils selected by the people, each with its own chairman. Most families live at or near the permanent settlements, where they can work for cash wages, use the medical facilities, and send their children to school. A number of clans congregate at each settlement, and this sometimes leads to friction. Because of this and a deep-felt need to live in their ancestral homeland, some families have moved to outstations in their clan territories where the sacred water holes and totemic sites of their people are located.

Whatever alternative is selected, the wise old men who lead the clans recognize that both time and patience are required to make the transition to an industrialized society. As Silas Maralngurra, a leader of the Gunwinggu people at Oenpelli said to me:

> We don't want *Balanda* [the white people] to go too quick. We do not know yet how to dig the holes to plant bananas and paw-paw or how to cut the shoots off the yam so a new one will grow. We have to learn how to fix our automobiles. What will happen if all the mail comes from Darwin and nobody knows what to do with it? We need the sister [nurse] to help us if we get sick.
>
> First *Balanda* must train us how to do these things. This will take time, but we will learn. After *Balanda* turns things over to us, he must stand by and watch us. If we make mistakes, he will help us. Like this, maybe in four or five years we will need only one or two *Balanda*—the rest we will do ourselves.

My own feeling is that rather than five years at least two and probably three generations will be needed to bridge safely the cultural gap between the Stone Age and the Industrial.

The aborigines regard the *Balanda* differently from *Yolngu*, the general term applied to their own people. First, the aborigines look upon moderns—their airplanes, canned food, and radios—with initial awe; this culture is so far beyond their own and so foreign to their understanding that they put it in a special category, exempting it from the conventions and taboos they would ordinarily follow. For example, the rock cod is a totemic fish of the Gubabingu people, but today they will eat filleted rock cod in fish and chips without demur unless an old man of the clan should "growl" and make an issue of the matter. Moreover, while aborigines rarely address each other by their personal names, they take it as a matter of course that the *Balanda* will do so. Aboriginal women are not permitted to see sacred designs or to approach certain taboo sites, but female government or missionary persons are readily exempted from these restrictions and, in fact, seem to be regarded as of a neuter gender.

These restraints are also eased in regard to the handling of bark paintings and carved wooden figures, or *rangga*. The aborigines show little concern in giving or selling sacred ceremonial objects to *Balanda*. At the conclusion of the ceremony, it is believed, the spirit that ani-

Moses Striking the Rock
by unknown artist.

mates the totem returns to the clan water hole. Although the power of
the object diminishes at this time, in normal use the bark painting or
figure would still be treated with some care and would either be
placed in the water hole or hidden in the bush to rot. However, exact
replicas of the sacred designs are painted on commission and sold to
Balanda with considerable alacrity by the same old men who create
them for religious purposes. The inference here is that outsiders are
exempt from tribal or clan restrictions.

Nowadays the aborigines recognize the value of money in buying
such items as food, radios, motorcycles, and autos, and, of course,
make bark paintings for pay. During one of my visits to Arnhem
Land, for example, the excellent artist, Malangi, happened to be on the
bush plane that took me from Milingimbi to Darwin, where he was to

participate in an exhibition of aboriginal painting. Jokingly, I asked him what he would do with all the money he was making.

"Buy boat," he replied unsmiling.

Sure enough, on my next trip I saw Malangi proudly steering a new outboard motorboat, its hull low in the water under a weight of wives, children, and vegetables as it glided into the pier of Milingimbi. He had saved his money for many months, a practice entirely foreign to his culture, where food, belongings, and money are ordinarily shared at once to satisfy prescribed kinship obligations. Unfortunately, tribal rules also required he share his boat with relatives, and soon it had been abused beyond repair.

Aboriginal Religion

Still alive and active in the aboriginal camps and settlements are old men who are the repository for the ancient traditions and ceremonies and who maintain them with some vigor today. From them, directly or indirectly, I have secured some of my information about the myths, bark paintings, carved figures, and totems. These old men are the last living link with the past. As youths, they underwent initiation rites and learned the myths and stories that have been transmitted, with inevitable changes but also without interruption, for thousands of years. This lore is rapidly disappearing. With the passing of the elders, its primary source will be lost forever.

Aboriginal religion rested on an explicit belief in supernatural ancestors who brought the world into existence, creating stars and sea, animals and birds, men and women. The events of the Creation and the values and behavior prescribed by the creators were passed down orally from one generation to the next in the form of myths. Learning and observing them were prerequisite to acceptance as a full member of society.

Even though the myths were an uncertain medium for communication—some were episodic, many overlapped, and details varied from one telling to another—they formed the core of aboriginal religion. The myths explained this religion to the clanspeople, related it to their daily lives, and were the vehicles that preserved and transmitted it to their children. The myths explained the world, they justified the relationships of people with other living things, and they provided each person with guides for living. In the face of uncertainty and danger, the myths offered constant support.

The aboriginal lived his religion. He could recreate the spirit ancestors and feel their presence, for they were part of his mind and world. When he approached a figure of the First Mother, Ngalyod, he did so with great reverence. When he danced, his feet were touching Earth Mother's flesh. His chants were not mere songs: their powerful words caused the kangaroo, for example, to mate and reproduce abundantly. As the story of the Wagilag sisters was retold in song, dance, and mime, the participants intensely experienced the return of these ancestors in an act of faith and a reaffirmation of the marriage and incest laws given by the sisters. Similarly, it was important that the great song cycles of the Wagilag, the Djanggawul, and the age-grading rites be faithfully repeated at the proper season, for the supernatural beings who created the world in a mythical era called the Dreamtime were immortal. They existed still and could be invoked by conducting the proper totemic rites; they caused the seasons to change, game to multiply, and children to be born.

Religious Totems

Everything in the aboriginal world—snake and gum tree, fish and insect, rock and star, man and woman—contained an essence or spirit that had its beginning in the Dreamtime. Each person was descended from one of these spirits and possessed some of its life force. Therefore

The Clap-Stick Man
by Madaman. The stories of the great myths were sung and danced to the beat of clap sticks.

he was of the same spirit and flesh as all other descendants or mani-
festations of that spirit. The aborigines painted images of the spirits
on cave walls and the interiors of their bark huts. They drew the totemic figures on their bodies and on the ground, and they carved them
in wood. When the proper words were sung or chanted, the spirit
could be prevailed upon to enter the painted or carved image. When
the spirit departed, the totem once again became a piece of wood or
bark.

The members of each clan believed that they were descended from
the same totemic spirit. For example, even today, Jama, of the
Gumaidj clan, *Duwala* language, believes he and every member of his
clan are descended from the Dreamtime crocodile, Baru. Jama will
not hunt or kill crocodiles. When he travels and meets other aborigines who are strangers to him, the first information he imparts is that
he "sings" the crocodile totem. Once his affiliation is known, he is
made welcome; a place is arranged for him by the fire, food is
brought, and he is treated as a family visitor.

The totemic spirits were celebrated in ceremonies and rituals, and
they played a prominent part in the myths. Each clan had one or more
primary totems and often secondary ones. These totems "belonged" to
the individual members of the clan, who inherited them and demon-
strated a special affinity to them in everyday life. When food was
scarce, the appropriate totemic ancestors were invoked to send plenty
of wallabies, opossums, or goannas (monitor lizards).

Naming the Name

Less palpable symbols than totems were also used to call forth the
ancestral spirits. The aborigines believed that the name of something
was not merely its symbol but was actually the thing itself. The names
of sacred beings or sites were accorded the same veneration as the objects they represented. The sacred name of the Great Rainbow Snake,
Julunggul, was uttered reverently, and the same taboos surrounded
this name as the snake itself. Inadvertent use of the sacred name was
avoided by substituting a second or even a third name.

A person's name was both the person himself and his spirit. To
speak the name was to call the person in his spirit. When a child was
named after a departed person, he was imbued with his ancestor's
spirit and character; when he was later initiated, the new name he was
given signified he had become a new person, with different status and
attributes.

The name of a dead person was not mentioned, for to do so would
bring back the spirit which the name represented. If the deceased
must be identified, an oblique reference would be made to "the one
gone." For example, after Dawudi, the great artist of Milingimbi, died,
I could not mention his name directly to his brother, Djawa, but was
obliged to refer to him as *bunakaka wawa*, "the departed one."

The Crow Man
*by Midinari. Clanspeople of the
crow clan believe they are descended from the Dreamtime's crow
spirit who became a man.*

Aboriginal Social Organization

The aboriginal peoples of Australia developed a complex social organization that was indispensable to their well-being. The ties that
bound aborigines to each other were multiple: blood, kinship, social
interaction, and economic dependence. If we study these relationships
as they exist today, they appear very complicated, for they reflect the
interpretations and changes that have occurred over hundreds of generations. Marriage, for example, introduced a fabric of well-defined
kinship ties. The aborigines married to form an economic unit that
was capable of sustaining itself and of bringing up children. When a
family, clan, or moiety (kinship group) gave up a girl in marriage, it
expected to receive a wife for one of its own members in exchange.
The alliance further cemented family ties, for the bride who came to
her husband's camp fire immediately entered into a new set of relationships with all his relatives, and he, in turn, with hers.

Mimi Spirit, *cave painting.*
One of the long, thin Mimi spirits
painted on a cave wall near
Oenpelli.

The Law of the Old Men

The traditions and laws, the myths and ceremonies, were held in stewardship by the older men and passed on by them to the next generation. When an aboriginal boy entered puberty, he was subjected to initiation ceremonies which retold the creative acts of the totemic ancestors. The old men dominated and controlled these rituals, imposing on the young men severe physical and mental ordeals such as circumcision, enforced isolation, and wilderness survival. The initiates listened with dread to the boom of the bull-roarer, a wooden device that simulated the voice of the spirits, and they learned of the powerful totemic spirits who created all things and laid down the rules that all must follow.

A unique feature of human evolution permitted the old men to command this initiation process: Although cultural characteristics evolve through selective preference just as physical traits do, cultural characteristics are not inherited; they must be taught. Since the male elders had the time, leisure, and knowledge, they became the teachers, passing on to the young what was advantageous for the elders to impart. The myths and ceremonies that they developed established roles and relationships for the young men that subjugated them to the will of their elders. The rituals and lore made clear each child's obligation to obey parents; suffering followed if he did not. The young men undergoing trials of initiation among the Murinbata people, for example, were taught the myth of Kunmanggur, whose son Jinamin disobeyed his father and eventually speared him. Jinamin, consequently, was turned into a bat that could be heard forever fluttering and squeaking his dismay in the dark of night.

Awed and frightened by the trials of initiation and the great mysteries that were imparted to them, the young men were bound to the commands of the old men for the rest of their lives. These ties were further strengthened every few years in age-grading rituals, in whose secret ceremonies the myths were repeated. But now they were enriched by even more profound mysteries that the celebrants were enjoined to hold sacred upon pain of death.

Actions that the old men felt it wise to forbid were taboo, or forbidden. Punishment for violation was meted out by the spirit beings who decreed the taboo, through their agents, the old men. Each generation repeated this process, the myths helping to create a continuity of values that preserved aboriginal society for thousands of years.

The loosening of personality traits through intense emotional catharsis and the substitution of new traits by indoctrination is a process that psychotherapists today identify as *unfreezing* and *feedback*. The techniques used by Stone Age people to "normalize" the personalities of their aberrant members were essentially similar to those practiced by contemporary group therapists.

The Expanded Family

Even more so in the past than today, tragedy stalked the aboriginal family in its primitive setting. Were the father incapacitated and unable to provide for his children, he would naturally look first to his brother for help. If he died, his brother was expected to act as surrogate father, securing food and protection for the children and often marrying the widow. Even in ordinary circumstances, should the father or mother leave for extended periods, a substitute was needed to care for the young. From necessity, the concept of the nuclear family expanded: the father's brother was regarded as father and the mother's sister was looked upon as mother, in almost the same way as the natural parents. Similarly, the grandfather's brothers and the grandmother's sisters were accepted as grandparents. Thus our idea of a "family" consisting of father, mother, and children really doesn't exist among the aboriginals, for they include in the family many other people whom they classify as father, mother, and children equivalent to the natural ones. Eventually, the entire web of relationships became formalized into complex social structures that permeated every aspect of daily life. The myths encouraged this process, preserving and transmitting the accumulated lessons of generations and providing a strong foundation for the development of social organizations.

Apart from the family, the smallest, most cohesive unit was the clan, a group related by blood who traced their descent from a common totemic ancestor, through either the male line (patrilineal clan) or, less commonly, the female line (matrilineal clan). Clan members shared the same myths, claimed the same water holes, and reserved a common territory, or "country," as their own. Clans provided the basis for social and ceremonial activities and frequently played a major role in hunting and fighting. Since membership was based on consanguinity, clanspeople considered themselves brothers and sisters; marriage and intercourse were prohibited among them and were sanctioned only with individuals of certain other clans. Unity was the underlying strength in clan structure: by blood ties, members were one with each other; by spiritual bonds, they merged with the common ancestor. This unity extended to all of nature, for the totemic beliefs joined people and animals, trees and rocks, sun and rain, in a common kinship.

In Arnhem Land the clans of a given territory joined together to form two complementary but opposing groups, the moieties. Because incest taboos applied not only to members of the same clan, but to members of the same moiety as well, the moiety system helped to regulate marriage patterns. The choice of a suitable marriage partner might be limited even to one particular clan in the opposite moiety. Each moiety included the same number of clans as the other, and each reserved exclusive rights to certain designs, colors, substances, and myths. In northeastern Arnhem Land, for example, white was a *jiridja* moiety color and red belonged to the *dua* moiety. Forked lightning was *dua*; sheet lightning, *jiridja*. The rainy season "belonged" to the *dua*; the dry season, to the *jiridja*. Each moiety had its own myths, which were shared by the clans of the moiety. The Wagilag and Djanggawul myths were "owned" by the *dua* moiety clans, while the Laindjung myth was told by the *jiridja* moiety clans. The *jiridja* people are innovative, the *dua* conservative.

Primary Function of the Myths

The myths were the vehicles that helped preserve the clan and moiety structures and transmit religious beliefs through them. This

The Tortoise Man
by Biragidji. Minala the tortoise is shown resuming his human form in the Dreamtime.

lore conveyed the wishes and commands of the creator ancestors that had first been voiced in the Dreamtime. The myths, then, were not just stories; they taught the lessons that guided all human actions.

The myths were remembered to the smallest detail and passed on from one generation to the next. They formed the primary theme, not only of song and story, but also of ceremony and rite. The art forms of the aborigines—bark paintings, carved figures, cave paintings, and rock engravings—were not primarily aesthetic forms, but rather in part a method for depicting and preserving the myths and for bringing back the Dreamtime spirits of which they told.

The substance of the myths also was retained because many secular versions were sung around the camp fires at night. This was—and still is—the most common form of aboriginal entertainment, one which included the women and children so they, too, might learn some of the great stories. These many individual memories contributing to the transmission of the myths resulted in a continuous cross-checking which preserved the primary themes and much of the supporting detail.

Secondary Functions of the Myths

The myths played a variety of roles in aboriginal life. In a culture where concepts of buying and selling were foreign and the idea of personal ownership rudimentary, the myths were yet a form of property; as such, they could be inherited or stolen, or legitimately used only with the owner's permission. Also, the myths had great power: Those who knew them and the ceremonies surrounding them became familiars of the spirits and could thus secure their help and support. The old men acquired the larger share of this power and taught it to the younger men in exchange for their obedience and support. As the initiates mastered this esoteric knowledge, they hoarded and preserved it—and then passed it on for their price.

The myths were also medicine. When a person fell sick, the aborigines had virtually no drugs or potions to treat the virus or infection. Instead, they treated the bad spirit that had invaded the patient. The old man who acted as "doctor" chanted portions of a myth, or an invocation from it, to exorcise the evil spirit.

The myths, finally, were mysteries, with layers of meaning disclosed to the young men as they learned the stories and understood their significance. They had to prove themselves worthy of acceptance by obeying the injunctions of the ancestor spirits; then they were accepted as men equal to other men. After this threshold of maturity had been crossed, other doors of knowledge opened that enabled the clansman to uncover added meanings, each more profound, with broadened implications and a source of greater personal power.

The myths of the people tell what they sought and what they found: food, security, sex, and satisfaction. Elemental in their expres-

Magpie Goose Totemic Figure *by Bininjuwi. Totemic figures of the Dreamtime spirits, such as this magpie goose, were made to ensure the fertility of the species for hunting.*

sion, overlaid by countless centuries of cultural veneer, the myths speak in their own patois, but they say that these primitive people sought essentially what we still seek, and that in their hearts and minds no less than in their bodies they were much as we are now. For example, the legends indicate that security was a driving need in aboriginal life and that fear of things seen and unseen was a constant motivation. Where we fear losing the jobs that enable us to buy our food and drink, the aborigines feared losing the last dregs of muddy water that seeped into their water hole and meant life or death.

We fear and venerate the spirits of the dark as much as the aborigines. To dispose of our deceased, we conduct religious ceremonies that have clear antecedents in Stone Age mortuary rituals: A hollow log preceded the modern casket. We, too, take off our shoes so our bare feet can touch the flesh of Earth Mother. We may chant our songs to the beat of piano or guitar instead of tapping sticks and drone pipe, but we seek a satisfaction beyond our senses as did the aborigines. No less than they do, we today seek to commune with spirit beings, through prayer and contemplation, seance, or self-hypnosis. The myths that tell of the departed spirit's journey to a place of unending happiness differ in little except language from our own. Where the aboriginal created magic as a ritual means of dealing with evil, death, and the unknown, many moderns participate in religious ceremonies to evoke the help of their spirit beings. Even the most determined atheists and agnostics often, almost unconsciously, knock on wood, avoid walking under ladders and use the once-magical gesture of shaking hands with friends.

These needs are as clearly expressed in our motion pictures and on our television screens, in our advertising, and our literature as they are in our houses of worship. We all know the detergent that is a magic whitener and the pill that miraculously cures headaches. Whatever their mode of expression, our present-day myths serve much the same purposes as did those of more primitive peoples.

Aboriginal myths tell of creator beings who gave their territories to the first people. To this day their descendants jealously preserve their lands, spearing trespassers who cross without permission. In time the myths solidified the territorial claims by recounting the feats of such remote ancestors as the Wagilag sisters, and the Djanggawul brother and his two sisters—beings who created the "territory" in the beginning, made all the living things it contained, and named all its physical features.

Like the aborigines, we have the same clear need to maintain a personal living space, to preserve our own "territory." We put up fences to keep intruders off our property, become infuriated if a neighbor's dog leaves his droppings on our lawn, and are exercised by the automobile driver who cuts into the lane ahead of us to occupy space that is "ours."

We can learn from a people who have preserved a paleolithic cul-

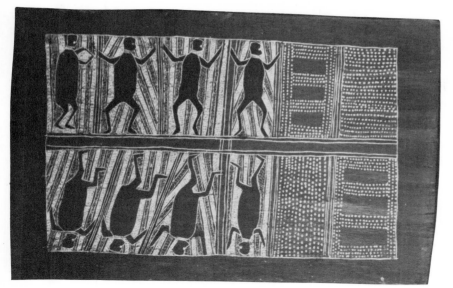

Trip to Sydney
*by Mawulan. The artist paints his
impression of his visit to Sydney
by air.*

ture almost to the present day. As we watch the reaction of the aborigines to an industrialized society and as we see the recoil and response,
we gain insight into the trauma and even the disintegration that occur
when cultural change outstrips biological capability. If we keep in
mind that the biology of today's city dweller has changed little, if at
all, from his Stone Age relative's, it becomes clear that in many respects the massive cultural changes whole societies are now experienc-
ing are an extrapolation of what the aborigines are passing through.

Is there much difference between the forces acting on the black
and naked young man I saw babbling to himself on an Arnhem Land
beach and those at work in the white youngster with long, tousled
hair and ragged jeans I observed staring at the wall in a drug recovery
center in Chicago? The aboriginal had been initiated in the traditional
rites of his clan, then had been urged to leave the bush and abandon
everything he had learned in order to adopt a new way of life. As an
Australian friend of mine remarked of the aboriginal, "He cracked.
The old men were strong, but the new ways were stronger."

The drug addict in Chicago had come from a religious family. He,
too, had been indoctrinated into one kind of life, then had entered
another, with different standards and rules in which he had no experience. He also had cracked. Is the way back similar for both?

More than anything else, we gain from our understanding of the
aborigines a feeling of confidence that the slow and sometimes chaotic
unfolding of the human story is purposeful; that the purpose is fulfill-
ment; and that it will be realized when societies as well as individuals
recapture the ability which the aboriginal clans once had to live in
harmony with their environment.

Regions and Art Styles

ALTHOUGH even the casual observer will have little difficulty identifying a bark painting from Arnhem Land, careful observation will reveal distinct stylistic differences that mark the work of six regions. The differences among them—of historical and anthropological as well as aesthetic interest—developed from patterns of migration, the incursions of outside cultures, and the availability of particular pigments. Characteristics of the six regions and their art styles follow.

Western Arnhem Land: Oenpelli Region

The Oenpelli region reaches from the East Alligator to the Liverpool rivers and includes the Cobourg Peninsula, and Croker and Goulburn islands. Forested plains which flood in the wet season border the rivers, and lagoons teem with fish. The chief settlement, Oenpelli, is about sixty miles from the coast, near the East Alligator River. Although as a cattle station it dates back to 1906, it first became the site of a Church Missionary Society settlement in 1925. Nowadays, aboriginal life centers on the mission station, where cattle are raised and crops are grown.

The aborigines of Oenpelli are organized into tribes rather than the smaller clans and commonly trace matrilineal descent. Among them are the Gunwinggu and the Maung. In the western region occurs the rocky escarpment of the Arnhem Land plateau, fissured by chasms and dotted by caves. Evidence of human occupation as long as twenty thousand years ago is reflected in the cave paintings of Oenpelli and other localities whose isolation prevented significant intrusion until this century.

The style of Oenpelli art stems directly from the cave paintings. Commonly, the background of a bark painting is plain; a coat of reddish ocher may be rubbed in, or the scraped surface may be left the scorched color it assumed when the bark was straightened over a fire. The design typically consists of a single figure or a small group that is boldly outlined in white and stands out clearly from the background. Though there is a minimum of detail, the design is sometimes filled in with white crosshatching. The figures are distinguished by their roundness and their quality of movement. Some Oenpelli paintings exhibit a unique X-ray technique whereby internal organs—usually of animals, fish, or pregnant women—are depicted. Representations of the attenuated matchstick figures called Mimi are also primarily found in the western region.

Central Arnhem Land: Milingimbi Region

This region extends from the Liverpool to the Woolen rivers. Founded in 1918 and today a focus of aboriginal contact, Milingimbi was a mission station of the Methodist Church (now the United Church in North Australia). Mainly from the country drained by the Goyder, Blythe, and Woolen rivers, the clans here are closely related to those of the northeast region. Patrilineal descent is the common pattern among the people. Old Makasan camps are found on the coast, and south of Milingimbi lies the water hole of Mirarmina, home of the mythical Rainbow Snake, Julunggul.

The style of Milingimbi art is in some ways transitional between those of the western and the northeast regions. Milingimbi bark paintings frequently show plain backgrounds, almost always in red ocher. However, backgrounds entirely covered with crosshatched designs are also found. The figures depicting the myth are generally filled in with red, yellow, or white crosshatching, or with solid color. Dots and stippling are infrequently used. Although the figures rarely achieve the sense of lively movement characteristic of Oenpelli style, neither are they quite static. Within the limits of the tradition, they may even achieve a forceful, dramatic quality.

Northeastern Arnhem Land: Yirrkala Region

The northeast region reaches from the Woolen River to the Gulf of Carpentaria and south to the Roper River, and it includes both Elcho Island and The English Company's Islands. The area, though it encompasses groups from Blue Mud Bay to the Roper River, is largely the home of the Murngin, or Wulamba, people. Patrilineal clans are the basis of local social organization. Yirrkala was founded in 1934, also as a mission of the Methodist Church. Today the mission settle-

Stingray Totem
by Mutpu. Central-region painting has plain or figured background, more dynamic style than northeastern style, which it resembles.

Stingray Totem
*by Biragidji. The more formalized,
static northeastern style contrasts
with the central region.*

ment is quite active: Bauxite mining on Gove Peninsula has brought
industrialization to the area with a rush, and both mission and government officials are working to minimize the culture shock.

White beaches and rocky bluffs alternate on the shoreline, and the
interior contains stretches of open savanna, which become flood
plains in the wet season. The region faces the sea both to the north
and east, receiving frequent exposure in times past to migrants and
traders. The Makasans touched here regularly on their way to Groote
Eylandt. As a result, the myths and art of Yirrkala show the impress of
outside influences more strongly than other regions of Arnhem Land.

Paintings of Yirrkala have several characteristics. First, the design
is likely to be "framed," that is, enclosed with distinct boundary lines.
Within this area, the surface of the bark often is completely covered
with primary figures and background designs, as though the artist
abhorred empty space. The paintings themselves tend to be finer,
more elegant, more formalized—and also more static—than art from
Milingimbi, the most comparable region.

Many of the background clan designs found in Yirrkala paintings
were derived from the patterns of batik cloth brought by the Makasan

traders. Crosshatching is common both as a background design and to fill in figures, as are lines, dots, and stippling. The designs are often laid on in fine lines that resemble embroidery; in fact, observers frequently touch the paintings to feel the "threads."

Yirrkala paintings are sometimes made up of several panels, each depicting a different incident or figure. Some of the largest barks come from this region, including the rare "book" barks, with each bark serving as a "page" from a myth such as the Djanggawul.

Groote Eylandt Region

This region is composed of islands in the Gulf of Carpentaria off the coast of Arnhem Land. Groote Eylandt, the largest, lies thirty miles from the mainland, with the considerably smaller islands of Bickerton and Chasm in between. Trepang, plentiful in the waters surrounding Groote Eylandt, for centuries attracted the Makasans in their great, square-rigged *prau*. Otherwise, the considerable separation from the mainland precluded all but sporadic outside contact until recently.

Groote Eylandt is hilly in the center, with open woodlands and thick rain forest covering the coastal plain. Some twelve clans, divided into two moieties, inhabit the island. There is a mission settlement at Angurugu and a government settlement at Umbakumba. Manganese quarries and shrimping have attracted outsiders and hastened cultural change.

Paintings from the area most often show a solid black or, less frequently, a brown background, on which the primary figure is presented in strong white outline. Dots, dashes, and stippling are typically used to fill in the figures; crosshatching is infrequent. One or a few figures are painted, generally to represent a totemic animal, a person, or an incident from a local myth. In contrast to the barks from Yirrkala, these paintings do not exhibit "frame" lines, and their size is usually nominal. Carved and painted message sticks are also executed in the Groote Eylandt region.

The Barramundi Fish
by Kneepad. Groote Eylandt style features black background, prominent figures, dashed lines, or dots.

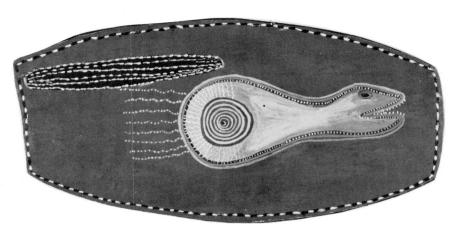

The Creator Snake, Kunmanggur
*by Indji Tharwul. Solid back-
grounds and strong figures or designs characterize Port Keats
region work.*

Melville and Bathurst Islands: The Tiwi Region

About thirty miles off the coast of Darwin, Melville and Bathurst islands are the home of nine bands, the Tunivivi, commonly known as the Tiwi. Although the islands lie along the course ships would logically follow from the East Indies to Australia, the Tiwi were notably hostile to intruders and tried to drive off visitors until recent times. European contacts, which included encounters with the Portuguese (who raided the islands for slaves) and the Dutch, were marked by continual strife. The strong tidal currents flowing between the islands and the mainland contributed to the isolation of the Tiwi people. Consequently, Tiwi culture shows little foreign impact. The boomerang and spear-thrower, for example, were not known on the islands, while the distinctive *pukamani* grave posts and elaborately carved ceremonial spears were unique to the Tiwi.

Aboriginal life now centers around the government settlement at Snake Bay, where lumbering is done, at the Garden Point Mission on Melville Island, and at the Bathurst Island Mission.

The region is best known for its *pukamani* burial poles, mentioned previously, which are intricately wrought and painted for mortuary ceremonies. Paintings are made both on bark sheets and bark baskets, as well as on the barbed spears. Designs are usually rendered in an abstract, often geometric style whose meaning is private to the artist. Backgrounds tend to be filled in with lines, crosshatching, or dots. The latter are often executed with a stippling tool unique to the region.

Daly River Native Reserve: Port Keats Region

Port Keats is situated in the northwest portion of Arnhem Land, between the Fitzmaurice and Daly rivers, in what is now called the Daly River Native Reserve. The region is fertile, well watered, and abundant in wildlife. Relatively isolated until quite recently, the aborigines now maintain effective contact with the mission settlement at Port Keats. The Murinbata is one of the largest and most important of the local tribes, a number of which maintain their own territories.

Believed to have migrated from the deserts of central Australia during a period of prolonged drought, the aborigines of Port Keats maintain some customs more nearly akin to those of the Aranda and other central tribes than to the northern clans. The migrants brought with them *tjurunga,* sacred objects fashioned from ovoid pieces of stone or wood and incised in geometric designs. *Tjurunga* served as the prototype for the paintings of these transplanted people, who cut the barks of their new land into the traditional oval shapes and designed them with intertwining spiral and curved lines, concentric circles, dots, and animal or bird tracks. Solid backgrounds, most often in brown, predominate.

The Artists and Their Work

No ONE KNOWS when or where aboriginal painting began. There is some agreement that the Australian aborigines came from a Veddoid ancestry originating in South India and Ceylon. Since the term *Vedda* is derived from the Sanskrit *Vyadha,* meaning a hunter or one who lives from the chase, we can assume that this also was originally a hunting culture. There is evidence that these hunters made paintings in caves, using ashes and turmeric mixed with spittle, possibly to bring success to their hunting. We can only conjecture, with no factual evidence, that the earliest migrants to Australia may have brought this custom with them.

The Arnhem Land bark paintings evolved from pictures of fish, animals, and people which the first inhabitants appear to have made in caves and rock shelters. We can assume that these designs of kangaroos, fish, and thin, sticklike spirits called Mimi were drawn for the same purposes as today: to depict the totemic ancestors so their help and support could more readily be invoked, to encourage game to reproduce and increase, to make magic, and to depict the limits or characteristics of the "country" owned by a clan.

Today some of the Arnhem Land clanspeople credit their painting skill and the designs they use to mythical ancestors. In western Arnhem Land, for example, the Gunwinggu tell of the master painter whose non-sacred name is Marwai, and who traveled about the country carrying his paints in a dilly bag hung from his neck. During his wanderings, he camped at cave sites on whose walls he drew many of the important designs that are still used. Marwai taught the tribesmen how to paint the sacred totemic figures. Today, the highest compliment for a painter of the region is to be told, "You paint like Marwai."

The custom of painting is commonplace among the aborigines, and the designs have many uses. Sacred designs are painted on the bodies of men preparing for initiation and participating in age-grading and other ceremonies. Bodies of deceased kin are similarly decorated to prepare them for final rites. The designs also are used in sympathetic magic: If a figure in a painting is depicted spearing a kangaroo or enjoying intercourse, a similar event can be made to occur by chanting the appropriate charms over the painting.

The paintings have traditionally served as history books and religious texts, to instruct young men in the myths and accompanying rituals as they prepared for circumcision and age-grading rites. Often the painting was laid on the ground, the initiates clustering around while one of the old men explained each detail. This custom explains why some of the paintings seem to have neither a top nor bottom but can be read from all sides.

Paintings served other practical functions in aboriginal life. At times they were used on message sticks or boards. When a man journeyed to a distant clan, he was frequently asked to carry messages for friends and relatives. To help him remember, he painted or carved a series of symbols on a piece of wood or bark. When he delivered the message, he "read" the stick or bark. A young person preparing for initiation traveled to other locations to notify relatives and invite them to attend. On occasion he carried a message board which was decorated with a painting of his clan totem. This identifying emblem assured him safe passage across the territories of strange or unfriendly clans and served as an invitation to kinfolk when he arrived.

The ability to paint was as universal as the ability to hunt or track, for there was continual need to paint designs on the bodies of participants in the ceremonies, as well as on bark and other surfaces. Some painters were recognized as better than others not because they were more talented in the aesthetic sense but because they rendered the totemic designs with greater precision and fidelity.

Since men owned the important totems and had primary responsibility for religious rituals, traditionally most of the sacred painting was done by men. As is true today, however, women were permitted to make secular paintings and to help fill in the designs of sacred ones, although they were never told the inner meanings of the paintings on which they worked. For example, Mawulan, an old man and great painter of the Riradjingu clan, *Dangu* linguistic group, *dua* moiety of Yirrkala, taught his daughter, Bangul, to help him. She is one of the few women painters recognized in her own right.

Each clan and moiety owned specific myths and designs that were passed down from one generation to the next. Every man owned a few designs that he inherited and were his exclusive property. He could obtain the right to paint other designs only by permission of their

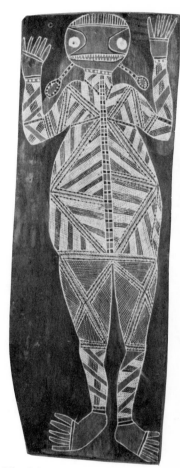

The Master Painter, Marwai *by Yirrawala. Marwai taught the tribesmen how to paint the sacred totemic figures.*

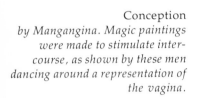

Conception
*by Mangangina. Magic paintings
were made to stimulate intercourse, as shown by these men
dancing around a representation of
the vagina.*

owners. Use of a design without permission invited trouble; in the old days such thefts prompted many spearings. As they passed through the age-grading rites, men progressively acquired full rights to the designs. Every father and his brothers, who were classificatory fathers, had both the right and the duty to transmit their esoteric knowledge to younger members of their lineage. Whatever their chronologic age, fully initiated men were known as old men. Each elder took on one or more learners, whom he taught to paint the designs in the sacred tradition. However, learners were never forced; they were taught to paint only after they showed their interest. As the neophytes completed each stage of the age-grading rituals, they learned more of the inner, hidden meanings of the sacred designs, and progressively acquired the right to add increasing detail to their paintings.

In some clans the learner was limited at first to two colors, but as he advanced in tribal stature he was permitted to use all four colors of the aboriginal palette. One reason for this restriction was that some colors, such as yellow ocher, were sacred. The deposits of yellow ocher had been laid down in the Dreamtime by one of the mythical heroes in places that could be visited only by initiated men who had the sole right to paint with the color. The right was conferred when the individual had passed the appropriate age-grading ritual.

While the old man was still alive, the learner was required to paint each design with some distinctive difference, acquiring rights to the full design upon the master's death. Often the master painted the outline and the learner filled in the detail. Sometimes only a few years separated a master from his apprentice; in other cases there was a wide disparity. For example, Nanjin of the Manggalilji clan was only four years older than Naridjin, whom he taught to paint. On the other hand, Djunmal of the Liagalawumiri clan, was separated by some thirty-four years from Bandarawui, who learned from him.

The bark to be used for painting is taken from the stringybark eucalyptus after the wet season has set in and the free-running sap makes it easy to loosen the bark. After the outer bark is removed, the sheet is heated in a hot fire to make it pliable, then it is worked

The Sea Gull Dance
by Bangul. One of the few paintings by a woman artist depicts a ceremonial dance.

The Yellow Ocher Site
*by Jama. The ocher sites were often
sacred and the men approached
with reverence to dig earth
colors for painting.*

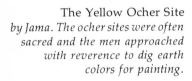

vigorously back and forth to straighten the curved surface. Finally it is held down by heavy rocks to cool and set into a fairly flat plane. When the painter is ready to begin, he coats the bark with a background color, generally brown or black. Sap from the tubers or stems of the Cymbidium orchid is rubbed into the paints. This acts as a fixative, holding the paints, which otherwise quickly flake off. Egg yolk and honey also are used as fixatives. Brushes are made by chewing the end of a twig to form a suitable tuft or by fastening hair to a sliver of wood. The primary figures are outlined, most often, in white, and the detail filled in patiently and deliberately. However, I have seen artists start at one end of the bark and work across, completing the design without outline and fully from memory.

Since every line and dot of a bark painting carries a traditional meaning, innovation is rare. Nevertheless, painters do develop distinctive styles. Bininjuwi, an outstanding Milingimbi artist, of the Djambarbingu clan, has a notably precise and beautifully balanced style. Malangi, also from Milingimbi, of the Urgiganjdjar clan, has a freer and more flowing, but equally harmonious approach. Today even the older painters are beginning to use commercial brushes rather than the traditional chewed twig. The result is a more delicate touch, with finer lines and more detail, and yet, overall, a distinctly "European-ized" look.

The paintings may depict a single figure, or they may illustrate one or a series of incidents. But they rarely present a complete story. The reason for this is that aborigines tend to think and talk in terms of separate incidents—things that actually happened—and not abstract ideas. Their stories, songs, and dances present individual events linked sequentially. Their speech is a series of statements, not a flow of narrative.

Work done for religious ritual is the finest of which an aboriginal is capable, for he believes the spirit of the totemic ancestor will enter into the painting during the forthcoming ceremony. When the singing and dancing are over, the spirit will depart. Thereafter, the work is considered merely a piece of painted bark that may be thrown into a water hole, abandoned, or, nowadays, sold.

Certain conventions hold in the composition of the work. First, although the aboriginal painter does not render planes to express the idea of linear perspective, he does indicate spatial relationships by size, showing nearby figures on a larger scale than figures meant to be farther away. For example, a large fish and a smaller one depicted on the same plane indicate that the one is swimming on the surface of the pool, the other in its depths. Distortion of scale to signify importance is another typical convention. Accordingly, the size of one figure in relationship to others in a group may be completely at odds with nature because the artist is stressing its primacy. Repetition is also a common device to indicate importance or degree of sacredness: A water hole repeated several times indicates it is an object of veneration. Color is used symbolically in aboriginal art. Depending on the context, white may stand for death or semen, red for blood or lightning, and black for storm or rain. Some conventions serve a purely practical function. If an artist's bark is too small to depict the full dimensions of a figure, he will foreshorten it or, perhaps, elongate one section. The long neck of an emu may be bent to accommodate its placement at one end of the bark; the tail of a stingray may curve to follow the border of the painting.

The aboriginal artist works slowly and methodically. If a line is not to his liking, he removes the wet paint at once with his thumb, which he wipes off on his thigh or on a stone. Although the painter does not set out to create an aesthetically pleasing object, the finished composition always has harmony and balance; the colors blend; the proportions are pleasing. In this, the aboriginal fulfills what I believe to be the basic test of real art: The work is beautiful, not in line and color alone, but because it perfectly expresses the artist's intended meaning.

PART II
CREATION MYTHS

CREATION MYTHS attempt to answer the perennial question: How did the world begin? In their lore, most primitive people tell of some cosmic event or of great, supernatural beings who created the earth and all it contains. There are endless variations in describing how this came about. According to the Maori, at first there was darkness and within it the sky lay upon the earth and from their union came the first people. Because women are the childbearers, in many cases the creator is a woman; for example, the Veddas of south India, from whom the Australian aborigines may have come, tell of a first mother by the name of Aditi. In some cultures, however, the creator is thought of as a male. The ancient Egyptians deified a masculine sun, whom they called Aten or Re. Judeo-Christian beliefs speak of God as the Father. In still other cultures, the creator contains both male and female principles or has no specified sex.

Australian aboriginal creation beliefs share this diversity; however, most have in common accounts of a period dim beyond memory called the Dreamtime or *wongar* time, during which spirit beings appeared and created the earth. These creator spirits had the form of animals, birds, and fish, but people did not yet exist. The Dreamtime period ended when some of these spirit beings turned themselves into human form and their descendants began to populate the earth. The creator spirits are eternal, they live now as in the beginning and will continue to exist forever.

Some Arnhem Land tribes speak of a male creator spirit, others a female. On the western coast, near Port Keats, for example, the Murinbata and related tribes say that the Old Woman, Karwadi, formed the land itself, but that people appeared only after the Rainbow Snake, Kunmanggur, created the first children by blowing them out the end of his *didjeridu* or drone pipe. Kunmanggur then changed himself into a man, took a wife, and raised a family.

The Rainbow Snake is most prevalent in aboriginal thinking, but its sex varies. The Gunwinggu of the western region speak of the Rainbow Snake as Ngalyod, a great snake that changed itself into a woman and created the people. Among the central and northeastern clans, the Rainbow Snake is called Julunggul and is both male and female. It carries within itself the eggs that became the first people, yet it is also the phallus that fertilized the eggs. The Groote Eylandt tribes tell of Jajaban, the snake that created their island. Only the Tiwi of Melville and Bathurst islands have no mythical snake; rather, they describe a female creator spirit, Mudungkala. Even when a mother figure is prominent in aboriginal creation myths, once she has performed her unique function of giving birth the male dominates. This we might expect, for men were the custodians and transmitters of the creation stories.

The creator beings not only formed the first people, but also gave them their language, their religion, and laws and rules to help them live peacefully together. They revealed to their people magic songs and chants which would enable them to call upon the spirit ancestors for help in times of drought, pestilence, and war. The creator spirits also marked out the territories which were to be the homelands of the people forever. The creation myths that are sung, danced, and mimed by the aborigines at birth, initiation, and death and during the various stages of the age-grading ceremonies serve as constant reminders of these all-powerful creator spirits and what they said and did.

Sisters of the Sun: The Djanggawul Myth, I

The Djanggawul myth tells how the first people came to Arnhem Land from an island called Bralgu, which lies to the northeast, roughly from the direction of Cape York and New Guinea. We can only assume that the myth reflects tribal memories of prehistoric migrants who crossed the Torres Straits from New Guinea and landed first on Cape York or, alternatively, drifted to Arnhem Land on rafts or canoes blown by the monsoon.

The myth, told by the clans of the northeast and central regions, gives the story in graphic detail. These people believe that their first ancestors were a brother and his two sisters, the Djanggawul, who lived on an island beyond the mists of the horizon. The Djanggawul brother, husband of Walu, the Sun Woman, committed incest with the sisters and, because of this, the three Djanggawul were banished by Walu. They journeyed by canoe to the mainland, landing at what is now Port Bradshaw. They wandered through the country, creating the water holes and naming all the natural features they saw. From their incestuous union came the present-day clans of the *dua* moiety. In their travels they encountered Laindjung, the progenitor of the people of the *jiridja* moiety. The sisters had kept for themselves the sacred totems which reserved the greater power to the women; however, these were stolen by the men, placing the women in the subservient role they have had ever since. "We bear the men, so we have the real power," the sisters console themselves.

The Djanggawul myth, together with the songs, dances, bark paintings, carved figures, and sacred designs, is the property of the *dua* moiety. From this basic theme emerge many of the other rituals and ceremonies of the clans of this moiety. The simple elements of the Djanggawul myth are known by all: men, women, and children. But as boys are initiated and pass through the age-grading ceremonies known as the *Dua*

Narra, they increasingly acquire lore that is kept secret and sacred, on threat of death. During a visit at Yirrkala, for instance, Midinari showed me a painting of the sacred *rangga* emblems of the Djanggawul myth. The bark stood facing the wall. Before he turned it, Midinari looked about carefully to be sure no women were in sight. As he described the work and its meaning, his voice lowered noticeably. When he finished, he again concealed the design.

IN THE TIME when the dreaming began, the land and the sky were empty and dark. There was neither bird song nor river sound, neither birth nor death. In the darkness of the cavern that lies beneath the earth, Walu, the Sun Woman, slept, her bright face hidden in her encircling arms. At last she arose and lifted her arms so that the darkness vanished. Then she climbed over the edge of the world and the land sparkled with her coming. Long she walked, casting light and warmth upon the land below. Her fingers stroked the hard earth as she passed, and soon it stirred and grumbled to itself and began to put on a covering of green and orange and yellow. Clumps of gum and acacia trees grew tall and sent out sheaths of leaves to drink in the sunshine. The leaves rustled in pleasure, chattering among themselves, and their fragrance filled the warm air.

In many places spirit beings appeared and began to shape the green earth. They created hills and trees, rivers and lagoons. They formed creatures that hunt and kill, that play and make love in the warmth of the sun.

Now the strength of Walu waned and she became faint and weary. "Where shall I rest?" she asked, but no answer came. Over all the earth she looked, seeking a place where she might draw her cloak of clouds about her, cover her face with her arms, and there, hidden in the darkness, renew her strength. Then she saw on the horizon a piece of land, green and soft in the encircling sea: the Island of Bralgu. On Bralgu she sank down and slept long, while darkness came to earth.

When she awoke, she found the land to her liking. So she dwelt there, shedding light and warmth. In her bright rays the plants grew lushly; fish and tortoise came to feast upon the lilies that bloomed in the river shallows. To this fair land came many spirit people from the Sky World and the underworld, and there they lived in peace and contentment.

Only spirits lived on Bralgu. In this time of the Dream they could turn themselves into any form they wished—into animals or stars or rocks. Often they went about in the shape of humans and lived as people do, but still they were spirits and never died. As the time of the Dream continued, far off across the sea the Great Rainbow Snake created human beings, who became many and spread throughout the land. The spirits on Bralgu knew of these men and women who dwelt beyond the mists and spoke often of them.

To Bralgu came the spirit Bralbal. In the form of a man he came, paddling strongly in his bark canoe. Tall and wiry Bralbal was, and he shouted of his coming as he drove through the heaving waves and ran his canoe upon the beach. He made his camp upon the shore, and every morning he pushed his canoe through the breakers, then leaped aboard and paddled out to the deep waters to poise his fishing spear. When he returned, his canoe loaded with mackerel, cod, and turtles, he made a camp fire on the beach and invited the other spirit people to eat of the catch.

To Bralgu came the spirit Barnumbir, who had the form of the morning star. Early each day as the camp fires of the star people faded in the sky, Barnumbir rose above the treetops into the Sky World, her gentle beams caressing the hills as if coaxing them from the shadows. The cool wind blew in gusts from the sea; it whistled at Barnumbir and flung showers of spray toward the beach, tempting her to venture out over the deep waters. But Barnumbir feared the mighty waves that crashed and fought among themselves, and she never strayed over the sea but kept always above the island of Bralgu.

When Walu, the Sun Woman, began her daily journey across the Sky World, Barnumbir returned gratefully to her home. By day she was a girl, pleasant and comely, who made her camp in a sheltered cove where the hills fell softly to the sea. She spent much time with her friends among the spirit people, and often she wandered alone along the beaches and in the forests of gum and banyan trees, for she loved the fresh smell of the earth and the sound of the waves and the wind.

To Bralgu also came the Djanggawul, paddling out of the mists of the sea in their bark canoe. Three of them there were. Ganjudingu, the brother, leaped into the surf and pulled the canoe ashore. Muscles stood out on his arms, and his shoulders were broad and strong. His two sisters followed close behind to help him beach the canoe. The elder was named Bildjiwuraroiju and the younger, Miralaidj. Bildjiwuraroiju carried over her shoulder a netted bag that contained sacred totems: carved wood figures that represented the parrot, the goanna, the porpoise, and the ant. With these she could call up great power. Only the two sisters knew the secret songs that could call up this power; their brother, Ganjudingu, did not know.

The Djanggawul made their camp upon the shore. Ganjudingu often ranged in the forests and hills to hunt wallaby and opossum. These he brought back to the camps of the spirit people to share. Ganjudingu and Bralbal became friends and often went together beyond the breakers to spear fish. At times they saw sharks prowling the water near their canoe; at times a mighty whale set their canoe rocking in its swell. But they stood fast with their long spears drawn back and their strong arms ready so that no harm came to them.

The sisters camped with their brother. So often were the three together that the other spirit people called them the Djanggawul, as if they were one person. Everything the Djanggawul shared, save for

The Sacred Fish
*by Madaman. Tribesmen feast on
a fish left by the Djanggawul at
the water hole Gundalmirri.*

one thing: the power of the totems. One day Bildjiwuraroiju and Mira-laidj called together the women of Bralgu and taught them the sacred songs and dances that would give them the special power only the sisters possessed. They permitted the women alone to participate in these rituals. If the men came near, silence fell and the women would begin to talk idly among themselves. Jealously Bildjiwuraroiju guarded the totems, keeping them always within her reach so that no man might take them and gain the power.

Often Ganjudingu asked that Bildjiwuraroiju teach him the songs, but she refused. "The men are stronger. They will beat us and take what we have if we do not keep this secret power for ourselves," she said. Ganjudingu dwelled in his mind on how he might steal the totems, but always Bildjiwuraroiju was alert and he could not find a way.

Despite all this, Bildjiwuraroiju grew even closer to Ganjudingu. She was with him constantly, even when he and Bralbal went fishing. Bralbal objected. "Fishing is for men," he said when Bildjiwuraroiju climbed into the canoe. "A woman grows tired and she must return to land to pass her blood." Bildjiwuraroiju heard, but she stared past the men to the sea and kept her place in the canoe.

Miralaidj, the younger Djanggawul, cared little for the company of men or for their pursuits. She had just passed her first blood and preferred to go with girls of her own age to find shellfish in the streams and to dig for yams and lily bulbs. Her favorite friend was Barnumbir, with whom she spent happy hours searching for mussels and crayfish on the beach and for palm nuts and yams in the forest.

The Sacred Fish
*by Wandjuk. The same theme
painted by another artist of the
same clan.*

By day, Walu took the form of the sun, hot and bright. She walked from Bralgu across the Sky World to the western horizon, and from there she returned to her island home to rest and sleep. The Djanggawul brother noted her coming and going and became enamored of her. Soon he prevailed upon Walu to lie by his camp fire at night. She became his wife.

Each day now, Ganjudingu waited impatiently for Walu to return, for the heat of his desire was very great. In his eagerness, his penis grew long. Soon it reached the ground and everyone who saw this marveled. The men were jealous and the women longed to lie with him.

The days were empty without his wife. Ganjudingu grew restless and lonely. Often he stood on the high cliff that overlooked the western ocean and gazed toward the massed clouds that marked the land only Walu knew, for over its breadth she passed each day. Bildjiwuraroiju came to her brother in his loneliness and looked also to the distant clouds. "Walu says that much of the land is dry and flat. She aches for its emptiness. There are people, but they have little. The land waits for more water holes and green grass, for shade and coolness," she said.

One day Ganjudingu, accompanied by Bildjiwuraroiju, went high into the hills to hunt wallaby. Much time they spent before the brother's spear found its mark. The Sun Woman had traveled far over the ocean as they turned toward camp. Hot and dusty, they came to the sand that borders the sea. There they put down their catch to frolic in the cool waters of the bay and to lie upon the sand to rest. Now

*The Promised Land
by Wandjuk. The Djanggawul
brother stands on a high cliff and
gazes toward the mainland.*

Ganjudingu felt his desire rise, and he turned toward his sister, placing his hand on the soft hair that shielded her place of pleasure.

"What are you doing?" Bildjiwuraroiju asked, her eyes not unwilling.

"Walu travels far across the Sky World," replied Ganjudingu, "and I cannot wait for her to return by night. Come lie with me."

"Walu will be unhappy," Bildjiwuraroiju objected, but her hand was light upon his and she came to him.

Walu knew. Three times the moon grew round and fat, died and was born again. Watchfully did Walu observe how closely Bildjiwuraroiju followed Ganjudingu. She saw the tender glances they exchanged, more tender than those of just brother and sister. Watchfully did Walu see Bildjiwuraroiju begin to swell.

Walu knew and sorrowed. When she came to Ganjudingu's bed at night, she refused to lie with him saying, "You have been unfaithful. You must leave Bralgu. You shall take your sister with you and find food and shelter for her when the child comes."

Now Ganjudingu went often to the height overlooking the western ocean. One day he said to Walu, "I shall go to the land in the west. I shall make many water holes and streams so there will be trees and green grass for the people. There Bildjiwuraroiju shall give birth to many children, and they shall fill that country."

"That is good, for the land is empty," Walu replied. "Take digging sticks and sleeping mats. Bildjiwuraroiju shall take her sacred totems so that her children can call the spirits for help. Thus shall they be content."

When she learned that Ganjudingu and Bildjiwuraroiju would leave, Miralaidj was distressed. "Do not go, sister. I shall not know how to live without you," she said.

But Bildjiwuraroiju feared to take her younger sister. "The land is strange; there may be much danger. Stay with your friend Barnumbir and the people you love," she said.

Miralaidj still longed greatly to go. She talked to her friend the morning star; but Barnumbir smiled gently and put her arm about the girl. She talked to the man Bralbal, but he just grunted and told her to stay home. In the dark of night Miralaidj wept as she lay upon her bed of soft bark, wretched that her sister would soon leave her. She could see the embers glowing at Ganjudingu's fire, a spear's throw away, and his long form stretched on his bed.

Miralaidj rose and crept toward him. She lay down beside him, pressing her body to him until he awoke. Close she clung and moved her loins against Ganjudingu. "Lie with me, brother," she begged. That night they knew each other many times. In the morning Miralaidj told her sister what had occurred. "Now you must take me for I, too, shall have a child," she said.

Walu also knew. "You must leave with both your sisters," she told Ganjudingu. "The voyage is long and the canoe will be heavily loaded. To help you, I will watch over you by day and light your path

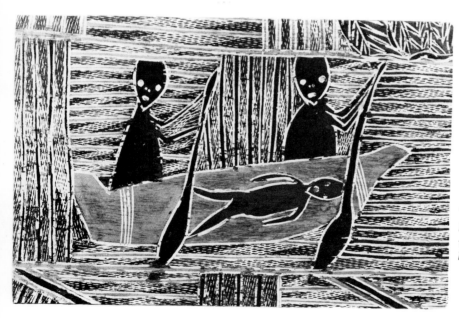

The Canoe Voyage
by Wandjuk. Two of the Djanggawul paddle while one rests on the bottom of the canoe.

across the waters with my rays. So shall you travel in safety to the new land.''

Early in the morning, Ganjudingu and his sisters loaded their canoe. They took food and water and circular mats of woven fiber, the *ngainmara,* to serve both as a shelter and a bed. The sisters took also their *rangga,* among them the *mawalan,* or digging stick, with which to make water holes, and the *djuda* pole, from which trees would grow. Both of these *rangga* had strings of bright feathers hanging from them. On their backs the Djanggawul slung woven bags for carrying food. Bildjiwuraroiju placed in her bag the sacred totems and laid them carefully beneath one of the woven mats. Then the sisters climbed into the canoe, and Ganjudingu pushed off and jumped in.

With the wind blowing strongly from the island, the three paddled smoothly. Soon the land faded behind them and was lost to sight. Now they followed the bright path that Walu cast on the water as she climbed through the Sky World before them. Three days passed, during which the Djanggawul took turns paddling; when they wearied, they rested under the mats on the bottom of the canoe. At night they followed the stars, but in the early morning, when the camp fires of the sky people flickered out, they had no guide and often lost their course until the sun's first rays lit the horizon.

The fourth day, in the chill blackness that precedes the dawn, Ganjudingu was paddling when he saw the pale light of Barnumbir. He gazed in wonder as he saw her appear and climb directly overhead. Never before had the morning star's beams marked the course for the canoe to follow. Ganjudingu turned the canoe toward this path of light, then woke his sisters. Together they sang a song of thanks to Barnumbir. She flickered and nodded her pleasure.

Then Walu, the Sun Woman, mounted the sky and showed them the way with her bright rays. Strongly they paddled; with shoulders bent and hips that swayed from side to side, steadily they moved toward the low clouds ahead. Flocks of birds skimmed by; a whale blew a great plume into the air; a giant sawfish threatened to overturn the canoe.

At last, after many days, the cloud bank began to dissolve. Now they could see sandhills behind the beaches, and waves running high on the incoming tide. Paddling hard, they drove through the spray and beached the canoe on the sand. They pulled up the canoe beyond the tide and unloaded it. Then they looked around. The sand ran in rippling hills far inland, and everywhere the Djanggawul looked the rays of Walu shone. The land baked in the heat.

"This land is strange; we do not know what we will meet," said Bildjiwuraroiju. "We need much power to protect us." She rubbed her hand under her arm so that sweat covered her palm, then she rubbed her sweat on Miralaidj's chest and arms. "My sweat will give you strength," she said.

As they crossed a sand dune, Ganjudingu saw a monitor lizard, a

The Lizard Design
by Lardjanga. The Djanggawul were enchanted by the trail left by the lizard in the sand.

djanda, running across the sand. The pattern left by the little rivulets of sand that ran from its feet enchanted him. "This shall be a sacred design: our children shall see the *djanda* and its mark, and they shall remember us," he said to his sisters.

Long they walked, but then their footsteps lagged in the heat. "I am thirsty," Miralaidj said. "But there is no water."

"We will make a water hole here. We will cause the *djuda* tree to grow," said Bildjiwuraroiju. "We will drink of the cool water and rest in the shade."

She thrust the *djuda* pole in the ground, and a towering *djuda* tree sprang up, its spreading branches making pools of shade to which the Djanggawul retreated. Then Miralaidj took the *mawalan* pole and pushed it into the sand. Deep she thrust it, then deeper. She moved it back and forth, and slowly began to draw it out. A rush of clear water filled the hole. The sand caved in before the spreading water, and soon a water hole had formed. Grass grew on its banks and parakeets flew in to perch on the branches of the tree. Gratefully the Djanggawul rested. They watched Walu's rays grow faint as she walked toward the horizon.

"This land is ours. We shall make it a good place for our children," announced Bildjiwuraroiju confidently, and then fell quickly asleep.

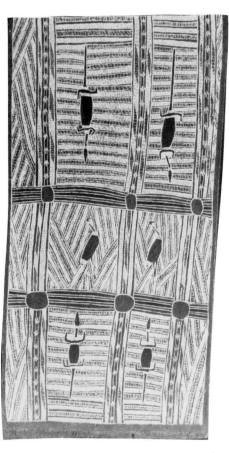

Lizards and Birds
by Lardjanga. Lizards and birds were among the first living creatures the Djanggawul saw after they came ashore.

The Lost Power: The Djanggawul Myth, II

THE COCKATOOS awoke as the pale light of Barnumbir, the morning star, touched the treetops; their raucous outcry soon had the Djanggawul stirring. By the time Walu thrust her head above the horizon, they had gathered their belongings and set out to explore the new country.

They walked north, following the sand dunes along the coast, with Ganjudingu taking the lead and his sisters following. Each carried a woven bag and a circular mat. Bildjiwuraroiju shared her totems with Miralaidj, but to Ganjudingu they gave none. Each held a pointed *mawalan*. Whenever they stopped to rest, they thrust a *mawalan* into the ground and watched as the hole grew large and deep and filled with clear water. On the banks of these water holes they caused *djuda* trees to spring up; their branches reached out and cast a shade over the water.

Everywhere they went, Ganjudingu and his sisters made many things and gave them names. At one place, Bildjiwuraroiju took a yam totem from her woven bag and carefully planted it in the ground. Leaves and tendrils shot up and soon a patch of yams grew where there had only been sand. And as they walked, they named the hills and bays, the rivers and inlets.

Now Bildjiwuraroiju and Miralaidj were both heavy with child; travel became ever more difficult for them. They came to a country that stretched flat to distant hills. Thick grass matted the ground, interrupted by stands of cycad palms. They filed through the rough grass that grew shoulder high beside the lake. A flock of blue-gray birds passed overhead, tightly bunched, then separated as they turned on the wind to land in the shallows, their feet pattering on the water as they came to a running stop.

Suddenly Bildjiwuraroiju stopped and doubled over. "The child comes," she said. She looked about for shade in which to lie, but everywhere the rays of Walu glared on the sand and rough grass.

Seeing her sister's discomfort, Miralaidj thrust her pointed *mawalan* into the ground. Immediately water gushed forth, forming a large spring from which the water ran in a rivulet to the beach. "Now I will make shade," she said and again placed the *djuda* pole in the ground. Where it penetrated the earth, a tree quickly grew, casting deep and pleasant shade.

Ganjudingu and Miralaidj spread one of the mats and helped Bildjiwuraroiju relax upon it, for her birth pains now came closely together. "Sister, open your legs a little," instructed Ganjudingu. Then he put his finger inside her womb and brought out a male child. He placed the baby in the rough grass, reached in again, and brought out a female child. He drew together some soft grass, placed the baby girl upon it, and covered her carefully with a woven *ngainmara* mat.

Several more children came from the sister's womb. The boys Ganjudingu laid in the rough grass, the girls he placed on soft grass and half covered them with the mat. "When the boys grow up, they will have much hair and whiskers, and their skin will be tough from

The Unknown
*by Wandjuk. The Djanggawul
brother surveys the unknown land
he and his sisters will explore.*

·The Sister Gives Birth
*by Wandjuk. The Djanggawul sis-
ter supports herself on the yam
sticks as she gives birth.*

the harsh grass,'' he said. ''But the girls will have little hair, and their
skin will be soft and smooth, for they are protected under the sacred
mat. Thus shall we always treat children when they are born.''

The Djanggawul continued their travels, exploring the new country, creating water holes and trees. The sisters gave birth to many
children, who grew to men and women much more quickly than they
do today; and before long these children bore children of their own.

Now the camps of the people were many in the land, and men
began to quarrel with one another. ''This is my country,'' one said,
''and there are only enough kangaroo and opossum for my family. The
rest of you must stay away and hunt elsewhere.'' Soon there was
throwing of spears, and people were killed as they fought over the
land.

Ganjudingu saw this and was troubled. ''This is not good,'' he
said to his sisters. ''We must help our children live peacefully
together.'' So the three Djanggawul went among the families and gave
them the laws and rules they must follow to live in peace. To every
man they apportioned his country. ''Here you shall hunt, for this land
is yours and none shall trespass,'' said Ganjudingu to each.

The Djanggawul also taught the people to paint the sacred designs, but only the sisters could teach the power songs. And these
were made known only to the women. ''You shall gather together

when the rain goes back to the Sky World and the land becomes dry,"
Bildjiwuraroiju told the women when she called them together away
from the men, "and you shall repeat the words I have given you so the
spirits will come and cause the fish to increase and the kangaroo to
multiply. I shall teach you songs and dances so that you will remember what I have said, and you shall teach them to your girl children. But to the men you shall not give them."

Many times Ganjudingu asked his sisters for the sacred totems
and emblems they kept in their bags, for they contained much power
that he wished to share with the men. But the sisters refused and insisted on teaching the songs only to the women. Ganjudingu's eyes
burned in anger as he saw the women go far off by themselves so the
men could not hear them. At each place the sisters left some of their
sacred totems with the women. "Soon they will give away all the
totems and the power will be gone," the brother thought. But to his
amazement, the sacred totems renewed themselves as often as the sisters gave them out. "Here is great power indeed," thought Ganjudingu to himself. "It belongs to the men and they shall have it."

The Djanggawul continued their travels, naming all the places and
creatures they met, and making water holes and trees. Wherever they
went, the sisters sang the sacred songs and performed the ceremonies
while Ganjudingu hunted for food with the men. Each night the
brother slept with his two sisters, so Bildjiwuraroiju and Miralaidj
continued to bear many children.

At one place they walked away from the sea and traveled inland
for many days. They entered a dense mangrove swamp and slowly
picked their way through the interwoven roots that laced the heavy,
warm land.

"Brother, I am hungry," Miralaidj said.

They came to a river in which they saw many fish darting back
and forth. "We shall catch the fish and eat them, for they are strong
food," Ganjudingu declared. The Djanggawul built a fish trap, using
branches and plaited fiber; then they camped and ate the fish they had
caught. They left the trap in the river so the people could learn to use
it.

"When our children come they will find fish and thus learn how
to make traps for themselves," Bildjiwuraroiju said.

One day they came to an island. "This island is a sacred place,"
said Bildjiwuraroiju. "We shall camp here until we are rested." As
they approached, they saw smoke rising through the trees. On the
wind they could smell the aroma of sea slug being cooked. Men of a
light brown color were tending the fires, each wearing a length of
woven cloth wound around his middle. The Djanggawul stopped and
counseled together. "These strange men are fierce. They carry long
knives and spears," Miralaidj said.

Bildjiwuraroiju spoke calmly. "They are Bajini who come from
across the water. They are strong men and great fighters, but they seek

Children in the Grass
*by Djunmal. The girl babies are
put in the soft grass and covered
with a mat, while the boys are
placed in the rough grass so their
hair will be thick and their skin
tough.*

to trade and will not harm us." Then the Djanggawul approached the
Bajini and identified themselves. "This place on which you camp is
sacred," announced Bildjiwuraroiju. "It is forbidden to those not of
our blood. You must leave if you wish to return in peace to trade for
more sea slug." The sisters grasped their long poles firmly. Ganjudingu placed the cord of his spirit bag in his teeth to give him strength
and courage. Then the Djanggawul waited silently, for they did not
know if the Bajini would retreat.

The brown men spoke to one another in their strange language.
They saw the Djanggawul were not to be frightened, and so went
away to the mainland, leaving behind their fireplace and the cooking
pots and spoons they had been using to prepare sea slug. Miralaidj examined these utensils with interest; in handling them, her hands became black with charcoal. "This shall become a sacred color for our
people, and it shall be used for painting the sacred designs," Bildjiwuraroiju decreed. Ever since, only the people descended from the
Djanggawul have the right to use the black color of charcoal.

The Djanggawul made camp where the Bajini had been, and then
spread out in search for food. Ganjudingu and Bildjiwuraroiju waded
out into the surf to catch fish while Miralaidj wandered off to find
yams. Ganjudingu was standing in the water, poised to spear one of
the stingray that came to feed in the surf while, closer in, Bildjiwuraroiju searched for crabs. Suddenly Miralaidj ran up to them

breathless. "A man is on the other side of the island," she said. "His body is painted with sacred designs, but the patterns are not those we gave our children. What shall we do?"

Ganjudingu looked at Bildjiwuraroiju. "We will go speak with him," she said, and together the three strode toward the stranger's camp. They approached cautiously, making noise with their feet and circling the area so the stranger would see them. They recognized him immediately as a spirit being, for on his body was painted a sacred diamond design. Below his white beard, ridges of flesh stood out on his chest, and white bands of parakeet feathers encircled his head and arms.

"We are the Djanggawul," said Bildjiwuraroiju. "We come from Bralgu."

The stranger acknowledged them and replied, "I am Laindjung. I have come to aid my people, even as you show your children how to find food and how to live justly. Let us do our deeds in peace."

The four spirit people sat by the fire, sharing food and speaking of their experiences. At last the Djanggawul rose to leave. "You have taught the laws and ceremonies to your people," said Laindjung. "Now I will teach them to the people of my tribes so our people, yours and mine, will live in peace together."

Laindjung then gave his friends a gift of string made from opossum fur and white feathers that his tribespeople wore. In return, the Djanggawul presented Laindjung with a waistband and a string of red parakeet feathers unique to their tribespeople. Laindjung had traded with the Bajini for a piece of their batik cloth. This, too, he now offered to the Djanggawul; but they were afraid of the power of this strange material and refused it. Ever since that time, when the descendants of the Djanggawul and Laindjung meet for ceremonies and consultation, they exchange similar gifts.

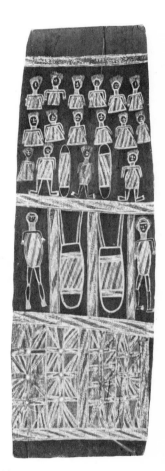

Children in the Grass
by Djunmal.

Again the Djanggawul continued their journey. The wet season came on, and they camped in caves or under large rocks to escape the rain. While they waited for the rain to cease, the Djanggawul painted designs on the cave walls telling of their travels. These designs later became the sacred patterns of the clans and were painted in the huts and on bark.

Still the two sisters kept the sacred totems to themselves. Day by day Ganjudingu's anger grew that they would not share their power. One night, while the sisters slept, he went to the dilly bag and tried to steal the totems. But Bildjiwuraroiju and Miralaidj straightaway awoke, as if the totems had called to them. In great anger, Bildjiwuraroiju leaped upon her brother and beat him with her digging stick. "Only the women shall have the totems. They are not for the men," she loudly declared.

One day the sisters went out to gather food while Ganjudingu hunted kangaroo. They searched deep in the forest for berries and nuts. Unknown to them, they were being followed by three men of their clan. The men had been camping near the Djanggawul's fire and had crept close at the first light of dawn to see who was there. From their place in hiding they had seen Ganjudingu leave with his spear to hunt for kangaroo. From their place in hiding they had seen the sisters make ready to search for food. From their place in hiding they had seen the bag that Bildjiwuraroiju carried.

"There are the sacred totems," one of the watchers had whispered. "Maybe we can get them so the men will have power over the women." When the sisters went into the forest, silently the men followed.

The sisters had strayed apart as they searched through the undergrowth of the forest for berries and nuts, when Miralaidj stopped and called, "Sister, I have found a bee tree. Come help me make a bark container. Then we will climb to the nest." Bildjiwuraroiju looked carefully around, saw nothing to alarm her, and so took the net bag from her neck and hung it on a tree.

When the sisters returned with their honey-laden container, the net bag had disappeared. Frantically they searched every tree and bush. But the totems could not be found. Bildjiwuraroiju's eyes scanned the ground: she noticed a place where the grass had been bent and had not yet sprung back. She found a pebble that had been recently turned over, for its bottom was still moist. She discovered a damp stretch where footprints showed fresh in the mud. "Three men have been here, sister," she said. "They have stolen our totems. Let us run after them. We must get them back!"

Quickly they followed the tracks of the men to catch them before they could open the bags and invoke the power of the totemic spirits. But suddenly through the forest came the rhythmic beating of singing sticks and the voices of men chanting. Bildjiwuraroiju grasped Miralaidj by the arm, beat her breast, and cried aloud, "Sister, the men have stolen our power. Now we have nothing!" Miralaidj moaned in her grief.

The sisters concealed themselves in the bushes and crept close to the group. Among the men they saw their brother, Ganjudingu, who had returned from the hunt and had joined the men performing the stolen ritual.

"Let it be, sister," said Bildjiwuraroiju with resignation. "There is nothing to be done. The men have stolen the power of our totems and will never return it. But all is not lost: we have the greatest power of all, and it cannot be stolen. For only from our wombs can children come. All men must come from us. And we know the songs already. These we will not forget. So we will let the men keep the totems and conduct the ceremonies. From this time on the women will gather the yams and bulbs and make palm nut bread. We will gather food to nourish the children and the men. We will comfort them, for we know we have the greater power."

And so it has been ever since.

The Good Man: The Laindjung Myth

The Laindjung myth, which is told by the clans of the *jiridja* moiety, parallels the Djanggawul myth of the *dua* moiety. Nevertheless, Laindjung emerges more as lawgiver than creator ancestor, more Moses than Adam. The myth tells us that human life came from spirit beings that lived in the water—specifically, from a barramundi fish that took the form of a man known as Laindjung.

Laindjung came to help the people of the *jiridja* moiety, bringing them the sacred rituals, songs, totems, and customs that have distinguished them ever since. Envious men killed Laindjung, but his spirit rose again in the form of Banaidja, his son. Banaidja returned to carry on his father's good work, only to meet a similar fate.

In studying aboriginal myths, one runs the risk of overextending coincidences. Still, some aspects so closely replicate similar stories in other parts of the world that it is difficult to avoid comparison. There are striking resemblances in the Laindjung myth to other accounts of rebirth and redemption, from the Egyptian legend of Osiris the Good, killed by the evil Set and subsequently resurrected, to the story of the death and redemption of Jesus Christ.

There were many different versions of the myth, as I was able to document them from different informants at different time periods. Some versions added a third person, Barama, to fill various roles, and some interchanged the identities of Laindjung and Banaidja. When and how these figures appeared, the details of their lives, and the manner of their deaths all differed markedly.

I have selected from my notes portions of differing versions that I have heard or read, consolidating them to provide one coherent story and filling out the narrative with cultural information that should be helpful to the reader.

LONG, LONG AGO in the country of the Daii people who live near the sea, a great drought fell on the land. The trade winds blew steadily, licking the moisture from the earth. Everything turned brown in the fires of the Sun Woman, who marched across the sky day after day. The game moved far away. Roots and berries became scarce. The people were very hungry and looked everywhere for food. Only the Koolatong River ran full and strong, for it came from deep springs in the hills. Many fish swam in the river; big fish lurked in the roots by the shore, little fish darted back and forth in the shallows. There were many fish, but the people did not know how to catch them. They threw spears at the fish, but the fish were never where the spears struck. They tried to catch the fish in their hands, but the fish swam quickly away. The children cried; the bellies of the people were empty; the mothers had no milk. And still many fish swam in the cool water of the river where the people could not catch them.

A spirit lived in a deep lagoon called Gululdji near where the Koolatong River widens before emptying into Blue Mud Bay. This spirit could turn into any form he wished, and most of the time he had the appearance of a barramundi fish who swam in the cool depths of the pool. But even there this spirit heard the hungry cries of the children and the sorrow of their mothers. And he grieved, for these were people of his totem and he did not want them to suffer.

One day the barramundi swam from the lagoon down the Koolatong River and into the waters of Blue Mud Bay. There, where the combers came rolling in great swells to the shore, he changed himself into a man who called himself Laindjung. In his arms he carried *rangga*, sacred totems of the tortoise, the kangaroo, the wild bee, the orchid, and the lily. These he would give to the people so that the spirits of the *rangga* would help them.

It so happened that at this time the man Galbarimun was fishing in the deep tide pools that are found along the shores of Blue Mud Bay. In his hand he held a long spear. It was attached to a spear-thrower that had a tassel of human hair fastened to the end. Everywhere among the people this spear-thrower of Galbarimun was known, for it had been given to him by the spirit of his departed father. The hair of the tassel was his father's hair, and it caused the spear to fly straight and true. But Galbarimun was tired and discouraged, for he had fished all morning with his spear and had caught only one small groper. Even this was bony and hardly worth eating.

Now Galbarimun glanced up and saw a figure rising from the surf. He was startled, for all morning he had seen no one on the beach, or in the water, or on the rocks. "This is magic," Galbarimun thought. And he stood still, his spear in hand, watching the stranger's head, shoulders, and thighs appear through the breaking waves. White foam ran from the man's hair down his face. White, too, was his beard, and white the bands of feathers that decorated his face and arms. Seemingly unaware of Galbarimun, the stranger strode through the surf onto the beach. He was a strong man and tall, and he walked like one who had much power. Galbarimun turned and moved cautiously through the water toward the newcomer. He held his spear in his spear-thrower so the stranger would know he had to prove his intentions. As he approached, Galbarimun noticed the totemic figures the stranger held in his arms. "This is a spirit man," he thought, "for he brings totems."

"Your face is welcome," said Galbarimun in formal greeting. The stranger stood easily, letting the salt water on his body dry in the hot sun and looking at Galbarimun in a friendly manner.

"I am Laindjung. I come in friendship," he said.

Galbarimun liked the man's relaxed manner and open look, his quiet speech, and the warm voice that prompted a friendly response. "We have little food, but I have caught a fish. Come share it with me. We will eat at my camp fire," Galbarimun said, pointing to the grouper fish he had placed on a rock.

Together they went to the camp where Galbarimun's wife, Neiri, was busy at the fire. "This is Laindjung. He will eat with us," said Galbarimun, handing the fish to his wife. Neiri looked doubtfully at both fish and stranger, but Laindjung nodded in a friendly way and said, "I am pleased."

"Where do you come from?" Galbarimun asked the stranger as his wife occupied herself cleaning the fish.

Laindjung swung his arm in a broad arc. "I am of the barramundi totem and I come from the river and the sea," he replied.

While they stood talking, the boy Nguni, the child of Galbarimun and Neiri, came to the fire. Nguni looked with interest at the stranger. "I climbed a tree and found honey," he announced holding up sticky fingers on which traces of wax still remained. Then he noticed the patterns made by the dried sea foam and salt water on Laindjung's chest and back. "The salt water has dried and it looks like the honeycomb," he said, pointing to Laindjung's body.

Galbarimun patted his son's head. "Maybe it is a sign that now there will be more food so we can share it with our friend," he said, nodding at Laindjung.

"There will be more food," the stranger said with assurance. "The turtle and fish will multiply in the river, for the totemic spirits are my friends." Laindjung looked at the dried diamond pattern on his skin. "As a sign, I shall make these designs on my body sacred," he told them. "And this shall be your totem."

Galbarimun and Neiri heard and were pleased. They knew Laindjung was a spirit man and that he had power. But this was not unusual, for spirits commonly turned into people in those days. However, the spirit people were often indifferent or unpleasant to those they encountered. Sometimes the spirits became mischievous and brought harm to the people. But Galbarimun and Neiri could see that Laindjung intended only good, and they were happy.

Laindjung
by Mahkarolla.

But soon it became clear that not all in the camp welcomed the stranger. Each day Laindjung took out the sacred totems where the people could see them and sang power songs so the fish and kangaroo would multiply. Even the women heard, and some of the men scowled and muttered among themselves, for it was forbidden that women should see the sacred totems and hear the songs.

Muru, a big man with three wives and many children, stopped Galbarimun one morning. "Send the stranger away," he said. "He sings the sacred songs to the women and this is taboo. Much evil will come. Besides, we have too little food as it is, and this man Laindjung has not even a spear. He will eat food that we need for our women and children."

But Galbarimun defended his friend. "He has shared his totem with me. He is my tribal brother. He comes from the barramundi spirit and soon will cause many tortoise to appear in the river."

But Muru scoffed and spoke against the stranger to his friends. That evening, as Laindjung sat with Galbarimun and Neiri eating, a number of men took up their spears and joined Muru. They gathered together, shaking their spears angrily and glancing toward Laindjung. Then they walked toward Galbarimun's camp fire. Laindjung looked at them calmly and waited without speaking for the hostile group to approach.

Galbarimun feared for his friend. "Take my spear, it is yours," he said, placing his long spear in Laindjung's hand. "Here, also, is my spear-thrower with the hair attached that makes the spear fly straight and true." Galbarimun gave up his treasured weapons and picked up another spear for himself. Men feared the magic power of the hair tassel, and he knew Muru and his friends would hesitate when they saw it in Laindjung's hands.

While Muru threatened and blustered, Galbarimun held his spear firmly. Laindjung was silent. "There is not enough food for an extra mouth. The stranger is not welcome," shouted Muru, and then slunk away with his group.

The next morning, Laindjung invited Galbarimun and Neiri to the pool, saying, "Come to Gululdji, for the totemic spirits will cause the tortoise and the fish to increase greatly, and there will be food in plenty."

Within a few hours they caught several tortoise. There were many fish in the water, some large and fat, but they swam swiftly and escaped the spear of Galbarimun. Laindjung did not spear the fish, for they were of his own totem.

After a while, Laindjung said, "I shall show you how to make a fish trap so you can catch many fish." At the mouth of the pool, where it narrowed to run into the river, the spirit man drove sticks into the river bottom to form a fence, leaving an opening in the center where the deepest water flowed. Then he wove branches and leaves into the fence until it was tight. Together, Laindjung, Galbarimun, and Neiri made a paperbark raft, which Laindjung submerged with stones across the opening of the fence so that its top was barely below the surface of the water.

"Now we will drive the fish onto the paperbark," said Laindjung. The three took pandanus branches and, starting from one end of the pool, beat the water vigorously to drive the fish before them. The fish fled toward the mouth of the pool, encountered the raft, and attempted to jump over it. But most failed to get across, and soon a harvest of fish lay thrashing on top of the raft.

The delighted couple thanked Laindjung warmly as they gathered the fish. Laindjung pulled out one of the stakes, the *golertji,* saying, "This also shall be a sacred totem to you. You shall pass it on to your children, along with this song, so they shall know how to catch fish in the river." And then Laindjung taught them a song that tells of the making of a fish trap from *golertji* stakes.

Laden with food, the three returned to camp. Shouts of welcome greeted them, and soon the smell of broiled fish and tortoise rose from the camp fires. Only Muru and his friends were dissatisfied. "We have fish and tortoise, but no kangaroo or wallaby," Muru growled. "A man needs red meat to remain strong." However, he ate heartily with his friends, even though it was clear he would not be pleased.

The moon died and was born again. As Laindjung promised, the tortoise increased in the river shallows and the fish became even more plentiful. And now the people could catch them. The children grew plump, their voices ringing out happily as they played. The grateful people brought gifts to Laindjung so he would know he was welcome. Only Muru and two friends held aloof, angry at Laindjung's success.

Now that he had won the confidence of the people, Laindjung taught them many things: He gave them the sacred totems and told them how to protect these *rangga;* he showed them how to perform the sacred ceremonies, the songs, and dances to call up the power of the spirits and cause food to be plentiful; he told them how to live peacefully together and how to settle quarrels when they arose. And so the people came to admire Laindjung greatly.

But it was not so with Muru and his two friends. The more Laindjung was honored, the more bitter and frustrated they became. "He is not as powerful as Manjili the magician," scoffed Muru. "He deceives the people with his tricks."

The wind changed to the northwest, bringing banks of dark clouds. From them fell the rain, spilling over the cliffs and flooding the river. The land teemed with kangaroo and the rivers with fish, which the people caught easily with the traps Laindjung had taught them to make. "Laindjung is a good man. He has brought food," they said to one another. To honor him, they held an initiation ceremony in which the men painted Laindjung's honeycomb design on the backs and chests of the boys who were to be circumcised. "This shall be a sign for our young men, so they will remember the wise words of Laindjung," they said.

But Muru closed his ears to the accounts of Laindjung's deeds. When the other men of his age group met to take counsel with the good man, he found reason to set off on hunting trips.

Muru's mind darkened with hatred and his tongue injected poison into the minds of his friends like the fangs of a brown snake. When the sun came out and the land steamed, he sat with his friends in the shade of a gum tree and said, "We will lie in wait on the path he follows to the pool. When he comes, we will spear him."

The next day, as the Sun Woman climbed high in the Sky World and the heat became oppressive, the people slept or sat talking in the shade. Laindjung set off down the path to the sacred pool, Gululdji, where he often went to talk with the barramundi, the tortoise, and the frog. Seeing him depart, Muru and his two companions quickly ran ahead and lay in ambush.

Muru hid in a tree beside the trail, his short stabbing spear in his hands, his tongue dry with hatred. When Laindjung walked by, Muru drove his spear into the good man's back. Laindjung staggered and fell to his knees. Now the others drew back their spears and let them fly with deadly aim. Though sorely wounded and heavily bleeding, Laindjung tried to fight back. But again and again his enemies speared him. He staggered backward until, step-by-step, he came to the banks of the pool. There, with a great shout, he leaped into the water.

And so Laindjung returned to the cool depths from which he had come. The cool water softened the bite of the spears bristling from his body. The cool water drank the blood that poured from his wounds.

Thinking they had killed him, Muru and his friends congratulated each other. They carefully covered the blood of Laindjung that had spilled on the ground, for they did not want the people to know of their deed. Then they returned to camp.

But Laindjung was not dead. Down through the waters of Gululdji he sank, down to the bottom, where the cool water eased his pain. The tortoise swam from the warm shallows to where he lay. From the reeds by the bank the frog dove down through the water to his wounded friend. From all sides came the barramundi fish to nibble at the spears that lodged in Laindjung's body.

Laindjung called upon his powers to dislodge the spears and pressed upon the wounds to stanch the flow of blood. He rested then, waiting for his wounds to heal. After several days, his strength returned and he spoke. "The man Laindjung is dead, speared by his enemies. But I am a spirit; I cannot die. I shall return and help my people live in peace."

So saying, Laindjung changed himself into another man, calling himself Banaidja, son of Laindjung. His face was wise and kind, his eyes sad, his glance strong. In the early light of day, Banaidja rose

The Laindjung Story
by Biragidji. At the bottom Laindjung rests after being speared by his enemies; at the top, he emerges from the water hole as Banaidja, with the sacred designs on his body.

through the waters of Gululdji and walked to shore, sacred designs gleaming on his body in the sunlight. As he made his way through the swampy ground up the trail to the camp, a·flight of white cockatoos rose from the grass. The sun caught and held the flaming red of the water lilies.

Galbarimun and Neiri were preparing for the day, and the aroma of their broiling fish filled the air. They had missed Laindjung, but had accepted his absence, assuming he had gone to another place. Banaidja walked noisily to attract their attention. Galbarimun looked up at the approach of the stranger and immediately noticed the honeycomb design on the man's body.

"I see your face," he said. "You bear the totem of Laindjung."

"I am Banaidja, son of Laindjung," replied the stranger.

And so they welcomed him, offering yam bread, honey, and fish. Soon others heard of Banaidja's arrival and they crowded in from all parts of the camp. Only Muru refused, saying, "The son of Laindjung comes to cause us trouble, as did his father." To his friends he muttered, "We will spear him, as we speared Laindjung."

Banaidja reminded the people of the lessons his father had taught, and many new things he taught them: how to soak the bitter yams in water so the taste would leach out; how to take a digging stick, sharpen it on both ends, and use it to pry sheets of bark from the paperbark tree; how to make huts from the bark to keep out the rain. Much good Banaidja brought to the people.

Muru waited. He spoke against Banaidja, but once again the people would not listen. Muru waited. He traded a wallaby for flint spearheads and he made new spears. And he waited. He fashioned a club from a tree root; he sharpened his throwing stick. And he waited.

He talked to his friends. "This man is worse than Laindjung," he said. "He has made a charm so the women follow him as the eye of a snake follows a bird. He must die."

Now the flowers hung from the gum trees like white bells, and the magpie geese flocked to the drying swamps until the shores became a ribbon of black and white. One day, in the time when the wind of the monsoon was soft, Banaidja left camp and walked down the path toward Gululdji. Muru motioned to his friends and quickly gathered up his spears.

The white cockatoos rose shrieking from the grass and the water lilies glowed flame red in the sun as Banaidja made his way down the path toward Gululdji. Suddenly a spear was thrust mightily into his back, followed by a rain of spears, heaved from all sides with deadly accuracy. Spears flew and made their mark until shafts bristled from Banaidja's body like the spines of the echidna and blood flowed like streams. On the banks of Gululdji, Banaidja was dead.

Quickly, to hide their deed, Muru and his companions carried the body into the deep bush where mangrove roots twine like snakes. A white egret rose from the reeds with slow-beating wings. The red

Banaidja
by Libundja. Banaidja, the son of Laindjung, is shown with cicatrices on his chest and arms and the sacred design on his body. The Vandyke beard is typical of the central-region style for this figure.

shoulder of a parrot flashed against a ray of sunlight. In the darkness of the mangroves they laid him down and left him. "He will no longer trouble us," they said with satisfaction.

But Banaidja's spirit was the spirit of Laindjung and the spirit of the barramundi fish. His spirit had existed since time began and would live until sky and earth were no more. This spirit returned to the sacred pool, Gululdji, where it once again took the form of a barramundi and swam in the cool water.

The body of Banaidja died. But it did not disappear. It turned into a paperbark tree, sending roots down into the earth at the side of the sacred pool. There it grows to this day. When the people seek bark for their shelters, they sharpen their digging sticks on both ends and paint on them the sacred honeycomb design, as Banaidja taught them. When the men remove the bark from the gum tree, they see on its inner side a pattern of lines that resembles the honeycomb of Laindjung. When the people celebrate the memory of Laindjung and Banaidja, they take paperbark and tie it in bundles. Then they dance and beat the bark bundles until their sound is the sound of the barramundi fish that leaps high in the air and falls back in the water. When the people paint totemic designs given by Laindjung, they remember the words he spoke to their fathers in the creation time. The people hear and remember. They obey the words of Laindjung and his son, Banaidja. And they know the spirits of the good men still live in the sacred pool, Gululdji.

The Sisters and
the Snake:
The Wagilag Myth

The snake has been featured in mythology since earliest times. From the snakes depicted in the cave art of France and Spain to the snake in the Garden of Eden, it is a favorite of artists and storytellers. Both male and female, a symbol of procreation as well as fertility, the snake is an important religious object for most tribes of northern Australia. It appears as a Great Rainbow Snake in the myths of all the tribes except the Tiwi of Melville and Bathurst islands, and in the Wagilag myth, here recounted, it is known as Julunggul.

The Wagilag sisters are the most important legendary ancestors of *dua* moiety clans, both in the central region and in parts of the northeast. In this myth, the sisters flee after one commits incest. Carrying their babies, they reach the home of Julunggul, whose water hole the younger sister inadvertently profanes. Julunggul rises from the pool and vengefully swallows the women and children—a forbidden act, because they are of his own moiety. To make amends to the other totemic snakes, Julunggul reveals secret and powerful rituals.

Although the different versions of the Wagilag myth, which are full of detail, conflict at numerous points, there is substantial agreement on the broad, general theme. This I have tried to preserve by combining elements derived from both the central and northeast clans, and then adding cultural and geographic material to maintain a continuous narrative. The version of the myth given here was reviewed orally and checked by Djawa and several other clan leaders at Milingimbi.

IN THE DREAMTIME, in the country of the *Liagalawumiri* people, near the top of the Woolen River, was a water hole small but deep, whose waters flowed from huge caverns in the center of the earth. Rushes and reeds crowded its brim; trees and grass grew around it.

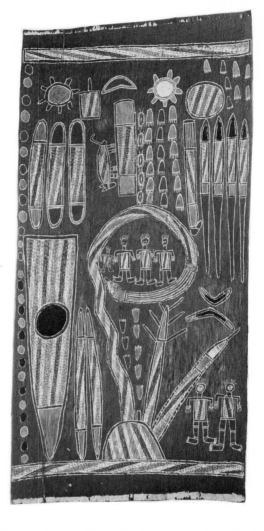

The Sacred Pool
*by Dawudi. The Rainbow Snake
encircles the sisters preparatory to
swallowing them.*

Here dwelt Julunggul, the Great Rainbow Snake. Both male and female, and most powerful of all spirits, this giant snake had created the world and everything in it.

Many spirits lived in the pool with Julunggul, where they swam about in the clear green water as tiny fish. At times they changed themselves into other forms: to bandicoots and opossums, to yams and water lilies. And they went forth to live upon the land. When these forms died or withered, the spirits that inhabited them returned to the water hole.

Occasionally the waters of the pool stirred and heaved as Julunggul rose from his coil in the black depths and reared into the sky. From his towering height the mighty python could see north to the islands of the sea and south across the bush to the great deserts. Tall in the sky, he called to the other totemic snakes and spoke with them, his voice echoing like thunder from the clouds.

People had not yet appeared in this country. On the coast, far to the east, a man named Ganjudingu had come with his two sisters in a canoe. From a place beyond the mists of the horizon they came, fleeing their own people, for the Djanggawul brother had committed incest with his sisters, an act that was forbidden by Julunggul. The Djanggawul sisters gave birth to many people, who became the clans on the coast. Some people traveled to the south, and now families began to appear along the Roper River.

Among these children of the Djanggawul that reached the Roper River were the two Wagilag sisters. Garangal was the name of the elder; Boaliri, of the younger. Although their form was human and they lived, talked, and bore children like women of today, the Wagilag sisters also had special powers. Both were strong and comely, with white teeth and ready smiles, and they wore girdles to hold their swelling breasts. From place to place they traveled with their people, Garangal carrying her son in a paperbark cradle and stopping from

The Wagilag Sisters
by Dawudi. The elder sister (left) and the younger sister (right), both with sacred caterpillar designs on their bodies.

time to time to suckle him at her breast. Finally the sisters came to a round hill, where they found every known kind of plant, animal, bird, insect, and reptile. The sisters camped there a long time, giving to the people of their clan the plants, animals, and other creatures that were to be their totems, and naming them with their sacred names.

One day Boaliri dove into the shallow waters of a pool to gather water-lily roots. Her skin gleamed in the sun. A man of her clan came by and stopped to watch. Finally he called her name. "Come, Boaliri, and talk with me," he said. The Wagilag sister hesitated. A man called a woman by name only if he had serious intentions, so she knew that he liked her and wanted to make a proposal. But they were of the same totem; to have relations would be incestuous. "I'm too busy," she called back.

"I will sing the magic song of love and you will have to come," he teased her and began to sing the words of longing. Boaliri smiled and came from the water, for in her heart she desired him. They went into the bush and tarried a long time.

Over many days they met secretly to avoid suspicion. Then the man left on a hunting trip. One day Boaliri came to the camp fire where her older sister was cooking yams. "I am with child and by a man of our totem," she confided. "The child is forbidden. Our clanspeople will surely kill me if they find out."

"We must go away at once," Garangal responded.

The two women began to collect their things: stone-tipped spears to kill game and stone blades to cut it up, sticks to dig roots and bulbs; dilly bags woven of pandanus fiber to carry their food. Then they set out, Garangal cradling her baby in his bark wrapping.

They walked northward, for to the south stretched vast deserts. This was new country where the sisters saw strange animals and birds. They gave each a name so it would have power and thus be as a sacred totem for their children.

Boaliri's child began to stir within her. One day while the sun was still high, at a place called Woimare, she stopped and built a small fire. Garangal understood something was about to happen, for only at nightfall did they usually stop to make a fire. "My womb opens," Boaliri said. "Soon the child will come out." She dug a hole in the ground with her stick. Over this she squatted while her sister massaged her neck and shoulders to ease the pains.

A baby girl was soon born. The mother cut the cord with a sharp stone and held the baby over the smoking fire so the moist skin would dry and the new spirit be sealed within until death. Since the navel cord had magic power, she wrapped it in paperbark and put it into her dilly bag. The next morning the sisters again set out, each carrying a baby wrapped in paperbark. Blood from Boaliri's afterbirth still flowed occasionally, but this did not delay the women for long. As they walked, they could see clouds floating high in the air on the northern horizon: They were approaching the coast.

The Yam Sticks
by Dawudi. The yam sticks carried in their travels by the Wagilag sisters.

Before long the country began to change. The dry plain gave way to clumps of trees that stood like islands in a waving sea of grass. As the sisters walked, threads of deeper green began to mark small streams. In the distance a flock of white egrets showed briefly against dark green mangroves. "We must be coming close to a water hole," said Boaliri. She shifted her baby in her arms, for she was tiring.

"Yes," said her sister and then fell silent until they entered a forest of tall eucalyptus. There she placed her baby under a tree. "Rest with the children, sister," Garangal said. "I will hunt food so we can camp at the water hole."

Garangal scouted the surrounding territory and soon caught a bandicoot in the deep grass. She hunted farther and caught an opossum. Then she unearthed some yams. When her dilly bag was full, she rejoined Boaliri. Together they proceeded toward the bright water they could now see gleaming through the trees.

As they approached, they saw a rainbow arch over the pool, its bright hues translucent in the sun. "This is a place where powerful spirits dwell," said Boaliri. She unwrapped the dried navel cord from its container, touched it to her own forehead and those of both infants, and then passed it to Garangal, saying, "Sing the power song with me, sister."

The Forked Stick
by Dawudi. The forked stick on which the Wagilag sisters placed a pole to build their bark shelter.

The Rainbow Serpent
by Midinari.

Rain and Water
*by Midinari. Another version of
the Wagilag myth, showing the
water hole, upper center, the billabongs that run into it, center,
the singing stick and rain, lower.*

In song they approached the pool, where many birds appeared to walk on the surface. "Is it magic that enables the little birds to walk on the water?" asked Boaliri.

But as they came closer, they saw that the birds perched not on the water, but on lily pads that grew beneath its surface. "The birds will be sacred totems to our children," Garangal decided, giving each a name. The pool also they named, calling it Mirarmina. The sisters set down their babies and proceeded to make camp beside the water. Garangal went off to cut poles and sheets of eucalyptus bark for a shelter, while Boaliri started a fire to cook their meal. When the fire was crackling, she fashioned a container from a piece of bark and walked to the pool for water. As she bent over to fill the container, some of her afterbirth blood flowed out and stained the water.

Soon all was ready, and Garangal put the bandicoot on the fire to cook. But to her amazement, the bandicoot leaped from the fire and scurried to the pool. With a shrill squeak, it jumped into the water and disappeared from sight.

"What has happened?" Boaliri cried.

"There is magic here, but I do not know what it is," Garangal answered.

Garangal placed the opossum on the fire and said, "We'll see what this does." As soon as it touched the embers, the opossum jumped up, ran to the water hole, and disappeared, just as the bandicoot had.

"Let's try a yam," Garangal said. "It cannot run away." But when she put one of the yams on the fire, its long, trailing roots stiffened into legs on which it scrambled to the pool and disappeared.

The sisters did not know that Mirarmina was the home of the mighty Julunggul and that Boaliri had profaned his sacred waters. On the bottom of the water hole, Julunggul stirred his great coils. Slowly he raised his head and sucked in a mouthful of the tainted water. The blood taste was strong. In mounting anger, Julunggul took a great gulp and spat it into the air. The sisters noticed the surface of the pool being sucked down. They watched fearfully as the spout of water shot into the sky. Soon a dark cloud formed, and a light rain began to fall. The moisture brought out other snakes from the holes where they had rested in the heat of day. Looking for food, many crawled on the ground near the sisters' camp. Darkness came quickly.

Now the sisters were very hungry. The babies cried for the breast. When the mothers finished nursing, it was too late to travel farther. "We had best try to sleep," advised Boaliri. "We will leave as soon as the morning light comes."

Garangal looked at the dark clouds overhead. "We must cover the babies carefully. I fear the rain will be heavy."

The sisters had no sooner closed their eyes than the storm broke. Floods of rain poured down, lightning crackled, thunder boomed. The shelter quickly flooded. "Sister, we must sing our power song to stop the rain," Garangal shouted over the noise. She stepped outside and began to dance and sing while Boaliri remained crouched over the two babies inside the shelter.

The rain eased a bit, but the lightning flickered back and forth, and came closer. Julunggul had lowered his head from the clouds, where he had been spitting out flashes of lightning, and drew near. Suddenly the lightning stopped; the Wagilag sisters saw above them the head of the great python, the coils of his body a huge mound in the dark.

"Sister, it is Julunggul, the sacred snake. He has come to eat us!" Garangal cried out. She began to dance more intensely than ever, loudly chanting the words of her magic song to keep the snake at bay. She heard him hiss in the darkness, but her songs had power. The snake came no closer.

In time the dancing exhausted Garangal and she called out, "Sister, take my place. I can dance no more for I am very tired."

They changed places, and as Boaliri danced, her blood again began to flow. Julunggul smelled it and moved forward, his head close to the ground, his tongue flickering. Terrified, Boaliri ran into the hut and huddled with her sister and the babies. Now Julunggul, his tail

The Great Serpent
by Midinari. The Great Rainbow Snake is shown in his home in the sacred water hole, Mirarmina.

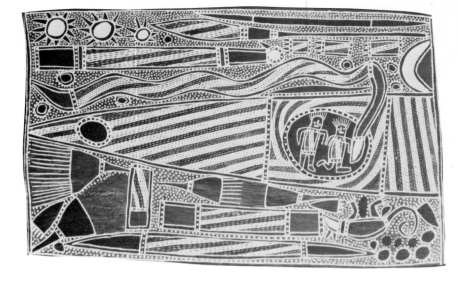

The Coming of the Sisters
*by Dardanga. The great Rainbow
Snake swallows the Wagilag sisters and their babies.*

The Great Python
*by Dawudi. A totem of the Rain-
bow Snake used in the Wagilag
ceremonies. The eggs from which
the people came are shown in the
snake's body.*

anchored in the pool, stretched and coiled his body around the shelter. Then he pushed his head through the opening. The sisters picked
up their singing sticks and began a new power song to repel him. The
snake heard the song and hesitated, for the words told him that the
women were of the same totem as himself. By his own decree, the
great snake was forbidden to eat of his own totem: The sisters were
taboo. But the smell of fresh blood was strong. The python opened his
mouth and sprayed saliva from his throat to make the skins of the
women and babies soft. Julunggul gulped down Garangal. He devoured Boaliri next. Then the two babies. It was done.

Uneasy that he had disobeyed his own rule, Julunggul reared his
immense body to the clouds. Several snakes who were the totemic ancestors of nearby clans had been wondering what had caused so much
noise and such a great storm. When they saw Julunggul stretch himself aloft, they, too, raised their bodies into the sky. All looked up at
Julunggul, for none was as tall as he.

"What have you been doing?" asked a rock python, his voice
echoing among the clouds.

"I cannot tell you," replied Julunggul, ashamed to admit he had
broken his own taboo.

"I have been eating a fish. Have *you* been eating something?" the
rock python persisted, volunteering this information in order to ob-
ligate Julunggul to reciprocate.

"Nothing important," answered Julunggul.

"Your voice is strong and pleasant to hear," a second python commented. "I have just eaten a wallaby. Maybe you will tell us what *you*
ate?"

This praise also set up an obligation so that Julunggul found it difficult to conceal what he had done.

"*I* ate a turtle," said a parrot snake, weaving his head back and forth. "I would like to know what *you* have eaten that is such a big secret."

"*I* have eaten a wallaby," said a fourth snake.

"And *I* have eaten some snails. Tell us what *you* have eaten," insisted a fifth snake.

Though greatly ashamed of what he had done, Julunggul was even more ashamed of his evasions. In embarrassment he raised his body high into the clouds until only the tip of his tail remained in the water hole. "I have done wrong," he admitted. "I ate the Wagilag sisters and their babies."

When they heard this, the other snakes drew back in astonishment, for Julunggul had broken his own law by eating people of his own totem. He looked from one brother snake to another. They stared back. Then Julunggul caused a great wind to arise as proof of his superior power. Still the snakes stared. Defeated and in humiliation, Julunggul plunged to earth. Like a giant tree his body crashed into the soft ground, gouging out a deep hole. There he lay, motionless and silent.

Soon Julunggul raised his head and looked at the other snakes who had clustered uneasily around him.

"I have done a great wrong," he repeated. "But I will try to make amends so this evil will not happen again. Therefore, I will reveal to you my most secret songs and dances. These you can teach to your people so they will follow the right way."

Julunggul produced his drone pipe, the *didjeridu*, and the song sticks. He taught the other snakes how to use them, how to keep time with the singing sticks, and how to conduct the dances and ceremonies that told the story of the Wagilag sisters. Taking some hollow logs, he stood them on end and painted each with sacred designs. Then he spoke these words:

"You shall teach the people to use the hollow log, in which they shall place the bones of those who die. And another log they shall use as the *ubar* drum. When they beat it they shall hear my voice. Still another log, *Badurru*, they shall make. It shall be a home for the spirits after they leave my sacred pool and are waiting to be born again of woman. So it shall be that the spirits will not wander about and bring harm to the people. Finally, you shall teach the old men to make the *didjeridu*. This is most important, for when the people blow it during the dance, it shall become my voice."

Julunggul sucked up a mouthful of water and sprayed it with great force into the air. Slowly he sank back to the bottom of Mirarmina, and a rainbow arched once again over the water, as it had been before.

The Didjeridu
by Midinari. The didjeridu *Julunggul taught the people to play. The snake is shown on the bottom of the drone pipe.*

The Snake Woman: The Ngalyod Myth

The Rainbow Snake is also the primal creator ancestor of the Gunwinggu tribe of western Arnhem Land. Here she assumes the form of a woman, Ngalyod, the Old Mother, who marries and has children, the predecessors of the Gunwinggu. Through precept and example, as well as by specific instructions, Ngalyod taught her people how to live. The Old Mother, as she is often known, traveled extensively throughout the Gunwinggu country, caring for her children, and the myths tell of many incidents in which she intervened to teach an appropriate lesson or to punish wrongdoing. The Gunwinggu dance, sing, and mime the story of these adventures in their ceremonies, so that all will remember what the Old Mother taught.

The Ngalyod story must be put together from a series of fragmentary episodes, which are all that remain today. Whether the myth ever had as much continuity as the Wagilag and Djanggawul legends, we do not know. The Ngalyod myth as given here was read to and checked by Silas Maralngurra, a leader of the Gunwinggu tribe, at Oenpelli. Ngalyod is also spelled Ngaljod with the "j" pronounced "y".

IN THE EARLIEST DAYS when time began, the sun brightened the earth and made it warm. Spirit beings lived then who sometimes transformed themselves into human form.

Chief among these spirits was the Great Rainbow Snake, Ngalyod, the Mother who created the world and who even today causes the plants and animals to multiply and the Gunwinggu women to bear many children. Sometimes, after the rain, you can see her arch her body and take on the colors of the rainbow where the water washes from sky to earth.

In the Dreamtime, Ngalyod turned herself into a woman called Waramurungundji and took Wuragog for her husband. The couple went from place to place in the Gunwinggu country, she carrying a digging stick and a net bag. Wuragog wished to have intercourse more often than Waramurungundji was willing, and they quarreled often about the matter. Finally, when Wuragog sought to lie with her, Waramurungundji turned herself into her snake form. However, Wuragog persisted, and from their union came the first people. The children grew quickly, and soon there were many camps of the Gunwinggu people. Waramurungundji continued to quarrel with Wuragog, but she cared for her children and tended to their needs even when they became men and women. "Be kind. Help one another," she told them as she traveled among their camps.

When drought came and her people hungered, Ngalyod sent food. When the water holes dried up, Ngalyod plunged her digging stick into the ground and spring water gushed forth. But this did not bring happiness to the people. They fought with one another, and the noise of their bickering was loud and unpleasant. Ngalyod heard and was concerned. "My children have not learned to live peacefully even though I have given them all they need," she said. She went to the camps to show them how to live together harmoniously. "I shall teach you songs and dances so that you may know how to live in peace," she told them. "You shall teach them to your children, and they also will know." So the people gathered and learned the sacred songs and rituals which their mother, Ngalyod, taught. But some quickly forgot her words.

Close by a tree-bordered lagoon lived an old man who had lost his wife. In the same camp lived a girl, his granddaughter, long of limb and firm-breasted. The old man hungered after her. One day he found a bee tree and brought back a bark container brimming with honey. "Come with me," he coaxed his grandchild. "You and I will eat the honey." They went into the bush, and the old man coaxed the girl into making love to him.

Ngalyod's anger was awakened, for this she had forbidden. She appeared to the old man in the form of the Rainbow Snake. "What you have done is bad," she rebuked him. "This place shall be taboo to you and to all men so that the people shall remember what I have said." So she drove him from that place.

The old man wandered about for many days. Finally, he encountered a group of people gathered to perform a sacred ceremony. The ritual was to last for a day and a night, so the people had caught many fish and cooked them in advance.

"These fish are sacred; they may be eaten only during the ceremony," the song leader announced.

The men danced the ritual dances, and the women sang the sacred songs far into the night. Their noise rose to a clamor. The mothers neglected to feed their children, who began to cry from hunger. Their

The First Mother, Waramurungundji
by Nguleingulei. The Great Rainbow Snake turned itself into the first woman and gave birth to the Gunwinggu people. She carried a digging stick and a bag in her hand and on her back.

Spirit Ancestor
by Jambalula. Ngalyod myth.

wails finally reached the hearing of Ngalyod. "This is not right," she decided and called to the people to moderate their noise and feed their children. But they paid no attention. The dancing quickened, the songs intensified.

A little orphan boy stood up and began to wander about the fire, sobbing from the pangs that gripped his empty stomach. Seeing the fish that had been prepared, he reached out for it. But one of the men caught his hand and pushed him aside, saying, "It is sacred. You may not eat it." All through the night and well into the morning the orphan cried.

Ngalyod saw the child's suffering, and her anger was great. She sent a flood to punish the people. The ground became soft and wet. The water rose higher and higher. The dancers stopped. The singers fell silent. The water became a flood. Some of the people climbed rocks, others trees, as they tried to escape. The old man scrambled up a tall ironwood tree and huddled in its highest branches. He continued to chant the sacred songs, trusting their power to arrest the flood.

Ngalyod came through the water to survey her handiwork. The old man broke off his song and clung close to the tree, hoping the great snake would not notice him. Just then a mosquito flew by and

The Mother Protector
by Nagurridjilmi. The Rainbow Snake protects a young orphan boy who has been denied food by the tribespeople.

began to buzz around his nose. The old man slapped at it as gently as he could, but even that small noise Ngalyod heard. She lifted her head and saw the old man. "You shall die, for you have done wrong," she pronounced and swallowed him.

Ngalyod, the Great Rainbow Snake, continued to travel across the country teaching her children. At one place, a river fell over a cliff and made a waterfall. A large pool had formed at the top where the people came to fish. Often an unwary fisherman would lose his footing on the steep banks of the pool and be carried over the falls to his death.

"My children must learn to avoid this place," Ngalyod said.

She went to the pool and swallowed the first fisherman she saw. Then she approached his companion and swallowed him. The third fisherman saw her coming and turned to flee.

"This place is forbidden to you and your people. You shall fish only at the stream below the falling water," called out Ngalyod after him.

From that time on, fishermen went to the stream below and never returned to the pool.

Ngalyod continued her travels among the camps of her children. At another place, two girls had gathered some round yams, *mangind-jak,* and had lit a fire to cook them. As they were slicing the yams, their brother stopped by.

"What are you doing?" he inquired.

"Cooking yams," they replied.

"I am hungry. I will share your yams," suggested the brother. He sat down and began to fondle one of the sisters. "Come into the bush with me," he invited.

The girl resisted. "I cannot. It is forbidden. You are my brother."

When he tried to force her, both sisters set upon him and beat him. "Let me be!" he cried at last. "I would do you no harm."

As soon as they released him, the infuriated brother ran to the pile of yams and urinated on them. "You are spoiling our food, brother," cried the girls. They picked up the yams and carried them to the stream to wash. But no matter how vigorously they scrubbed, the yams remained bitter and inedible.

The brother ran off into the bush, where he met Ngalyod. "Brother shall not lie with sister," she pronounced and promptly swallowed him.

Then Ngalyod returned to the sisters, who were still lamenting the loss of their yams. "Make a bag of reeds and place the yams in it. Put it in the quiet water by the side of the stream to soak. Tomorrow the bad taste will be gone." The sisters did as Ngalyod directed, and by morning the yams were once again sweet in the mouth.

Later, the sisters told their people what had happened. So well did they listen and remember that even today the story is repeated around Gunwinggu camp fires, and all know what their mother, Ngalyod, the Great Rainbow Snake, said and did in the Dreamtime.

The Death of the Father: The Kunmanggur Myth

In the northwest region of Port Keats, the Murinbata people tell of the Rainbow Snake who appeared in the form of the man Kunmanggur. Kunmanggur created the people and taught them how to live in peace. In this myth, Kunmanggur sends his two daughters on a trip. On the way their brother, Jinamin, forces one of them to commit incest with him. The sisters use magic to punish Jinamin, but he returns to camp and spears his father, Kunmanggur. Jinamin turns into a bat and Kunmanggur once again becomes the Great Rainbow Snake, who can be seen as one of the bands of color in the rainbow.

The Murinbata are unable to provide detailed accounts of the Kunmanggur myth; it is probable that much has been irretrievably lost. This version is based largely on information secured directly from tribesmen at Port Keats; also from published accounts of the Murinbata culture, the most complete of which is Stanner (1966) and from data that I have collected in conjunction with the bark paintings. I was fortunate to be able to discuss this myth with a number of the old men who have passed the initiatory and age-grading rites that entitle them to share in the lore and to read and check the version recounted here with one of the most knowledgeable, Harry Palada, of the Murinbata tribe.

IN THE DREAMTIME when the earth was young and people had not yet come to be, lived Kunmanggur, the first ancestor of the Murinbata people. Kunmanggur had the form of a python. His home was in a deep pool on top of the mountain, Wagura. By day he rose from the depths of the water hole and lay coiled in the sunshine, his scales glowing with all the colors of the rainbow.

Kunmanggur looked down from the mountaintop to the land that

The Sacred Mountain
*by Indji Tharwul. The water hole
on top of the mountain that was
the home of the Rainbow Snake.*

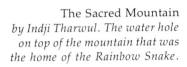

undulated green and brown to the sea. He saw there were no people. "I shall create men and women," he decided.

So Kunmanggur fashioned a *didjeridu*, which he called *maluk*, from a bamboo stalk and sang a song of power. Then he blew on the *didjeridu*. As the first resonant notes sounded, several flying foxes popped out of the *didjeridu* and flew off in a chorus of squeaks.

"I want to make people," said Kunmanggur. Again he blew, long and hard. This time a boy and girl emerged from the end of the *didjeridu*.

Now Kunmanggur was pleased. "I shall keep the *didjeridu*. It will bring much good," he said. He changed himself into a man and sat with the children on a rock that rose above the surface of the water hole. Swallows dipped and swooped in the sharp, clear air; a hawk poised on bent wing and hurled itself at a mouse; dragonflies darted back and forth in the sedge by the waterside.

And while these small events occurred, the two children grew to man and woman. Kunmanggur told them how to live in peace, then he sent them away to populate the land.

"I shall go live among the camps of my people," said Kunmanggur soon after, and he went to a place called Kimmul where the river brawls from the hills, levels through a plain, and flows quietly to the sea. Kunmanggur made camp near a grove of baobab trees, took a wife, and fathered two daughters and a son. The children were close in age, and they grew happily together until the boy passed the initiation ceremony and the swelling breasts of the girls marked their first blood.

The older girl, Biligmun, and the younger one, Ngolpi, were pleasant, attractive, and obedient. But their brother, Jinamin, had a headstrong nature that sometimes offended his father. So it was that Kunmanggur taught his daughters certain power songs with which they could work small magic—foretell the rain and summon small creatures like flies and wasps to do their bidding. But because his son displeased him, Kunmanggur taught Jinamin nothing.

The pubic hair had come to Biligmun and Ngolpi and their

breasts were large and full. The girls were ready for husbands. However, no suitable matches had been found, although from the time of their birth, as was the custom, Kunmanggur had urged their maternal uncles to betroth them. But a great plague had killed many men, and no young men in a marriageable relationship were available.

Jinamin, a year younger than his admiring sisters, was quick and alert. When he strode into camp with a wallaby over his shoulder, even the older women looked at him with desire. The pubic shield he wore indicated he had been circumcised. Still, he had not yet passed through the rites that qualified him to marry.

Jinamin and his two sisters were fond of each other. But now, when talking to them, he ceremoniously averted his face and eyes, for so he had been taught when he had entered the boys' camp to prepare for initiation. At times he still affectionately embraced his sisters, and they in turn often let their fingers linger softly on his arm when they talked to his averted face.

One day Jinamin came upon Biligmun picking figs among the mangrove trees. As she stretched to pull down a branch beyond her reach, Jinamin leaned over to help. Her body moved against his as she stepped back. In quick response, Jinamin put his arms around his sister and pressed her close.

"Come to the pool at the river and lie with me," he invited.

But Biligmun shook her head. "We are brother and sister; it is forbidden," she replied. "Our father will kill us if we disobey."

Jinamin walked away disconsolately. From the shade of the fig tree, *karrak,* the kookaburra or laughing jackass bird, cocked its head, eyed the youth and uttered a harsh, mocking cry. Jinamin winced, but his thoughts soon turned to Ngolpi, her swelling breasts and long, slender legs. He had seen her leave camp, and now he set off to find her.

"Your work is good," he said when he came upon her stripping sheets of bark from a paperbark tree. She placed more bark on the pile. "The bark is deep," Jinamin continued, sitting on a pile to test it. Ngolpi cut more bark and pushed Jinamin aside.

"I work and you rest. You could help me," said Ngolpi with irritation.

Jinamin caught her arm. "The bark is soft. Sit with me and try it," he replied and pulled her down beside him.

When his hand sought her breast, Ngolpi sprang up. "It is forbidden; you are my brother," she said.

"You have no husband and I no wife. Lie with me," urged Jinamin. But Ngolpi did not yield and drove Jinamin away.

At this time, the men were assembling spears, woven rope, and net baskets to carry for ceremonial exchange to the Fitzmaurice River, Djamanjung, which was several days distant. Frustrated and unhappy, Jinamin set off with the trading party. After some time, the sisters began to miss him, and they went to Kunmanggur for counsel.

The Rainbow Snake and Children *by Simon Ngumbe. Kunmanggur blows the first two children out of his drone pipe.*

"Father, we are sad," they explained. "We desire men but do not yet have husbands. What shall we do?"

"I have talked with the men of your mother's tribe," replied Kunmanggur, "and they seek husbands for you. But men in the proper relationship are few. It will take much time. To pass the days, journey to the land of your mother's people and take my greetings to them."

The sisters set out as their father advised. They followed the winding river, found groups of their kin, and visited with the women. For many days they traveled from camp to camp. Everywhere the suitable men were married, and their possessive wives hurried the comely sisters on their way.

Meanwhile, Jinamin had returned to the camp of his father and had learned of his sisters' departure. Again he grew restless. He thought of Biligmun and Ngolpi and the soft hair that grew to shield their places of pleasure.

"I go to visit our clanspeople," he told Kunmanggur. He tied an opossum band on his forehead and set out down the river, in the opposite direction from that which his sisters had taken. As soon as he was out of sight, he turned and swiftly followed the tracks of his sisters. As the blazing torch of the Sun Woman dropped toward the horizon, Jinamin killed a wallaby and began to look for a place to pass the night.

Nearby the two sisters had also stopped to make camp. Each stripped sheets of paperbark from the trees and placed them in a pile. Then they gathered firewood for the night.

"We will sleep here, sister," said Biligmun. "But now let us go find food."

While the girls were gone, Jinamin came upon their camping place. He saw the two piles of paperbark and the firewood stacked close by. Quickly, he put all the bark sheets in one pile, then removed his pubic covering and carefully pulled the bark over him until he was concealed. He poked a hole through the layers to breathe, then he waited.

When the sisters returned with fish for their supper, they immediately saw that the two piles of bark were now one. "The wind has blown our bark sheets together. We must sort them out," Biligmun said. They began to separate the sheets, but when they reached the last one, something began to move.

"Oh! There is something here," cried Ngolpi, backing away.

Jinamin leaped up and threw off the bark. "The trading party returned and our father sent me to find you," he said. "I will travel with you. Now let us share the wallaby I speared."

The sisters silently watched Jinamin clean the wallaby. "We will catch more fish while you make the fire," Biligmun finally announced and went with her sister to the river nearby.

"Jinamin intends to lie with us. What shall we do?" asked Ngolpi.

But Biligmun frowned and did not respond. They caught several fish and carried them back to the fire. Jinamin offered them the wallaby, but they refused the meat. "We will eat the fish," they said.

As the Sun Woman dropped below the horizon, Jinamin helped the sisters arrange their bark beds once again. "We will sleep here together," he said and went into the bush to relieve himself.

"It is not good for our brother to sleep here, for he means to lie with us," Biligmun whispered. But when Jinamin returned to camp he lay down between the sisters and prepared for sleep.

The night was filled with the laughing clamor of the kookaburras that congregated in the nearby bushes. When Biligmun stirred restlessly on her bark bed, Jinamin edged close to her and said, "Lie with me."

"I cannot, I am your sister," Biligmun replied.

Jinamin moved to the bark of the younger sister. "Lie with me," he again invited.

"I am too young; I cannot," came Ngolpi's reply.

Now Jinamin seized her roughly. "I will not hurt you," he said and forced himself upon her. Though she cried out in pain, Jinamin had his way.

The two sisters awoke to the racket of the kookaburras as soon as the morning star touched the treetops and in a few moments they were ready to leave. As Biligmun lifted her dilly bag over her shoulder, Jinamin sat up and yawned.

"There is no need to hurry. Tarry with me," he said.

The girls ignored him and quickly set off down the trail. "I will catch up with you," Jinamin called after them. He lit a fire and warmed the last of the wallaby meat for breakfast.

As they hurried away, Ngolpi said, "Sister, we must do something to stop him from following us."

Together they sang a magic song to call up a great cloud of wasps, which they sent to Jinamin, who had just left camp. The wasps settled upon his head, his neck, his shoulders, and began to bite. His face became puffy. His arms and legs reddened and swelled. But still Jinamin followed, the slits of his eyes bright with anger and desire.

"Hurry, sister! We must cross the river," cried Biligmun. When the girls reached the far bank, they waited for Jinamin to wade to midstream. "Come across quick," Biligmun called.

Then Biligmun sang a magic song to bring up the tide. The water rushed in, as Jinamin hurried forward, knocking him off his feet and carrying him away in its raging current.

Relieved, the sisters climbed a cliff that rose beside the river and stopped to rest. But when they looked down, they saw that Jinamin had been washed ashore and was now pulling himself onto the rocks.

"Sisters, help me!" he called.

They made a long rope of vines and lowered it over the cliff. "Climb up," they shouted.

Jinamin began to pull himself up with the rope. As he labored up the face of the cliff, he saw Ngolpi's pleasure place as she spread her legs to brace the rope. Jinamin became excited.

"Sister, tarry with me; we need not return yet," he shouted.

But Ngolpi, still in pain from the previous. night, became angry. She reached for a sharp stone that lay at her feet, severed the rope Jinamin was clutching, and watched in satisfaction as he crashed to the rocks below.

The sisters lost no time in returning to their father's camp and telling him all that had happened. "Jinamin did wrong," Kunmanggur said. "Now he is dead. He was your brother and we will forgive him."

But Jinamin had not died. Bruised and broken, he crawled to a hunter's camp at a place called Punyitti and after a time was healed. "I will return to my father," Jinamin decided. He took a sharp stone from the end of a spear and cut his face and chest so the blood flowed freely.

Jinamin returned to the camp of his father at Kimmul. His face was bloody and his body gashed and bruised. His spirit was filled with anger, for he had suffered much. Kunmanggur welcomed him, but gave him a stern warning to stay away from Biligmun and Ngolpi. At this, the son's anger grew, for he was determined to continue relations with his sisters.

To celebrate Jinamin's safe return, Kunmanggur arranged a great corroboree. Everyone danced and sang, while Kunmanggur played the *didjeridu, maluk,* and his daughters kept time with tapping sticks. Jinamin danced with the men. He danced the story of the water spirit and the man who fell in love with her. He danced close to the sisters and swung his hips provocatively. Kunmanggur observed Jinamin and blew hard on his drone pipe in warning.

"I'm going to kill him," Jinamin muttered, but he spoke in the language of his mother's people, the Jangman, which nobody else could understand.

"What did you say?" a woman asked.

"I'm thirsty, get me some water," Jinamin replied.

The woman brought a bark container of water to the edge of the crowd. When he went to drink, Jinamin took his spear and laid it on the ground.

The people danced and stamped. The dust rose. The shouting and singing grew to a din. Darkness fell. The people grew hungry. "Let us eat," they said.

Jinamin had not yet been able to approach Kunmanggur. "Let us dance the flying fox dance, the snake dance, and the fire dance; then we will eat," he called to his father over the heads of the dancers. To humor him, Kunmanggur agreed and began to blow the song of the flying fox on the *didjeridu.*

Now Jinamin danced toward his spear and began to push it over the ground with his toes. Gradually, he moved toward Kunmanggur.

"How many more dances?" asked Ngolpi.

"Two more," replied Kunmanggur.

"How many more dances?" inquired Biligmun.

"One," said the father.

Now Kunmanggur blew the melody for the last dance, the dance of fire. The singers' voices rose. The dancers' feet pounded the earth. The dust thickened in the firelight. Night fell.

Jinamin clutched the spear with his toes and lifted it to his hand as the dance reached its height. No one observed when Jinamin leaped from the shadows and thrust the spear with all his might into Kunmanggur's side. Blood spurted from the old man's wound and splashed down his legs. Kunmanggur uttered a great cry. He

The Speared One
by Rock Ngumbe. Kunmanggur
lies wounded, speared by his son,
Jinamin.

staggered. He lifted the *didjeridu, maluk,* that had brought good to the people; with his last strength he smashed it to the ground so it broke in two. Then Kunmanggur fell to the ground. Several men rushed forward. Quickly they broke off the point, removed the spear, and placed hot stones on the wound to stop the bleeding.

"Get the killer! Take revenge!" rose the cry as the men ran for their spears.

Now Jinamin feared for his life. With a thin, high shriek, he leaped into the night sky and was instantly transformed into a bat. To this day he has so remained, squeaking his fear and dismay through the night.

Though sorely wounded, Kunmanggur did not die. "I shall go among the people I have created, and once more I shall teach them to live in happiness and peace," he said. So Kunmanggur traveled among them. But his wound did not heal, though at each camp the people heated stones to stop the bleeding. Day by day the old man weakened. As his strength ebbed, he began to leave signs for the people. At a place called Miwa, he painted his marks upon the walls of a cave; at another place, he embedded the imprint of his foot in a large, flat stone. He taught his people many sacred songs but steadily he lost his strength, so that the strongest men had to give support to Kunmanggur's frail body as he walked.

At last, one day he wearily reached a place called Toitbur where the river forms a deep pool as it joins the sea. "Here I shall leave you," he said. "But with me I shall take the fire so that the people will know they have done wrong."

He lifted the fire stick from its embers and fixed it in his thick hair with the glowing end upright. Then he walked into the pool. The water rose to his waist, to his chest, to his chin. The water lapped at the fire stick.

"We shall lose the fire forever," cried a man called Kartpur in alarm. He jumped into the pool, snatched at the fire stick, and carried it to shore. There he set the grass ablaze so that fire would stay with them.

Kunmanggur disappeared beneath the surface of the water. Down he went, far down to the bottom. As he sank, the water welled up in great bubbles that expanded to the banks of the pool and broke. In the depths Kunmanggur transformed himself once again into the Rainbow Snake. Beside the deep pool where fresh and salt water meet, he fashioned stones in the shape of children and placed them upright in the shallow water near the banks. Thus he created all the spirit children, *ngaritj-ngaritj,* who became the ancestors of the people who live in that country.

Today, when the women hunger for children, they come to the pool of Kunmanggur. There they heat bushy twigs in a fire and strike them against the stone figures so that Kunmanggur will know their wombs ache with emptiness and will send them children.

The Speared One
by Rock Ngumbe.

The Old Woman: The Mudungkala Myth

The Tiwi tribe of Bathurst and Melville islands has been isolated until modern times from the mainland, which is about twenty-five miles distant. As a result, the Tiwi and their culture, mythology, and art developed separately. The mythical figures common to the mainland tribes are not found among them. Their creation story centers around a dimly recounted female figure, Mudungkala, who rose from the earth at the beginning, bringing the first people with her. Among her children—or at least among her early descendants—was the man, Purukapali, whose story forms the primary theme of much of the Tiwi *pukamani* ceremonies.

The identity of Mudungkala is not clear. An alternative name, Pukwi, is given to another female creator spirit who also is said to have formed the Tiwi and their country. I have used names largely from Charles P. Mountford's data. The piti piti, or Pita Pitui, are tiny spirits who enter a woman's body and cause her to become pregnant.

WHEN TIME BEGAN the earth was dark and cold. The mountains had not formed, neither the valleys nor the rivers. An empty sea left foam upon empty beaches. Above the earth the spirits of falling stars searched with blazing eyes for living things to devour. Beneath the earth stretched a vast cave divided by a deep valley and high hills. Here and there through this underworld wandered small groups of people.

Among them was an old woman, great in size, wrinkled, and worn with labor. Her name was Mudungkala, and on her back she carried her babies, two girls and a boy. One day she dug her way to the earth above. As she kneeled to rest, the children began to wail from hunger. Mudungkala had no milk. She looked about her for food and a place to lay her children. But there was nothing: no grass on which to lie, no water hole from which to drink, no forest in which to hunt game.

Mudungkala placed the babies in a string bag tied around her neck to protect them from the eyes of the devouring spirits of falling stars. Then she began to crawl north, her heavy body gouging a deep ditch in the earth, into which the sea rushed. She turned east, then south, and after a long time, Mudungkala reached the place where she had started. The sea closed in behind her and formed Melville Island.

Mudungkala crawled ashore and placed her children on the ground. "I will make grass for them to lie upon and trees and bushes for the wallabies to live in," she said. "I will form a rocky home for the snakes and the lizards. So shall my children have food." This she did. Then she created fish to swim in the sea and birds to fly above the earth. She made the heron and the magpie goose, the crocodile and the flying squirrel. In the ground she placed arrowroot.

The children must have light to know one another and to see the land on which they live, thought Mudungkala. So she called forth a woman from the world beneath the earth. In one of the woman's hands she placed a blazing torch and in the other a bark container filled with powdered red earth.

"You shall carry the torch across the sky to the western horizon," said Mudungkala. "You shall cast down light so my children can see one another and know warmth. When you reach the western horizon, you shall journey beneath the earth until you rise again from the east. So shall day and night, light and dark, warmth and cold come to pass."

Mudungkala shook some red earth powder from the bark bag. "Before you leave the upper world," she told the woman, "you shall throw this red powder into the air to signal my children to prepare for night. And in the morning, as you rise upon the earth, again shall you scatter the red dust, now to awaken my children with its soft glow."

So saying, Mudungkala disappeared, never to be seen again. Her two daughters, Paranala and Piangkala, and their brother, Purukapali, made their home in the new land, where they prospered for many seasons.

After much time had passed, Paranala became lonely, for each day she saw only her brother and sister. Her arms felt empty and her bosom ached. "I would have a child," she said to her sister, "so that its mouth might suckle my breast."

Piangkala also hungered for a child and replied, "What shall we do?"

They decided to seek the help of their brother. "I shall go search for children," Purukapali responded. Many days he searched, but he found no children. Then he noticed a small island offshore. When the tide was low he waded across and walked ashore. The first thing he

Purukapali and His Wife, Bima by Aurangnamirri. Bima stands on her husband's shoulders as they bathe in the sea during the early days of their marriage.

The Dragonfly
by Aurangnamirri. Mudungkala
created all the creatures of the
earth, including the dragonfly as
shown above.

saw was a man no higher than his hand who was standing on a rock watching him.

"I am Piti Piti, whom you seek," said the tiny man. "I shall change into a spirit and return with you to your home. There I will enter your sisters and become the children they seek. Whenever your people would have children, they shall call upon the piti pitis and our spirits will enter your women and be born as children."

And so it was. The sisters had many children who, in turn, had their own children. Purukapali married a young woman named Bima and they lived in contentment together. And all who were born grew to strength and happiness. None grew old and none died, none were ill and none maimed, for age, death, and sickness had not yet come to earth.

PART III
MYTHS OF
NATURAL FORCES

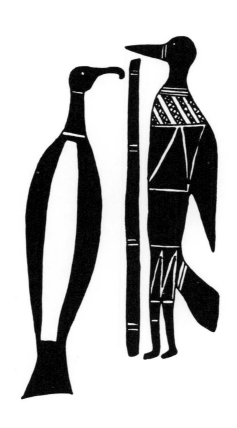

THE AUSTRALIAN ABORIGINES remained in the hunting and foraging stage of development until modern times. Inhospitable climate
and terrain, and the deficiency of cereal grains, discouraged even elementary attempts at farming. So it is that the attitudes of the hunter
pervade aboriginal thought and strongly influence many of the myths.

The lives of hunters and foragers are necessarily integrated with
the lives of the animals they hunt and the plants they gather for food.
Much like the wallaby or bandicoot, they make their beds in the open
or under a rock overhang. They pull fleshy bulbs and tubers from the
ground and gather berries and nuts from the bushes, eating them out
of hand as naturally as the opossum and kangaroo. No wonder, then,
that aborigines show a remarkable empathy with and an understanding of natural forces: they regard them as part of their own
world. Indeed, they easily visualize animals as people and people as
animals.

The aboriginal hunter was a keen observer of natural events. He
followed the course of the sun in the heavens and the waxing and
waning of the moon in the night skies. He identified the regular
course of the constellations and watched as meteors flashed across the
sky. The winds were especially important in northern Australia, for
the onset of the monsoon winds brought the rain and floods of the wet
season, whose plenty was followed by the drought of the dry season.

The aboriginal did not understand these forces, but like early men
everywhere, he sought to explain them with myths. Thus the sun was
a woman who carried a torch across the sky; the morning star was a
young girl who ventured over the waters of the sea to give light to her

friends; lightning was the flash of cliff-struck sparks from a spear thrown by a giant. These notions are not merely picturesque; within the framework of aboriginal culture, they are entirely logical and understandable.

The aborigines marked recurrent events on earth by the location of the sun, moon, or specific stars. Most important were the changing monsoonal winds that introduced the dry and wet seasons. Many aboriginal groups noted that their onset occurred when the constellation of Scorpio reached a particular position in the sky. In this way they learned to anticipate the changing of the seasons. Other important events, like the ripening of tubers and bulbs, the visits of the Malay trepangers, and the appearance of seasonal birds and game were noted to coincide with various positions of Orion, the Pleiades, and the Southern Cross. Thus the aborigines evolved a calendar based on natural time cycles. This method may be primitive compared to our more complex calendar, but it served aboriginal needs equally well.

The Constellation of Scorpio *by Lardjanga. The three stars are repeated in the three men at the camp fire and the two ibis and an opossum.*

How the Milky Way Was Created: The Catfish and Crow Myth

The Milky Way, the galaxy of stars and planets that spreads like a river of diffused light across the sky, was identified by the aborigines as a stream in the Sky World. Among the different clans the events that led to the creation of this river vary greatly. The following version centers on an adulterous act and the vengeance that followed. Here the formation of the Milky Way becomes a testimonial that wrongdoing brings evil in its train. Binyu is also spelled Binju.

THE MAN BINYU lived in his tribal territory near the place where the sea has eaten away the sand to form the long, folded bay we call Port Bradshaw. Binyu was not a man as we know today, for he lived in the Dreamtime, that time of the beginning of things when the Djanggawul brother and his two sisters came from the mists beyond the horizon, and when from their union were born the first people of the tribes. In that far time, when the hills and plains were new and the rivers had just begun to flow, from the south came the Wagilag sisters, naming the hills and streams, assigning territories to each of the clans, and bidding them to stay within their boundaries so there would be food for all.

Many things were the same in that time when our fathers' fathers first came to this country. Even as now, night followed day and the dry season the wet; men and women danced and ate and made love; children were born and old people died. But in those days also, many things were different. That was a time of great mysteries, when the totemic spirits could change into people, and people could transform themselves into emus, alligators, crows, or even rocks and trees. When the earth was new, spirit beings could move unseen through the air; they could travel to the underworld that lies deep and dark beneath the earth, or rise to the Sky World where the camp fires of the stars burn each night.

In this world of the first forefathers did Binyu live. He was broad of shoulder and quick of foot, with hands both swift and sure. Man he was and crow also, for he and all his people were descended from the crow spirit of the earliest Dreamtime. Sometimes Binyu flew among the treetops or stood in the river shoals spearing crawfish with his quick, darting beak. But he noticed the girls who went about their tasks in the camp; he saw their firm breasts and the soft curves of their thighs, and he changed from Binyu the crow into Binyu the man so he could walk beside the girl of his choice and tell her of the grassy glade by the river.

One day, the man Binyu stood in the shade of a milkwood tree near his camp and looked idly over the scrub pandanus that shimmered in the dry heat. As he watched a dingo run through the bush, he casually rubbed the weals of the ritual scars on his chest. Binyu had passed through the ceremony of the cutting of the scars shortly after his circumcision. The cuts had been filled with clay, and the ridges had healed in parallel lines across his chest. In this way he was marked as an initiated man, ready for marriage and qualified to participate in the sacred ceremonies, which were forbidden to the women and children.

Binyu's idle glance took in the distant clump of towering gum trees that marked the territorial boundary of his tribal brother, Moorka. Moorka belonged to a totem that traced its ancestry to the flying fox. He could become a flying fox at will, and when he died his spirit would unite with the fox's. Moorka had two young wives, sisters who belonged to the catfish totem. Their spirits came from the river, and there they could return as catfish if they wanted to.

As he gazed toward the gum trees, Binyu imagined Moorka's first wife, Bainan. She was tall and slender, her breasts pendulous with milk for the son she had borne some months before. But Binyu's mind lingered even more on the younger wife, whose name was Jalmar. No spirit had yet entered her womb; she was still childless. Binyu thought of Jalmar's rounded breasts and the curve of her thighs. Then he slapped his hand decisively against his chest.

"I will go visit my brother and take meat to him, for we have more than we need," he said to himself. He selected a plump, unskinned wallaby from the morning's catch, slung it over his shoulder, took up his spear, and set off.

Binyu arrived at his tribal brother's camp just as Moorka was beginning supper at the fire with his two wives. The moment he caught sight of the group, Binyu shuffled his feet noisily and walked slowly, for if a man wished to avoid a sudden spearing, he did not burst in unannounced upon people, not even kinfolk. The younger

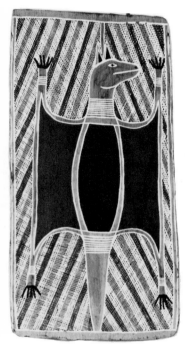

The Flying Fox
by Wululu. Moorka belonged to the flying fox totem.

wife, Jalmar, looked up and saw Binyu. She touched her husband's elbow.

Moorka glanced up and, seeing Binyu, called out, "Your features are pleasant and good to look upon. Come eat with us, my brother." Binyu placed the wallaby he had brought near a stump where Moorka skinned his game. Then he joined the group at the fire.

"Your hunting has been good," said Moorka. "Today I have not succeeded as you have. But the kangaroo will come out to feed when Walu, the Sun Woman, disappears, and soon I shall try again. Maybe you will join me?"

Binyu politely shook his head. "Let the kangaroo fall to your spear, brother," he replied, studiously avoiding the smiles of the women as he ate. Jalmar busied herself at the fire; Bainan tended her baby in his paperbark crib. But Binyu was quick to catch the sidelong glances of them both. From his acquaintance with them before their marriage, Binyu knew the women's interest in him was more than sisterly. This thought filled him with pleasure.

Bainan left her baby and brought a bark container of water, which she set before Binyu. "Drink," she said, brushing her arm against him as she turned away.

Jalmar brought a bark pan of honeycomb, tasty and sweet. "Eat, Binyu," she said, her hand lingering on his.

Soon Moorka took up a bundle of spears and left. Binyu sat by the fire and watched the women prepare for night. Much wood burned, and the flames were bright and hot. The image of Jalmar strong in his mind, Binyu remembered that when a man wanted to make magic so a woman would love him, he would sometimes sit thus and stare into a fire. Then he would call upon his totemic spirits to bring the woman he desired to him. As Binyu looked fixedly into the flames, he saw the bright eyes of Jalmar, her tilted breasts, and the curve of her buttocks.

But the vision clouded. Jalmar was the wife of Moorka, son of his uncle and his tribal brother. It was true that when a man traveled far, often a kinsman would offer his wife to the visitor. However, Binyu was unmarried and lived quite close, so he could not expect such courtesy. Moreover, there were two women at this camp fire, and Binyu could see that the eyes of Bainan were even brighter and more eager than those of Jalmar.

Jalmar came close and poked the flaming embers with her stick. "Wake up, Binyu," she teased. "Do you stare at the fire to make magic?"

Binyu started, irked that Jalmar had so quickly read his thoughts. He turned to look at Bainan, who had put her child to sleep and now approached the fire. "Yes," he replied, "I make magic so your sister will walk to the soft grass by the water hole and lie with me."

Bainan, hearing his banter, put her hand possessively on Binyu's arm and said, "The child sleeps. I am ready."

Dismayed at the turn his joke had taken, Binyu looked uncertainly at Jalmar, whom he really desired. Moorka's younger wife had heard: Her mouth turned hard, her eyes burned as bright as the flames, her fingers tightly gripped the fire stick as if to crush it.

"Come," urged Bainan, tugging at Binyu's arm. "Soon Moorka will return. My thighs are strong; they hunger for you. Come."

Trapped by his own words, Binyu reluctantly turned to follow Bainan. As the couple walked away from the fire, Jalmar suddenly let out a shriek and leaped at Binyu, jabbing and poking him with the flaming stick. Binyu threw up his arms to protect his face and stepped back. But he stepped too far; the fire log caught his heel. He tripped and fell across the flaming coals. As he reached out to catch himself, he seared his outflung hands in the embers. The smell of burned flesh was sharp in the air.

With a terrible howl, Binyu flung himself from the fire, pulled himself up, and lurched in agony toward the water hole. The air resounded with furious shouts as he fell in and thrashed about the shallows like a speared crocodile. Terrified, Jalmar and Bainan clung to each other and watched Binyu's desperate efforts. The baby awoke and began to cry loudly. Amid the din of wails and screams, Moorka ran into the camp.

"Binyu tripped and fell into the fire," Bainan shouted. "Help him."

Moorka hastened to help Binyu from the water and to support him as he staggered toward a paperbark pad. There he lay with clenched teeth. Moorka took some kangaroo fat and applied it to the burns. Silently and stoically Binyu endured the pain.

"What happened?" Moorka asked.

Bainan had prepared an answer. "Binyu tried to make love to Jalmar, but she resisted. He tripped and fell into the fire," she quickly responded.

Binyu painfully stood erect, his burned hands dangling at his sides and his eyes shining red in the firelight. Mute with rage and frustration, he glared at the sisters and then hobbled off into the darkness toward his own camp fire.

When Binyu reached camp, his condition was quickly noticed, and soon he had related his side of the story to the elders of the clan. The duplicity of the women grew in his telling, in proportion to his pain and frustration. His impassioned voice denounced the women: Moorka's wives had lured him on, he said. They had tricked him. They had lied about the incident to make him a fool.

The more he spoke, the greater seemed the injustice. Soon Binyu's kinsmen were as aggrieved as he. They gathered together and said, "We will seek revenge. We will kill the women."

The elders counseled with each other and agreed on a plan. One old man smoothed a place on the ground. He took a stick and drew figures of two women. Then he scraped some dead and scaling skin from Binyu's burns, mixed this with spittle, and placed a wad of the mixture over the heart of each figure. Because Binyu's hands were still raw and he could not carry his spears, the elders chose three men to go with him to Moorka's camp. While the old men sang magic songs, Binyu's companions repeatedly danced up to the two figures on the ground and thrust their spears into their hearts. "This is the way the women shall die," they shouted.

The vengeance party set out that night, traveling slowly so Binyu could keep pace. Soon Moorka's fire glowed dully in the darkness. Close by, in the windbreak, Moorka slept with Jalmar. On a pad at their feet stretched Bainan, the last light of the fire flickering on her face. At her side the baby, curled like an opossum, slept in his paperbark crib.

One of the avengers seized Moorka and pressed a spear against his throat so the captured man dare not move. The spears of the other two attackers thrust swiftly into Jalmar's heart. Just then Bainan rose in alarm and turned to her child, but the swift spears silenced her, too.

Moorka was allowed to live. Later, Binyu sat with him before the fire and told the story as it had happened to him. He had been shamed, he said, and so the women had to die. Moorka listened in silence and sorrow. Great anger burned in his heart, but he knew he could do nothing. To Binyu and his companions he said, "Come, you are hungry. We will share the food that remains."

The first rays of Barnumbir, the morning star, touched the treetops as they sat and ate. Binyu rose and carried a bark container to the water hole. As he bent over to fill the vessel, two catfish swam boldly from the sedge, approached the container, and nibbled at its edges. Binyu saw and became alarmed. He quickly retreated to the fire and told the others what had occurred.

"My wives were of the catfish totem," explained Moorka to Binyu. "Their spirits have returned to their home in the pool. Let them stay there in peace."

But shame and anger were still raw in Binyu's heart as he thought of the two dead women whose spirits swam in the pool. They were happy and free to enjoy themselves, more comfortable now than before. "It is not right," he said. "We killed the women, but they are not yet dead. Now I will make an end to them."

Binyu enlisted the help of his clansmen to build a fish trap, which they carefully positioned in the narrow mouth of the pool. Then the men waded into the pool and thrashed the water with branches to drive the fish before them into the trap. Binyu waited by a tree, his burned hands still tender. Suddenly he reached into the trap, scooped up the two catfish with his injured hands, and triumphantly shouted, "I caught them!" The men joined Binyu as he carried his catch to the fire, but the fish wriggled free and fell to the ground. There they flopped desperately, their gills working and their eyes open wide.

Moorka watched the gasping mouths of the fish and his heart filled with pity, for he remembered his wives, Jalmar and Bainan.

The Catfish
*by Malangi. Moorka's wives
turned into two catfish.*

Transformation of the Crow Man
*by Nanganaralil. A Dreamtime
spirit transforms himself into a
crow man, right, while the ibis and
spoonbill watch.*

Knowing the risk he was taking, he stood up and walked toward the fish, intending to carry them back to the pool.

"No!" shouted Binyu. He pushed Moorka aside and kicked the fish into the fire, where they began to sizzle.

Moorka picked up a spear and ran at Binyu, his eyes burning with hatred. Moorka thrust, and suddenly blood spurted from Binyu's chest. Binyu leaped once, his harsh scream tearing the air. But his knees buckled as they touched the ground, and he fell. Aghast, the kinsmen brought water in an effort to revive Binyu, but his spirit had already left his body. He was dead.

Sorrowfully, the people made ready for the funeral ceremonies. The men formed two lines and danced ritual dances to encourage the spirits of Binyu and the two women to return to their totemic water holes and not harm those they had left behind. A fire burned, dancing feet thudded against the earth, the cries of mourning were loud and shrill.

Then a crow with bright, beady eyes swooped down from the treetops and landed beside the fish, which had been removed from the fire and were now cooling on a stone. The clansmen watched this crow for none wished to confront it. They knew it was Binyu's spirit and feared the evil it might bring. As the crow began to peck at the fish, Moorka winced as though his own flesh were being devoured. Dancers' feet, singers' voices rose and fell through clouds of dust while the crow pecked on. Beak drummed against flesh until, suddenly, Moorka rushed at the bird. But the men pulled him back, and soon the bones of the catfish lay white and gleaming in the firelight.

Cawing hoarsely, the crow thrust its heavy body into the air and circled above the fire. Moorka watched the bird ascend, then suddenly dashed forward and seized the catfish bones.

"Take them!" he howled at the crow, throwing one bone after another high into the air toward the heavily flapping bird.

The clansmen watched in fear and amazement, for the bones did not fall back to earth. Instead, they continued to fly upwards, whirling end over end until they receded to faint points of light that finally disappeared in the darkness of the Sky World. The crow labored after the bones, its harsh voice cawing ever more faintly, until it, too, was lost in the night.

Thereafter, when the people look into the night sky, they see a black void. It is there, they say, that Binyu the crow roosts. Beside him spreads a broad swath of stars that are the catfish bones. The two women hover near, hungering for the lover they can never reach. When death comes, the people sing and dance the story of Binyu, and they remember that shame and anger burn even more than fire.

The Milky Way
by Mawulan. The stars of the Milky Way are the bones of the catfish Moorka threw into the sky; the black ribbon is a river.

The Wind Tree: The Barra Myth

The seasonal winds had a profound influence on the daily life of the aborigines. About December, the northwest monsoon swept in from the sea, bringing relief from the summer heat. Drenching rains fell intermittently until the land was awash with water. As the wet season became prolonged, the earth flooded, making traveling, hunting, and fishing difficult. Food became increasingly scarce. Fearing the rains might not cease, the aborigines called upon the spirits to bring back the sun and renew the hunt. By April, the retreating sun had allowed the land mass to cool, and the wind changed to the southeast.

As the southeast trade winds continued to blow, the land dried, vegetation sprang to life, and game became easily available. Ceremonies and rituals were conducted, and life was easy and pleasant until the dry season lengthened into drought. Then the blazing sun dried up the herbage and water holes, game migrated to more hospitable areas, and the land became dry and thirsty. Finally, the northwest wind once again brought welcome rain, completing the annual cycle.

The Groote Eylandters called the northwest wind Barra. The myth of this wind is the property of the Waningadarrbalangwa clan, but the rights of the story are shared with other clans.

DAY AFTER DAY the Sun Woman carried her fire across the sky. The land of the Waningadarrbalangwa people blackened. The spear grass in the swamps withered. The water of the Amakulu River meandered into threads among the rocks. The women held their children to slack breasts and waited in the shade of gum trees for the hunters to return with food.

"When will the rains come?" Dagiwa asked her mother-in-law.

Her husband, Galanga, had been gone for several days, vainly hunting wallaby and goanna. Dagiwa held her infant son in her arms. His protruding stomach barely moved as he panted softly in the heat.

"The Barra spirit, the spirit of the northwest wind, blows the clouds in from the sea," said the mother-in-law. "The clouds bring rain. But the Barra spirit hides; it comes when it pleases."

Dagiwa glanced at the trees; she looked at the rocky hills. "Where does the Barra spirit hide?" she asked. "If it sees how the child suffers, surely it will begin to blow and bring the rain."

"No one knows," replied the mother-in-law. "One day the wind blows, the clouds come in from the sea, and rain falls. Only this we know, not where the wind spirit has its home."

"My baby will die if the rain does not come," Dagiwa said. "Where may I seek the wind spirit that I may beg it to blow?"

"Go to *mabunda*, the hibiscus tree that is the totem of your mother, and ask its spirit to send the wind, that the rain may fall," replied the older woman.

So Dagiwa went to the place where *mabunda*, the hibiscus, grew beside a shaded lagoon. Dagiwa could hear the bees buzzing as they flew among the hibiscus blossoms. She stood beneath the tree and called upon the spirit for help. "Send Barra, the northwest wind, so the rains will come and we may have food. Help my child."

The leaves of the hibiscus rustled. "We cannot help, for the wind does not live with us," they murmured.

The yellow flowers that hung among the leaves nodded sadly. "We cannot help. You must go elsewhere," they agreed.

Dagiwa cried aloud in despair and turned away. The buzzing of the bees grew to a chorus that spoke to the young mother. "Go to the magician, Barunda," they told her. "Go to the clever man who makes magic."

Dagiwa did as the bees advised and sought out Barunda. "Help me find Barra, the spirit of the northwest wind, that I might ask it to blow and bring the rain," she begged.

But Barunda sorrowfully shook his head and said, "Each day I make my most powerful magic. Each day I call upon the wind spirit to blow. Each day I fail."

"My child is dying," replied Dagiwa, holding up her baby to him.

Barunda still shook his head. "I can do nothing," he repeated.

"Then tell me who can help," Dagiwa pleaded in anguish.

For a long time Barunda remained lost in thought. Finally he replied, "It is said that the night spirit, Wurramugwa, commands the winds; for always the winds begin to blow in the darkness. Go to the island of Maitjung which lies in the river, and there you will find the bloodwood tree, *undua*. Beside it juts a great rock that is the home of Wurramugwa." Barunda paused and then continued. "Go carefully, for there is much danger. Sit beneath the bloodwood tree and wait for darkness. Then light a fire and call upon the night spirit for help. Stay

The Wind Tree
*by Abadjera. The bloodwood tree
that is cut to release the wind is
shown repeated.*

always within the light cast by the fire, for if darkness surrounds you, the night spirit will kill you and your child. Then he will eat you both."

At this, Dagiwa tasted fear, for her people often told of the spirit with great sharp fangs. In the darkness, they said, Wurramugwa seized people and tore them apart with his teeth.

The baby cried weakly and Dagiwa put him to her breast. As the small mouth pulled, Dagiwa resolved to seek out Wurramugwa. Terrible though he was, he could save her child.

She set off toward the bloodwood tree that towered high on the small island in the river. Here the water ran deep and carried stinging jellyfish that paralyzed the flesh of their victims. Crocodiles also lurked in the deep pools, waiting to snatch the unwary. Tightly clasping her baby, Dagiwa waded into the water and made her way to the island and the great rock that was the night spirit's home. The branches of the bloodwood tree reached out over the river and cast a broad shadow in the fading sunlight. Weeping in fear and uncertainty, Dagiwa pulled herself up on a hummock. As she sat there gently rocking her child, the soft, new leaves of the bloodwood tree rustled, and their small voices filled the dusk.

"Do not cry," they whispered to Dagiwa. "Do not cry. All will be well, all will be well."

Dagiwa heard. She watched the shadows lengthen on the water. She felt a light breeze touch her face. She waited, but no help came.

Again her voice rose in wails. Now a small flock of plover flew to the grass beside the river, chirping as they settled down for night.

Darkness came. Dagiwa placed her son on the soft grass, lit a fire, and called upon the night spirit.

Fear was in her voice as she sang, "Cause the wind to blow, Wurramugwa. Cause the wind to blow so the rains will come and my child will live."

From the darkness beyond the fire came the harsh voice of Wurramugwa. "I can help. But first you must lie with me."

Dagiwa trembled. Her limbs shook. "I cannot. I lie only with Galanga, my husband."

"The baby will die. Come lie with me," urged the harsh voice from the darkness.

Just then the baby whimpered in his sleep, and his breath came quick and shallow. Hearing this, Dagiwa uttered a cry and stepped slightly away from the fire. The leaves of the bloodwood tree rustled anxiously.

"I will make the wind blow. I will save your child," promised the eager voice of the night spirit. Dagiwa heard his teeth grind; in bitter grief she took another step toward the darkness.

The long branches of the bloodwood tree tapped together urgently. The leaves cried out, "Do not go, do not go! We will help you."

The sound came to her like a sigh. Dagiwa stopped and turned.

"The Barra wind lives with us," said the tiny voices. "The great wind sleeps within our body." The branches crowded against each other; the leaves moaned softly. "You must cut into our trunk to free the Barra wind. It will hurt; we will bleed; but this you must do." The leaves fell silent and hung limply from their branches.

Wurramugwa shouted from the darkness, "They lie. Come with me if you would save your child."

Dagiwa hesitated and looked up at the leaves. "Trust us, trust us," they whispered.

Dagiwa glanced about. How could she cut through the tough wood of the tree?

"Galanga has returned. He has returned," said the leaves.

Dagiwa stared at the river. There lurked the crocodile and the deadly jellyfish. She stared beyond the firelight into the darkness. There waited Wurramugwa.

"Take fire and go," chorused the soft voices urgently.

Dagiwa pulled up tufts of thick grass and piled them on the fire. The smoke would help drive the evil spirit away. Then she picked up a flaming brand. Holding it in one hand and cradling her child in the other, she set off for camp.

To her joy, Galanga had indeed returned. Quickly she explained what had happened. Just as quickly, the men took up their stone axes and followed Dagiwa to the bloodwood tree. There they cut a great gash in its trunk. Red sap flowed like blood; the branches quivered; the leaves moaned painfully. The men danced and chanted:

We call Barra
We call the northwest wind
We call the wind spirit
We call the rain

The men danced around the tree, repeating the chant again and again. Soon a small gust of wind blew upon them. It freshened and strengthened. The bloodwood tree swayed. The leaves danced happily.

The next day the wind blew steadily from the northwest. Cloud banks appeared, and soon a constant rain began that filled the river and water holes, bringing back game that had fled far away.

Galanga took up his spear and his throwing stick and walked to the river. There he killed a crocodile and found a nest of turtle eggs. Everyone gathered for a great feast, Dagiwa had much milk, and her child grew strong and well.

Today the Waningadarrbalangwa call themselves "the Barra," that is, the people of the northwest wind. The bloodwood tree is sacred to them. Each year they gather before it, and as the sun sets, they cut a gash in its trunk. They sing the song of the wind so Barra will blow fresh and strong. And always the welcome rains soon follow.

The Wind Makers
by Abadjera. Tribesmen sing to encourage the northwest monsoon to blow and bring rain.

The Coming of Fire: The Goorda Myth

The aborigines probably knew about fire before they came to Australia, yet they retained a number of myths to account for this tremendously useful discovery. In addition to cooking his food and warming his body, fire served other important functions in the aborigine's life. In hunting, he set the grass aflame to drive game within reach of his spear. When he was injured, he or someone else cauterized the wound by the heat of fire and stanched the flow of blood by applying a heated stone. A woman in labor squatted over a small fire, whose heat facilitated childbirth. The newborn were passed through smoke to dry the mucus membrane and seal in the soul. Following circumcision, a boy stood over a fire so its smoke would heal him. The magician stared fixedly into a fire, like Binju at Moorka's camp, to pass into a trance. In this state he could communicate with the spirits and prevail upon them to carry out whatever tasks he set them. A person entering another clan's territory lit a fire and placed green branches ort it so the smoke would notify the owners of the territory that he was approaching on a peaceful mission.

The myths which explain the origin of fire often center around meteors that plunged to earth and set it ablaze. The Goorda myth of Arnhem Land is typical. Also known as Murriri, Goorda came to Arnhem Land to help the people but, instead, started a great bush fire that brought death and destruction. Some say that Goorda, or Murriri, came from Bralgu; some give his home as the Sky World.

LONG AGO GOORDA, the fire spirit, lived alone in the Sky World. His home was the constellation that we call the Southern Cross. There he had three camp fires, the Pointers, and he moved from one to the other as he hunted game. Goorda had many neighbors whose camp

The Fire Spirit
by Naridjin. The diamonds in the background represent fire, flame, and smoke.

Goorda Comes
*by Munggeraui. The fire spirit
leaps across the river to help the
people, but brings a fiery death to
them.*

fires flickered all around him. But they remained cold and distant; none came to Goorda's camp.

As time passed, Goorda said to himself, "It would be good if my neighbors came to see me." He stood and called loudly, "You are welcome at my fire. Come and share food with me. We will tell stories and sing together." But no one came.

Time passed. Goorda was lonely. One day he looked down at the earth and saw people hunting in the bush, walking together, and helping each other stalk game. He saw them splash and frolic in the water holes where they bathed. And he saw how they dug in the ground for bulbs and roots. "They enjoy being with each other," Goorda observed, and he called down to them, "Come, we will hunt together." Still no one came.

As Goorda continued to watch the earth people, he noticed that they ate the flesh of the goanna and kangaroo raw. "The people of earth have no fire to cook their food," he thought. When the sunlight faded and the shadows grew long the people began to huddle together for comfort from the cold. "They have no fire to warm themselves, while I have camp fires, but no one to share them," Goorda mused. "I will visit the earth people. I will bring them fire so they can cook their food. I will warm them at night."

Falling star spirits streaked across the sky through the upper world. From time to time they sped directly to the earth. Goorda remembered them now. "The falling star spirits come from Bralgu to visit the earth. Maybe I can go with one of them," he said to himself. When the next falling star shot by, Goorda called out, "Take me to earth with you." But the fiery star did not stop.

"I shall go myself," Goorda decided. He banked his camp fires so they would continue to burn during his absence, put on his waistband, and swiftly followed the course the meteor had taken toward earth. What looked like a flash of light speeding through the air was Goorda, the spirit of fire.

As he approached the earth, Goorda saw a group of people gathered on the banks of the Gainmaui River, near Caledon Bay. They had come to conduct a circumcision ceremony. Three men named Wirrili, Wueri, and Balangaltji were dancing. Other men were tapping their singing sticks and chanting. Nearby sat a group of boys waiting their turn to be circumcised and initiated.

"There are many people," thought Goorda. "I will go and make friends with them." He decided to land across the river from the people; this would show them he meant no harm. Just then, the three men ended their dance and knelt down so that their backs formed a single table. The first candidate for circumcision was being placed upon this table when Goorda reached the earth. "I am Goorda," he called to them across the river. "I can help you. Let me come to your camp."

But as soon as Goorda's feet touched the grass, it burst into flames. The people all stood up in wonder, for they had never before seen fire. The men crowded to the riverbanks in amazement, waving their spears. "They are welcoming me," thought Goorda with pleasure and cried, "I am coming." Catching the next gust of wind, he flew across the water and eagerly ran toward the people. Fire sprang up beneath his feet and flames leaped across the grass.

The people felt the heat of Goorda's coming. They panicked and turned to flee. "Wait!" shouted Goorda. "I mean you no harm." Even as he spoke, the flames spread wildly. Smoke, thick and blinding, mingled with the sparks and ashes that flew through the air.

The three dancers saw the fire coming. They fled to the river, jumped into a canoe, and paddled away as quickly as they could. They did not die.

The goanna saw the fire coming: "It eats everything. I must hide." He scampered into his hole, plugged the opening with dirt and there, in the cool earth, hid from Goorda. The goanna did not die.

Garwuli the spider saw the flames eating the grass and trees. Hur-

The Spider Man
by Munggeraui. The spider man hid from the fire in a cleft in the rocks.

The Spider Hides
*by Munggeraui. The spider makes
its home among the rocks.*

riedly he crawled into a deep cleft in the rocks and waited in the coolness. Garwuli did not die.

A man named Lualua felt Goorda's coming and saw smoke and flames all around him. He turned himself into a spider and, like Garwuli, crawled into a hole in the rocks. Lualua did not die.

The honeybees gathering pollen for their comb in the bee tree felt Goorda's hot breath. Swiftly they flew to a bee tree far away. The honeybees did not die.

The swifts circled high in the air above the sparks and smoke. There they caught insects which flew up to escape the fire. The swifts did not die.

But the boys who were to be circumcised crowded into the bark hut that the men had built for the ceremony. Goorda came close to speak with them, and the hut burst into flames. The boys wilted before Goorda's breath. They reddened. They blackened. They died.

Goorda raced here and there trying to approach the people. He ran toward the fathers who had come to circumcise their sons. They fled; they fell. He pursued the mothers and sisters. They burned also. He sought their kinfolk to reassure them. They, too, died at Goorda's coming.

The river began to steam. Black mud showed at the water's edge. The stingray fled in fear toward the sea. The shark dashed from one side of the river to the other, then sped away. The crocodile and barramundi swam in confused circles in the deep water.

All day the fire raged. When night came, Goorda looked around. Blackness and silence surrounded him. Little streams of smoke rose from the charred trees. The sweet, mournful cry of a curlew sounded from far off. A red-winged parrot flew heavily over the scorched earth, and finding no place to alight, squawked disconsolately and continued its slow-beating flight toward a distant belt of trees.

Goorda was tired and hungry. He looked about and saw the blackened body of a kangaroo that had been trapped in the fire. With a sigh, Goorda cut off a piece of the meat and sat down on a smoldering stump to eat. Almost at once, the stump burst into flames. Goorda chewed thoughtfully, then he said, "I must make friends with the earth people or after what I have done, they will never trust me." So Goorda changed himself into a spirit person and painted on his body a diamond design. "This design shall be my mark and I shall teach the people to use fire so they shall not fear me," he said.

The next morning a group of hunters came to explore the place of the great fire. Soon they came upon Goorda, who stood waiting and greeted them in a friendly manner. As they stopped, Goorda prodded the glowing embers of a stump with a stick. The stick burst into flame. Goorda raised it into the air and waved it, while the men watched the bright flame in wonder. "This is fire. It can help you," Goorda said.

Goorda picked up a piece of blackened meat, tore off a piece, and tasted it. "This is good!" he said, passing the meat to the men. They ate it cautiously at first but found it to their liking and were soon searching in the ashes for more, which they devoured with gusto.

Goorda then led the men away from the blackened area and showed them the secrets of fire. After clearing a space on the ground so the dry brush would not light, he took two sticks. By rapidly rotating one stick in a shallow depression that he cut in the other, he soon produced a glowing coal. "This is fire," he said. "Guard it carefully so it will serve you and not devour you." He then told them they might purposely set fire to the dry brush at certain times of the year so that the goanna and wallaby would be driven before the flames and easily fall to their spears.

"After the moon man has died once, new green shoots will appear among the ashes and the kangaroo and wallaby will come out to eat them," Goorda said. "Then you may spear them easily and food will be plentiful."

After the men had left, Goorda changed himself once again into the fire spirit and, with a great leap, returned to the Sky World. A trail of fire marked his path to the cold, empty plains of the Southern Cross, and soon his camp fires flickered again in the surrounding darkness.

The Circumcision Boys
by Munggeraui. The boys waiting to be circumcised in a ceremony are burned.

The Circumcision Boys Burn
by Munggeraui. Boys waiting to be circumcised are burned in the fire.

The Thunder Man: The Djambuwal Myth

Thunder and lightning are among the most dramatic natural occurrences. Primitive peoples in most cultures developed myths to account for them. The myth of the giant Djambuwal is told primarily in northeastern Arnhem Land by the people of the *dua* moiety. The myth accounts not only for thunder and lightning, but also for rainbows, meteors, and the water spouts that occasionally appear off the Arnhem Land coast.

The story of Djambuwal is of special interest because it is one of the few myths that incorporates information about the Makasan traders.

The Thunder Man
by Lardjanga. Djambuwal holds his great spear over his head and urinates to cause the waterspouts.

IN THE DREAMTIME, east of the Wessel Islands, lived the giant Djambuwal. Tall as a tree, his arms thick as their trunks, he stalked the length and breadth of his territory, jealously guarding its beaches, from which he drove trespassers with his great spear, Larrapan.

One day he sighted a Makasan *prau* offshore. He watched as it glided toward his island, its great square sail full in the breeze, the gulls wheeling and crying above its mast.

"Go away!" thundered Djambuwal, and he waved his spear, which made a bright path like a rainbow in the sky.

But the Makasans came on, riding hard the incoming tide to reach the shelter of the bay. Djambuwal urinated with full force into the sea to form waterspouts which whirled in the path of the *prau* and forced it to veer off. But as the spouts passed, the ship righted itself and came about. The sailors waved their swords and shouted threats from the deck. Angrily, Djambuwal waded into the sea to pull the boat ashore. In alarm, the Makasans attacked, cut off his hands, and beat a hasty retreat. But as the *prau* headed out to the open sea, Djambuwal's hands magically rejoined his arms and he pursued the intruders through the water, his strides throwing up great waves that rocked the *prau*. He seized the stern and began to drag it toward shore. To stop him, the sailors threw the anchor overboard but, seeing this maneuver had no effect, grabbed their oars and desperately began to row.

But Djambuwal pulled with such might that the boat lifted from the foaming water. The sea ran from its decks, and the barnacles on its hull shone white in the sun. Desperate now, the Makasans dropped their oars and furiously hacked at Djambuwal's forearms until his hold loosened and the boat crashed into the water. Djambuwal staggered; blood gushed from huge cuts in his forearms and flowed to red pools in the sea. Then Djambuwal took fresh hold on the plunging boat and again dragged it toward shore. Once more the sailors renewed their attack, and this time they cut off his forearms.

Djambuwal fell back in the water, but then, with a great shout, he summoned his magic powers and rejoined the severed arms. By now he had lost so much blood and was so weak and exhausted that he staggered to shore and lay down to rest. The Makasans took this opportunity to flee. The great sail of the *prau* filled and lifted the ship through the waters toward the horizon. But Djambuwal once more recovered, and with a final burst of strength seized the ship in his mighty hands and strove to drag it to shore. Grasping their swords, the sailors attacked in a howling mob. This time they hacked off Djambuwal's arms at the shoulders. The blood spurted in a red flood as the giant dragged himself through the water and onto the beach. As his strength waned, for the last time Djambuwal's great voice thundered through the air.

"Listen all! When I die, I will ascend to the sky. In every storm you will hear my voice."

Since that day, at the beginning of each wet season the giant Djambuwal stalks the beaches he loves so well. Every so often he picks up a handful of white stones and hurls them across the whitecaps toward the horizon. These build up to thunder clouds that float lower and lower as they move toward land. Then Djambuwal leaps into the sky and rends the air with a voice of thunder. As the storm breaks, he urinates mightily into the sea and waterspouts appear.

Djambuwal hurls his great spear, Larrapan, at the codfish coming in before the rain. A fiery shooting star marks its path as it flashes through the air. But sometimes he misses his mark, the spear glances off the rocky cliffs, and sparks fly off in flashes of lightning. Then Djambuwal mounts the clouds and releases into them spirit children called *djurtu*, who enter the raindrops, fall to the land, and there penetrate the foods eaten by the *dua* peoples to bring them strength and power. At times the giant shatters the rocks on the ground with his great club. Wherever the rock splinters land, yams grow; these the people use in their sacred ceremonies and eat for food.

Today, at the place where Djambuwal lived, channels in the face

Master of the Storms
by Lardjanga. Another version by a younger artist who had to secure permission from Biragidji, owner of the design and paint it differently.

of the cliff mark the path of his urine; on the shore lie black splinters of rock from the blow of his club. But neither man nor woman nor child comes here, for Djambuwal has declared it a sacred place where only he may walk and gather the white pebbles to toss toward the horizon.

The Thunder Man's Wife
*by Lardjanga. Djambuwal's wife
holds the clubs she strikes together
to cause the thunder.*

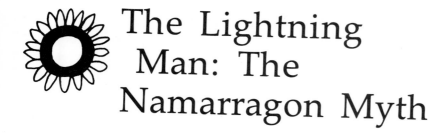 The Lightning Man: The Namarragon Myth

Lightning evoked myths among most primitive peoples. Lightning bolts are often thought of as fiery spears and the accompanying crash of thunder as the sound of a great hammer or ax striking the earth. The Arnhem Land tribes have many stories about the origin of lightning. The Namarragon myth, told by the Gunwinggu people of the western region, is an interesting contrast to the Djambuwal myth.

IN THE DREAMTIME, Namarragon, the Lightning Man, lived in the Sky World. In each hand he carried a spear of lightning and on knees and elbows he fastened stone clubs within easy reach for throwing. Most of the year Namarragon lurked far from sight in the reaches of the sky, where he basked in the beams of the Sun Woman, absorbing her radiance until he, too, shone like fire.

When the wet season came, Namarragon dropped down and rode the masses of clouds that moved from the sea toward the land. From this vantage point, he kept watch on the people below. When he saw a man and woman in adultery or brothers attacking one another in hot blood, the voice of Namarragon rolled in thunder across the sky. "Do no evil," he said.

But sometimes the people forgot. Then the voice of the Lightning Man would hiss and crackle and he would hurl his spear in a streak of fire across the sky. Sometimes it split a great tree, other times it shattered the ground. The people, seeing the warning, would grow fearful and cease to do evil. But occasionally a warning was not enough. Then Namarragon would aim his mighty ax at the guilty one, take aim, and strike him dead.

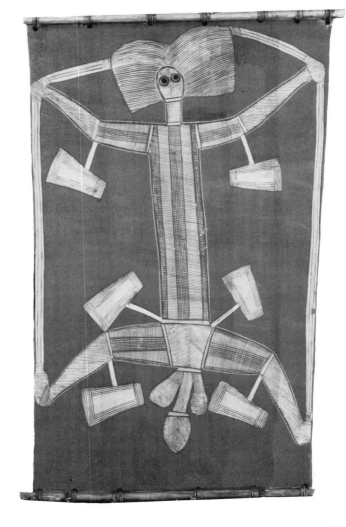

The Lightning Man
by Nameradji. The band surrounding the figure is the lightning; on his knees and elbows are the stone axes he throws to the ground. This painting is by a younger artist in a modernized style.

Among the Gunwinggu lived a medicine man, Marili. The people said he was a special friend of Namarragon, the Lightning Man, for at one time he was possessed by spirits that carried him into the Sky World. There Namarragon had greeted him and shown him a great magic, and from that time, Marili was able to call Namarragon to earth when he wished. Marili had found a hidden cave near the Gunwinggu camp. He took earth colors to his cave and over them sang the magic words Namarragon had taught him. With the colors he painted the figure of the Lightning Man on the wall of the cave; he painted the lightning bolts and the axes and with each line he chanted the magic words of Namarragon. The people knew of this; they whispered to one another and looked at Marili with respect. "Namarragon comes at the bidding of Marili. Marili has great power," they said. But Marili used his power only rarely, for he knew the sudden anger of the

Lightning Man and he feared to call him except when his need was very great.

Such a time soon came, for there was in the Gunwinggu country an old man called Namool, who was married to a young woman. Namool's beard was white, his limbs withered, his strength spent. He was beyond the years of satisfying his young wife. Namool slept so often alone that the young woman grew restless and began to look elsewhere for a man to share her bed. It was not long before the strength and vigor of the young hunter Manjuga filled her thoughts. And it was not long before the two were meeting secretly in the bush.

Namool knew. He knew and felt the weight of obligation to accost Manjuga and reprove him; but the fire had died in the old man, and when he went to Manjuga he growled with little conviction. However,

The Lightning Woman
by Anchor Barlbuwa. This is the traditional style found in the cave paintings.

other men of the camp knew of the affair between Manjuga and the wife of Namool. They came to the old man and began to taunt him. "You are weaker than a woman, for your wife cheats and you do nothing," they said, hoping to arouse him to revenge, for if Namool's wife went unpunished, their own women might do as she.

Again Namool bowed to custom and confronted his wife's lover. But Manjuga saw Namool's blunt spears, his broken club. The hunter threw back his head and laughed. Humiliation awakened Namool's slumbering anger. But he was shrewd in his age and weakness; patiently he waited and watched. He found the place where his wife and Manjuga met. He saw where their bodies had crumpled and twisted the grass. He took a handful of this grass and then another, and these he brought to the cave of Marili the medicine man, the cave where the figure of the Lightning Man was painted on the wall.

The medicine man took the grass and walked to the image of Namarragon. He began to sing. He sang a magic song. As he sang he folded and twisted the grass. He bent it this way and that, and he tied it with banyan string so that its form came to resemble the figure of Namarragon. He took twigs and pebbles and these he fashioned into axes, which he tied to the knees and shoulders of the figure. Into the figure the magician sang the spirit of Namarragon. Into the figure he sang the lightning bolt that kills. Into the twisted grass and string he sang the sheet lightning that blinds, the hiss and crackle of the voice of lightning.

As Marili sang for Namool, Namarragon, the Lightning Man, came. The air crackled when he came. The grass burned and the earth turned black. The magician sang words of power against the wife of Namool. He sang words of power against her lover. He sang words that called Namarragon to seek the woman and the hunter.

The Lightning Man searched the grassy banks of the water hole, and he looked in the hidden places of the bush where the couple often met. In these places he did not find them, for they had gone off to hunt. They had killed a wallaby; they had skinned it and lit a camp fire to cook it. Now the rich smell of roasting meat rose from the fire that the wife of Namool tended. It drifted past a bark container of water and a pile of water-lily bulbs and berries placed nearby. It drifted toward Manjuga as he lay on soft bark pads and waited for the food that Namool's wife prepared.

Here Namarragon found them. Like a great snake he came, snatching the stone ax from his right knee. A sheet of fire leaped from his hand and struck Manjuga in the head. His face blackened; his body burned. Namarragon unfastened the ax tied to his left knee. His voice crackled through the bush as a bolt of fire found its mark, cleaving the body of Namool's wife. Only the sizzling of the meat broke the silence that followed.

Though Namool is older and feebler than ever, the men of his camp taunt him no more.

PART IV

MYTHS OF
MEN AND WOMEN

RELATIONSHIPS among aboriginal men and women were often uneasy, just as in our own "modern" world. Myths played an important part in delineating the roles of each sex, for the behavior of the ancestral beings provided a model that was followed implicitly. Men were dominant because they had gained ascendancy in the earliest times; women were the childbearers because the Great Mother had so decreed.

Often the lessons of the myths applied impartially to men and women. They set forth the proper behavior for each during betrothal and marriage, admonished both to be faithful, and made clear that punishment followed incest and adultery. Sometimes, however, there is a female bias, as if the women were warning the men that their supremacy is still open to dispute; for example, a woman spirit dances her male antagonists to death and eats them.

Since men were the mythmakers, some stories view things from a distinctly male viewpoint. For example, they make clear what happens to wives who are quarrelsome or unwilling to have intercourse as frequently as their husbands desire.

The rules and standards of behavior were preserved and transmitted when the people sang and danced the myths before their camp fires. Here they brought to life an unseen world that was as real to them as the one they could see, taste, and feel. From the mythical heroes they learned how to behave in daily life. The lessons were not parental admonitions, but conclusions that all could draw from the mythical episodes.

So it was that young people readying themselves for initiation and elders participating in the age-grading rites shared common experiences that varied primarily in depth and intensity; each relived the experience of the first ancestors, and reinforced his learning in the process. Intuitively, it appears, these people used methods of experiential learning and behavioral conditioning that we look upon as modern educational discoveries.

The Lost Love:
The
Balada Myth

Among the aborigines, marriage was more than a convention for holding families together; it also was the basis for social organization, a means of uniting groups for hunting, ceremonies, and war, and it provided some guarantee that young men would be available to help protect and feed the old people.

Children in the proper kinship relationship were betrothed to each other from their earliest years. The boy's uncle and the girl's mother and maternal uncle usually assumed the responsibility of arranging their marriage according to the strict kinship rules governing conjugal alliances. The potential spouses had little choice.

Violation of the marriage taboos brought punishment or death, for it threatened the properly affianced relationships and, therefore, the kinship system itself. The Balada myth tells of a misalliance and the violent deaths that resulted.

BALADA lived high in the Arnhem Land escarpment. His camp was with his father and mother, but most of the time he roamed the high plateau, hunting wallaby and kangaroo. He came to know the rough, rocky country as well as the palm of his hand. He could find his way unerringly through the chasms that wound in and out; he knew the deep pools where the fish lurked. Many nights he made his bed on a heap of soft paperbark in the shelter of a boulder.

Balada was as much a part of his country as the trees or stones. When a hawk dropped like a spear through the bright air and bore aloft a goanna writhing in its talons, Balada was elated with the fierce triumph of the bird, but also his stomach shrank against his backbone, for he could feel the nails biting into his own vitals. When he saw the bee, Manjal, busily seeking nectar in the plum blossoms, he spoke to it softly. "Gather much honey, Manjal," he said, watching it wing heavily aloft, "for I shall share it with you soon." Then he followed the bee to its nest.

Balada's mother's brother, Awur, always had been as close to him as his own father. When Balada was a stripling, it was Awur who showed him the way through the winding crevasses and the great heaps of tumbled boulders that littered the escarpment. And it was Awur who one day took him to the Great Tree. In a hidden place far back in the hills, they came to a pleasant glade where a rivulet trickled among the rocks and the grass grew thickly. To one side, a black boulder loomed, its granite face split by a gum tree, gaunt and white, that towered against the sky.

Awur advanced with Balada until they stood before the tree. "I have brought the boy, Ngaba," he said. "Help and protect him."

Awur spoke to the tree as to his father, for in the Dreamtime his first ancestor had turned himself into the tree. "The Great Tree is sacred to you," he said to Balada, "for it is the spirit of your father and of his father before him."

They went forward and saw that a cave reached back to darkness among the boulders from which the Great Tree sprang. "Sit in the cave and let the spirit of the tree come to you," Awur said, leaving the boy to sit in the warm sun of the cave mouth.

Much later, when he returned silently to the glade, he was pleased that Balada still sat, a look of contentment on his face. "You have felt the spirit of the Great Tree," Awur said.

Now the time came for Balada to participate in the age-grading ceremony which would permit him to marry. Awur was to be Balada's sponsor. Daily the dark clouds massed on the horizon to signal the onset of the wet season; the time had come for Balada to enter the womb of the Mother in the *ubar* ceremonies that would bring him to manhood.

One night when the moon was full, his uncle hid with him in the bush, sitting silently in the darkness with two other initiates and their sponsors. Balada shivered in the warm night as he heard the tapping of a single pair of singing sticks. The spirit of the Mother was approaching the hollowed log that was also the *ubar* drum. Other sticks joined the tapping; then the high voices of the women caught the refrain in shrill jubilation: the Mother had entered the *ubar* log.

Awur touched Balada's shoulder. They rose from their hiding place and went with the others to where the fire gleamed through the pandanus. Balada listened in fear and respect as the old men chanted the secret myths. Always Awur sat comfortingly behind him, his voice in Balada's ear to instruct him, his fingers pressing the boy's arm to guide him. And when the Mother spoke with the terrifying voice of the bull-roarer, Awur covered Balada's testicles with his hand to protect his manhood.

The women stayed apart throughout the *ubar* rites, for its secrets were forbidden to them. Afterward, there was feasting and relaxation, and it was then that Balada first saw Waiula. She was among a group of women preparing special food for the initiates. He was taken by her bright eyes and flashing smile. As she handed him slices of yam to eat, his glance strayed to her long legs and the soft turn of her thigh.

He inquired of Awur, but his uncle shook his head. "Waiula is not for you," he said. "You are promised to Nama, who is in the proper relationship to you. You have taken gifts to her. You have shared meat with her father. She is your betrothed. You will marry her after you have seen the highest totems in the *mareiin* ceremony."

Balada said nothing. Nama was a short, heavy girl, pleasant and willing. But he felt no stir in his blood when she came close; his glance remained cool as he gazed upon her. Balada determined he would have Waiula, not Nama, as his wife.

When evening drew close, Balada waited until Waiula went to the lagoon to fetch water. He watched as a flock of heron flew in formation over the sword grass, then dipped in unison and coasted to their night perches in the mangroves. The birds were not frightened; probably the girl was alone. Balada quickly followed the path she had taken. Soon he saw her returning, heavily burdened with bark colanders of water. Balada ran forward and took the containers from her. "I will help you," he said.

In the morning he brought a choice portion of wallaby to the girl's camp fire and sat with her while she ate. But Balada's mother scolded him. "The girl is your kin. Stay away from her; she is forbidden to you."

Waiula took a bark basket and went to search for shellfish in the stream. Balada followed and soon he was kneeling beside her in the sun-dappled water, enjoying the touch of her shoulder and thigh as they bent to turn over the rocks under which crayfish hid. A glossy ibis, shimmering in its nuptial plumage, waded sedately in the shallows. Suddenly, its wings beat the air and, crying harshly, it labored above the trees. Awur appeared, a bundle of fish spears in his hand. He stopped as if surprised to see Balada and Waiula together, then came closer.

"Come help me fish," he called to Balada, reproving Waiula with his eyes. She rose and moved off down the stream. "Waiula is of your blood. You will cause great trouble if you pursue her," Awur advised. "Nama is betrothed to you. Give her your attentions."

But Balada had thoughts only for Waiula. The next morning the camp awoke to find the young couple gone. Waiula's father came to Awur. "There will be much trouble unless the girl returns. The women say Balada made magic to steal the girl. They say you did not try to prevent them from running away. The men take up their spears," he announced.

Awur sent out a party of men to find the couple. But Balada knew

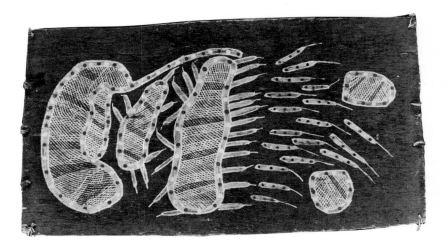

The Fight
by Balirlbalirl. The attackers at the right throw their spears at Balada, center, and Waiula behind him. The cave with the great tree reaching out is at the far left.

the rocky terrain so well that his trail was soon lost. By midday, two large groups of men had gathered and were shouting threats at one another. Occasionally, one man ran into the open space between the groups and brandished his spears, urging his companions to attack. In the background, the women added their screams to the melee.

Awur drew aside. "Soon much blood will be shed. Many will die," he said to himself. In his mind he saw the cave among the rocks from which the Great Tree grew. He remembered the trickling stream. He could see Balada sitting in the cave entrance, his face contented. Awur knew where Balada had gone with Waiula. He approached Waiula's father. "There will be no killing. I will lead you to Balada," he said.

Awur's people gathered and followed him down the ravine; Waiula's people banded together and walked behind. After much difficult travel, they came to the banks of the stream. Awur pointed, then held up his hand to indicate silence. Like shadows the two parties advanced through the trees. Like shadows the leaders came to the edge of the clearing. Like shadows they filtered through the heaps of boulders to the grassy glade that fronted the cave.

In the twilight of the cave a figure moved. Then a second. Balada came out, spear in hand. To his left stood Awur and a band of his kinfolk. At his right Waiula's father was ready, spear arm cocked. His kinsmen filed out of the trees behind him.

Whoosh. Thunk. Whoosh. Thunk. The spears flew through the air. Balada staggered and fell to his knees. *Whoosh. Thunk. Whoosh. Thunk.* Balada was dead. Awur watched in grief, his spear lax in his hand.

The shadow of the girl moved in the cave. The voices of Balada's kinfolk rose in grief and rage. Spears drew back. Arms flashed in the sunlight. *Whoosh. Thunk. Whoosh. Thunk.* Waiula screamed. Then all was silent.

Sorrowfully Awur and his people lifted the body of Balada. Sorrowfully they pulled out the spears, gathered paperbark, and carefully wrapped the dead man. Then they set out along the path to the sacred place, the *mareiin,* where the bodies of the deceased were placed. Behind them Waiula's people walked, bearing her wrapped body. Soon the women came from the camp, rending the air with wailing as they joined the line of mourners.

In the thin, clear air of the high plateau loom two rocks. Here once rested the bodies of Balada and Waiula, who turned to stone so that the people would forever know that evil befalls those who love unwisely.

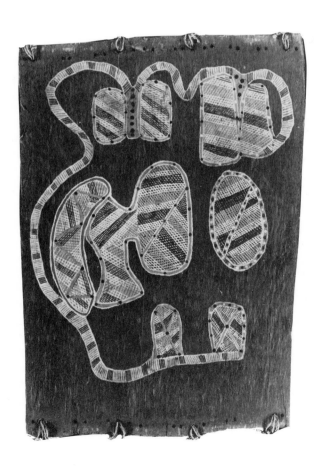

The Burial
by Balirlbalirl. The mourners carry the bodies of Balada and Waiula into the mountains for burial, following the snakelike trail.

The First Wife: The Dolphin Myth

In the Dreamtime, say the Wanungamulangwa people of Groote Eylandt, their earliest ancestors were the dolphins, the *indjebena*, who lived and raised their families in the deep waters between Chasm and Groote islands. In those days the earth was inhabited by spirit beings who had the form of animals, birds, and fish, and sometimes turned themselves into humans. It was they who became the first ancestors of the clans.

THE *indjebena* spirits enjoyed their lives as dolphins, carefree in the cool, clear depths. Schools of small fish that swam by could be easily snapped up for food. Huge strings of seaweed offered hiding places for the young dolphins, who swam in and out of its winding lanes. Often the dolphins swam up to the surface, where they delighted in the warm rays of the sun and the fresh breeze that blew foam from the waves. Repeatedly they thrust themselves into the air and dove back down, playing for hours in the sparkling sea.

The dolphins were fast and agile; they relished turning and twisting and chasing after one another, swimming far down in the green waters where the coral grew. There the shellfish, the bailer shells or *yakuna*, lived. They built strong shells within which they concealed their soft bodies. The *yakuna* had a muscular foot, which they thrust from their shells when they wanted to move about. Most of the time they fastened themselves to the coral to wait for prey. When a sea worm or small fish or a clam approached, the *yakuna* ate it with relish.

Dinginjabana was the leader of the dolphins. He was bold and strong, and the water churned to froth as he sped after small fish and snapped them up. On the contrary, his wife, Ganadja, was timid. The *yakuna* were her friends, and she often visited them to tell of the sun and waves and the things she saw on the land. The *yakuna* would thrust out their long feet and wave them to show their pleasure.

Ganadja greatly loved her husband and took pride in his speed and strength. But Dinginjabana scorned the *yakuna* because they could not move about like the dolphins. "Don't spend your time with the *yakuna* or you, too, will fasten yourself to the sea floor and become as they," he said to his mate. Then Dinginjabana would tease the *yakuna*, swimming close to them, swishing his powerful tail, and laughing as the sudden current made them clutch frantically at the rocks.

"The *yakuna* wish to be your friends," Ganadja objected. "Don't tease them, for they do not like it."

Although they waved affectionately to Ganadja when she came to visit them, the *yakuna* had no love for the male dolphins. These they would see swim by, chattering at a great rate. All the dolphins talked at once, and no one listened to the others. Hearing them, the *yakuna* would comment among themselves. "The *indjebena* have no sense at all," they would say loudly. "They talk all the time because they love the sound of their voices, not because they speak wisdom." Hearing them, the dolphins would simply toss their sleek heads.

One of the shellfish, named Baringgwa, was particularly loud in his criticism. "Here come the noisemakers," he would shout to a friend so that the dolphins would overhear.

"Yes," the friend would reply equally loudly, "we can hear their empty chatter as far as we can see them."

One day Dinginjabana decided to frighten Baringgwa. He swam up behind the *yakuna's* shell and bumped it hard enough with his nose to dislodge it. Baringgwa turned over helplessly. "Be quiet or I will toss you onto the land and leave you in the hot sun," the dolphin said to Baringgwa. The other *yakuna* heard and were greatly alarmed,

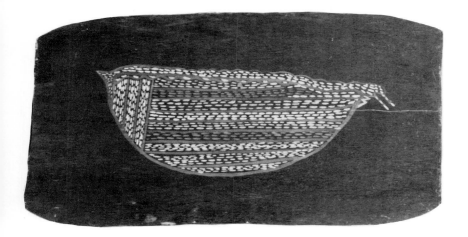

The Bailer Shellfish
by Bunaya. The bailer shellfish became angry when the dolphins teased them.

for they feared that the *indjebena* were swift and agile enough to carry out their threat.

"Don't take us away. We will be silent," they chorused. But their anger at Dinginjabana grew.

The more Dinginjabana teased the *yakuna*, the friendlier Ganadja became with them. She brought tidbits of food and dropped them within the *yakunas'* reach. She tried to reassure them, saying, "Dinginjabana means no harm." But the *yakuna* only waved their feet in reply.

Sometimes from the open sea came Mana the tiger shark, the enemy of the dolphins. Lean and powerful, with a row of sharp teeth in his underslung jaw, the shark would cruise like a black shadow among the coral beds until he could rush upon a careless *indjebena*, catch it in his jaws, and slash the life from it. In an effort to frighten off the dolphins, the *yakuna* often called out, "Mana the shark is close; go quickly or he will catch you!" But so frequently did the shellfish repeat this device that soon the dolphins made light of their warnings.

One day, when the fresh wind roughened the waters and the sun shone bright and warm, a school of dolphins cruised leisurely through the water. The mothers idly waved their fins as they suckled their young, while the male dolphins frisked among the waves. Soon the *indjebena* tired of their play.

"Let's go visit the *yakuna*," Dinginjabana suggested.

"Yes, we can play games with them," another said.

Ganadja overheard the plans and strongly objected. "Do not torment the *yakuna*; they are my friends." And she swam swiftly off to the coral beds to protect the shellfish.

But Dinginjabana was not to be foiled. "Let's knock one loose and threaten to leave it on the shore. We will bring it to the surface and then let it go," he said.

"Yes! Let's knock Baringgwa loose," they all chorused, swooping down through the green water. Ganadja tried to fend them off, but Dinginjabana made light of her opposition and would not let her interfere. Within a few minutes, Dinginjabana had dislodged Baringgwa from his hold on the rocks.

"Stop!" Baringgwa shouted in anger. "Let me be or I will call the sharks."

"Call away, foolish one," responded the dolphin as he balanced Baringgwa on his nose, then deftly caught him on his head and swam to the surface. The other dolphins streamed gleefully behind.

Before long, the *yakuna* was the object of a new game. One dolphin would catch Baringgwa on his nose, then toss him up and balance the shellfish on his head. Immediately another dolphin would rush in and scoop up Baringgwa, starting the process all over again.

Baringgwa was infuriated. "Let me go! Let me go!" he screamed. But his efforts were in vain; the dolphins only shouted and laughed the more as they dashed back and forth, sporting with Baringgwa.

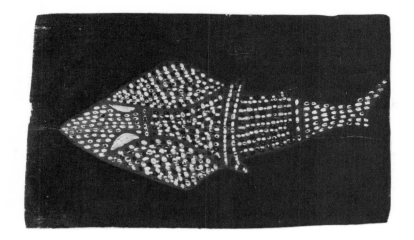

The Shark
*by Mini-Mini. The tiger shark that
attacked the dolphins.*

On the fringes of the crowd swam Ganadja, futilely protesting to
the other *indjebena*. Suddenly Baringgwa screamed. "The sharks are
coming! Swim for your life!"

"You can't fool us with that old trick," Dinginjabana sang out.

But a school of sharks had in truth heard the commotion of the
dolphins' game. First one black shadow sliced through the water, then
another and another. The clear green water clouded with blood as one
dolphin after another died. Sharp jaws sliced Dinginjabana in half; his
head and tail floated toward the surface as the shark made off with the
rest of his body in its jaws. Ganadja screamed in fear and dismay.
Frantically she tried to escape. But a black shark pursued her remorse-
lessly as she twisted and turned.

Baringgwa, floating down through the water, saw Ganadja's
plight. "Go to my brothers. They will help you," he called to Ganadja.

Ganadja fled desperately to the bottom of the sea where the *yakuna* lived. They made room for her among the coral and clustered
around so their heavy shells hid her from the sharks.

Thus was Ganadja saved. However, she missed Dinginjabana
sorely and in her grief sought comfort from her friends, the *yakuna*.
They counseled her, saying, "He has become one of the two-legged
creatures who walk upon the earth. He has become dry and hard. He
is no longer of the *indjebena*. Be patient and you will find another husband."

Ganadja could not be comforted; alone she roamed the waters.
Then, one night when the moon man had become great and round,
she swam close to the shore where Dinginjabana now lived in a new
form. The soft breeze carried the warm odor of earth to her. She heard
the hoot of an owl from a paperbark tree. Thrusting herself upon the
shore, she worked her way toward the dry sand with mighty heaves of
her flippers. At last, with a glad cry, she took the form of a woman
and stepped out upon the land to find her husband, Dinginjabana.

The Faithful Wife: The Tortoise Myth

Among the Australian aborigines, as in most primitive societies, the males were supreme. The myths constantly reiterated the theme of women's subjugation: They had lost the sacred totems and must obey their husbands. The overly possessive woman—a figure that appears briefly, but graphically, in the myths—also found disfavor.

Magic was used extensively among the aborigines. The medicine man, or clever man, exercised a special *mana,* or power, which he called up and caused to do his bidding. One of the medicine man's most potent techniques was to sing incantations that described in detail the event he wished to occur. This became a self-fulfilling prophecy: The anticipated event actually took place.

The figure of a person to be harmed or helped might be painted on bark, stone, or a cave wall; a wooden representation might be carved or painted. If the medicine man's intent were malevolent, he might thrust thorns into the image or whip it with banyan-root strings to cause the desired misfortune. He sometimes gained control over a person's spirit by overpowering him or her when asleep, then cutting into the body to obtain blood from the heart, which the aborigines believe is the source of life.

I have again drawn upon the lore that surrounds the practice of aboriginal magic to describe how a possessive wife turned her inattentive husband into a tortoise and then, in remorse, became one herself so that she could join him.

This myth, from the central region, provides an interesting comparison with the dolphin myth. Both deal with the same theme: the faithfulness of a wife to her husband.

LONG AGO on the mainland near the Crocodile Islands lived a woman named Barok. One day she went to the water hole of her clan at Kalabai to bathe and refresh herself. She had dug yams and picked berries all morning. Now she was hot and thirsty. The other women had not yet arrived, so Barok splashed and enjoyed her solitude in the warm shallows of the pool. Finally, she lay down to rest in the soft grass at the water's edge and dozed off.

Walu, the Sun Woman, had walked only a short way across the sky when Barok felt a soft touch on her leg. She stirred, sleepily opened her eyes, and saw a freshwater tortoise, its long neck outstretched, crawling up her leg. Barok lazily shook her limb, but the tortoise crawled on. She shook it again. This time the tortoise slipped, but it righted itself at once and headed back up her leg. She was about to dislodge it with a firm kick when her eyes widened with sudden understanding: Bornga, her husband, was of the tortoise totem. Surely this was the reason for her visitor and its unusual behavior. Carefully Barok lifted the tortoise from her leg and set it on the grass. Then she hurried to the camp to tell her husband what had happened.

Bornga thought on her words, then said: "We will have a child, for the tortoise spirit has entered your womb. We will call the child Minala, for that means tortoise."

As her husband predicted, Barok became big with child. When her time drew near, Bornga went to a place removed from the camp. There he made a shelter of paperbark sheets and piled up fire wood. Barok's mother came to stay with her daughter for the childbirth, bringing food, water, and soft paperbark pads. Three days later, a son was born. Barok dried him in the warmth of the camp fire and rubbed him gently with softest ashes to protect him from evil spirits. She put the navel cord in her dilly bag, for it contained the power of the tortoise spirit and was to be carefully guarded.

According to custom, Bornga could not approach his wife and child for several days. Barok gave one of her brothers the dilly bag containing the navel cord to take to Bornga. "Tell him the child has a long neck and a short foreskin. Truly he is Minala, the tortoise child."

As the tortoise spirit had commanded in the beginning, Bornga carefully sought out a paperbark tree near the water hole. He sang the sacred song of his clan as he cut down the tree with his stone ax, then removed a section of the trunk. From it he carved a figure of a tortoise, fashioning it with the ax and the edge of a mussel shell. With earth colors for paints and a chewed twig for a brush, Bornga carefully decorated the totem with a sacred design given by the tortoise spirit to his father and his father's father. He placed the totem on the ground and sang the power of the tortoise spirit into it, a song of the water hole that tells of the tortoise basking in the sun, its body warm in the soft mud. He sang of the little fish that frisk in the clear water, and of the tiny crayfish that burrow in the sand. As Bornga sang, the tortoise spirit entered the totem and brought power to it. Now Bornga chanted an invocation that the tortoise spirit's power might make Minala wise and strong.

The Tortoise Totem
by Djikalulu. Bornga carved a wooden figure of the tortoise and painted it.

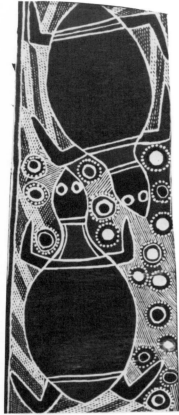

Tortoises in the Water
by Bininjuwi.

So it was that the tortoise child was born.

And the winds blew, clouds piled high on the horizon, and rain flushed the sky. Then Julunggul, the Great Rainbow Snake, showed himself in a multicolored arc against the sun, and the rains ceased. The land smiled. The young made love. Time flowed like water, and no one noted its passing. Minala grew.

When he was seven, the voice of the great snake again called from the clearing by the river. That year Minala was circumcised with the other boys of his age group. Shortly after he had healed and had returned to the camp, he departed with a band of men to learn the craft of stalking and killing the kangaroo. Upon his return he was met by his cousin Wimu, the daughter of his maternal uncle. She was a girl he had noted only casually in the past. Minala did not yet know that his father and his uncle had been discussing the two young people at length: The time had come for Minala to be betrothed.

Bornga called together the young couple. "Wimu will be your wife after her blood flows," he announced, and gave each a portion of kangaroo that had been roasted on the fire.

Wimu was shy, but her mind was made up: "I shall be a good wife," she promised Minala, and sat beside him while they ate their meat.

Minala was strong and swift. His eye was sure as he hunted the kangaroo and wallaby. Meat was always at his fire. He learned the sacred rituals. The raised scars on his chest marked the ceremonial cutting. He became a man.

Now Wimu's breasts began to swell. One day she retreated to the bark shelter in which unmarried girls pass the time of their first blood-flowing. When she returned to camp, her mother prepared the bridal camp fire, cut soft paperbark, and spread it for the nuptial bed. And so Wimu and Minala became man and wife.

Before long it became apparent that Wimu was very possessive of her husband. All the women were attracted to him, and the unmarried girls cast bold eyes in his direction. Since it was customary that a man have two or more wives, Minala clearly would not lack opportunity.

But Wimu was determined to keep Minala for herself. When women came to their fire, she drove them away. When they casually followed Minala into the bush, pretending to search for roots and bulbs, Wimu confronted them and said, "Seek another man. Minala is mine."

Everywhere Minala went, Wimu followed—even when he hunted. When Wimu set out to search for bulbs and roots, somehow her path always found Minala's. No matter where he went, she soon appeared.

Minala grew restless with his wife's possessiveness. Though he spoke sharply to her, she was not deterred. His anger toward Wimu increased: Was he not a man? Was it not right that he should satisfy other women who came to him like bees to honey? Why should one woman—particularly one who followed him everywhere like a

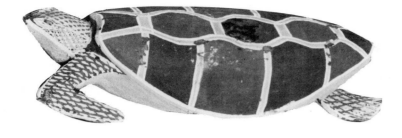

The Tortoise Totem
by Yuwati.

shadow—claim all his attention? "My wife loves me too much. She drives away other women who would also love me."

He thought long on the matter. Then he decided. "I shall make magic to turn my wife against me." This was a very strange thing to do; ordinarily men made magic to attract women, not to drive them away.

Minala knew he had to escape from Wimu long enough to place a magic spell on her. He sought out the song leader of his totem, an aged magician who knew how to invoke the power of the tortoise spirit, and told him his wish. Minala promised to bring choice portions of kangaroo if the magician would help him. Although the song leader was feeble with age, and this was a strange request, he agreed to help.

So it was that the song leader went to a cliff hidden in the jumbled hills that rose behind the camp. There he drew out a piece of bark on which was an old, faded painting that depicted a man turning into a tortoise. This figure represented the most distant ancestor of the clan. The song leader carefully repainted the figure so that its colors were fresh and its outline strong. When he finished, he sang a magic song and then made his way back to the camp. He called Minala to him and gave him instructions to transform Wimu into a tortoise. She would not be harmed, the magician told him. She would live peacefully in the river, where she would no longer bother him. He would be free to seek the arms of the girls who yearned for him.

The next morning Minala went into the bush as if to make water. As soon as he was out of sight, he circled the camp and made his way to the cliff face. There he sang the power song that the magician had taught him and directed him to repeat each day until Wimu had become a tortoise.

But Minala had reckoned without Wimu. As was her habit, she followed him and had seen him perform the magic. Barely had he completed his song and started back to camp than Wimu stole from the clump of trees where she had concealed herself. She went directly to the cliff face and spat on the tortoise figure that was propped against it. Then she gathered dry grass into a pad and urinated on it. She rubbed the pad over the freshly painted ochers, leaving the figure streaked and stained, its outline barely distinguishable.

That night Minala was unusually attentive to his wife. When the comely daughter of his brother brought a portion of game to the fire, he did not laugh and joke with her, or comment on her ripe breasts, as he usually did. When the couple finished eating and night fell, Minala did not suggest that they join one of the other groups to sing around their camp fire. Instead, he looked at Wimu and said, "Come lie with me."

The moon was born again. As it walked across the Sky World, the camp fires of the star people burned out and disappeared. Feeling something move against her leg, Wimu stirred in her sleep, awoke, and sat up. Minala was gone from her side! But the movement continued, and she heard a rustle in the paperbark bed. A long neck poked out from the sheets, followed by a round shell. A tortoise crawled from the bed and made its way through the grass toward the river.

Wimu rose and followed it to the bank, but it disappeared into

Tortoise in the Grass
by Libundja. The tortoise, Minala, moves through the grass to the river.

The Tortoises
by Daudaingalil. Minala awakens beside Wimu, his wife, who has also become a tortoise.

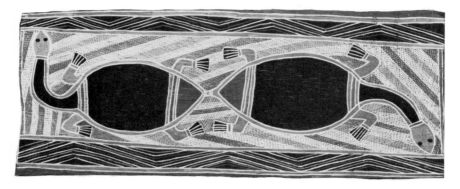

Tortoises Mating
*by Bininjuwi. Minala the tortoise
and his wife copulate beside the
river.*

the water. She stepped into the river as if to pursue it, then bent and
stroked the water where the tortoise had vanished. Slowly Wimu returned to her bed by the fire. In the dark night she clasped her arms
around her body and rocked back and forth as tears ran down her face.

Wimu knew that Minala had become a tortoise. It was her fault
because she had profaned his magic, and so it had turned against him.
Minala would now live in the reeds and sedge with his totemic kin.
He would lie in the mud by the river, where Wimu could never join
him.

Morning came. The people of the camp did not comment on Minala's absence, for they assumed he had gone hunting. Wimu rose and
walked to the river. She stared down at the water and the lilies that
grew in the shallows. But she did not see the tortoise. When the fire of
the Sun Woman began to heat the day, Wimu made her way to the
cliff, carrying a bark container filled with fresh water. Gently she lifted
the painting she had despoiled and washed off the smeared ochers so
only the faint outline of the figure beneath remained. Then she went
to her maternal uncle, who was also a song leader and a powerful
magician. "Minala my husband has been changed by magic into a tortoise. Uncle, help me to bring him back, for I miss him greatly."

"Minala is of the tortoise totem. He has returned to his ancestors.
There is no magic strong enough to bring him back," replied the
uncle.

"Then I must go to him. Make magic so that I, too, may become a
tortoise."

The uncle went to the cliff face, took the picture, and painted
afresh the figure of the human becoming a tortoise, but with one difference: now the body was round and full breasted. The uncle sang
the magic song, spoke the invocation, and returned to camp.

So it was that while Minala slept that afternoon on the bank of the
river, a second tortoise crawled through the grass and settled beside
him. The sun was hot. Insects flitted in the sedge. A stork poked in
the mud for food. In the warm, soft mud, Minala awoke and copulated
with Wimu the tortoise, who was his wife.

The Tempted One: The Mimi Myth

The Mimi were long, thin spirits who lived in the rocky fastness of the Arnhem Land plateau. They made their homes in caves and had wives and children. They hunted wallaby and kangaroo with spears and ate wild potatoes, yams, echidna, goanna, and other food. The Mimi were so light that a strong wind would blow them off the ground or even break their long, thin necks. If a Mimi saw a human approach, the spirit would split a boulder by blowing on it and pass through. Then he would blow again and the boulder would close behind him.

The aborigines of the western region believed that a Mimi would sometimes lure an unwary person to his cave among the rocks and there tempt the stranger to eat food or to have intercourse with a wife or daughter. If he succumbed, the visitor himself became a Mimi and could never return to human life.

The basic story of the myth was told to me by Sam Manggudja.

TALLER THAN human beings but thin and light as straws were the Mimi. They dwelt in secluded caves in Arnhem Land, among the rocks where the winds rarely penetrated, hunting wallaby and kangaroo in the hills and living much like the people they resembled.

In the Dreamtime, a hunter named Djala lived with his wife near the Mimi country. One day, when they were expecting their first child, Djala said, "I go to hunt the kangaroo so you and the child will have meat." Patting his wife's protruding stomach, he added, "You are hungry always, for you eat for two. I shall spear a large kangaroo."

"Return with haste, for soon my womb will open," replied the woman.

Djala set out and before long came upon the tracks of a large kangaroo. He hastened to follow the trail, for he hoped the game would fall to his spear before nightfall. The tracks led him deeper and deeper among the rocks.

In their camps the Mimi, too, were feeling the pangs of hunger, for none of the hunters had dared venture forth that day. They feared that the winds, which had blown steadily since morning, would hurl them through the air and dash them against the rocks if they left their caves. But at last, in the late afternoon, the wind had died. Kaman took up his spears and set off to hunt.

As the light began to fail, Kaman picked up the tracks of a large kangaroo and set out to pursue him. When the trail grew faint, he climbed upon a tall rock to scout the terrain. Ahead of him grazed the kangaroo. Without hesitating, the Mimi leaped from the rock and ran forward. The kangaroo lifted its head; the Mimi lifted his spear and let the weapon fly. The kangaroo bounded once, then fell dead to earth.

As the Mimi advanced to retrieve his game, Djala jogged noise-lessly into view, his spear ready. He took in the scene with a glance and saw he was too late. Night was falling. His wife would go hungry.

At the sight of the Mimi, Djala's first impulse was to retreat, for spears had often flown between his clanspeople and these spirit folk.

Mimi Hunter and Kangaroo
by Nguleingulel.

The Greeters
*by Manggudja. The Mimi's wives
greet the hunter, Djala.*

But hunger emboldened Djala and he came forward. "You are a strong hunter. Your spear flies straight and true," said Djala formally to the Mimi.

Pleased at the praise, Kaman lifted the kangaroo to his shoulders and replied. "It grows dark. Come to my camp and I will share the meat with you."

The hunter held back in uncertainty, for if the Mimi came to possess his spear or his belt, a few hairs from his body, or even his spittle, or should he eat any food they prepared, their magic would possess him. Against this danger he weighed the custom that permitted him to share game with the Mimi, since he, too, had hunted it. Besides, he was hungry, and so was his wife.

"I will go with you," replied Djala, "but this night I must return to my camp. The womb of my wife is about to open."

Kaman nodded and started off along a trail that led deep into the lands of the spirit people. Djala followed close behind. Abruptly the trail ended at a great rock. Here the Mimi stopped, drew a deep breath, and blew upon its face. At once the boulder split open and Kaman passed through. Djala, ashamed to show any sign of the fear that gripped him, followed his guide through the cleft. The Mimi turned, blew again, and waited while the rock closed behind them.

They found themselves in a grassy glade. At one side several kangaroo fed on the herbage; they lifted their heads as the newcomers appeared but quickly returned to their feeding. Before them loomed a large cave. Near the mouth a fire burned and around it a group of Mimi were dancing and singing.

"Aiee!" Kaman called out. "I bring a man."

The Mimi looked at them. Some called out. Kaman's three wives danced forward to greet them. Mimi women were larger and fuller than their men. The eyes of Kaman's wives were bright, their forms comely, their breasts large and firm. They smiled at Djala as Kaman eased the kangaroo from his shoulders. Then they drew forward pads of bark and invited the newcomers to sit.

"Bring food. My friend is hungry," Kaman instructed one wife. She motioned to the other wives, and the women went quickly to prepare food.

"I will take a portion of the kangaroo and hurry to my camp. My wife is with child," said Djala as a reminder.

One Mimi woman returned with yam on a pandanus leaf, which she placed before the visitor. Djala thought quickly. If he ate this food, he knew he would never leave the Mimi camp. If he refused, he would offend them. Finally, he said, "I will take this food with me to eat it as I journey home. Now, perhaps, I can help you skin the kangaroo."

But Kaman put him off. "No, you are tired. Rest by the fire while we skin the kangaroo and cut your portion," he said, drawing together more pads of paperbark and gesturing Djala toward them.

Reluctant once again to refuse, Djala stretched out on the soft bark. The Mimi began to sing. The fire flickered on the cave walls and played over the breasts of Kaman's wives sitting nearby. Djala closed his eyes and fell into a deep sleep.

He awoke to feel fingers stroking him. A soft body snuggled against his left side. Against his right side there was another. Djala opened his eyes, but he did not move. The coals in the fire glowed. The Mimi slept—all except two wives of Kaman who had drawn up their bark pads and now lay close, as their husband had bidden. A tender hand brushed the hair on Djala's chest, while another softly pushed aside his pubic covering, and still another lightly stroked his thigh. Djala lay still and clenched his teeth. Should he give in to desire, he would be transformed for all time into a Mimi and never could return to his wife. As the hands caressed, his excitement rose. Still, Djala did not move. The hands stroked his stomach. Djala thought of his wife, her belly swollen with child, and lay still.

After some time, the Mimi on his left grew tired and yawned. The Mimi on his right let her arm fall to her side. The breathing of the women grew deep and regular. The wives of Kaman slept.

Djala was wide awake. Carefully he drew up his limbs and raised himself. Silently he stepped over the sleeping figures, stole past Kaman, and left the cave.

When he was outside, he went quickly, for even now the morning star danced over the treetops and the birds chirped. In the first light of dawn, Djala made his way through the rocks and started down toward camp. He kept watch for a feeding kangaroo to spear and carry back to his wife.

In the cave of the Mimi, Kaman was the first to awaken. As the early light filtered through the smoke holes above him, he sat up, yawned, and stretched his arms over his head. He remembered the stranger and smiled in satisfaction, for now that the man had eaten Mimi food and had given his seed to Mimi women, he was one of them. Kaman turned toward the paperbark bed where the man had rested. The yam lay untouched on its pandanus leaf. The sleeping wives huddled together for warmth against the morning chill. But the place where the stranger had slept was empty. With a snort of disappointment, the Mimi snatched his spear and threw it at the empty space where his intended victim had slept.

Before the Sun Woman had walked to the middle of the sky, Djala sat with his wife by his own fire and cleaned the kangaroo he had speared. Today there would be much meat for the three of them.

Mimi Women Wait
by Namirrki. The Mimi women wait invitingly to make love with the hunter, Djala.

The Time of the Dream
by Malangi. *The sacred waterhole that is the home of the
Dreamtime spirits who created the
plants and creatures of the earth.*

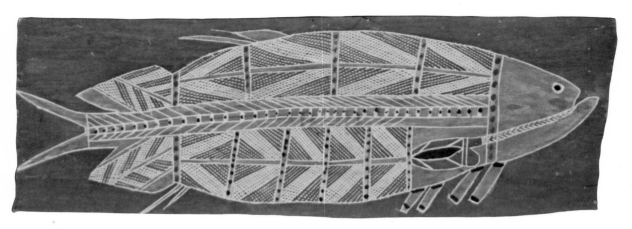

The Barramundi Fish Totem
by Yirrawala.

Mimi and Kangaroo
*by Yirrawala. The smallness of the
Mimi spirit hunter indicates his
distance in the background.*

The Djanggawul Brother
*by Madaman. Djanggawul, as he
came ashore on Arnhem Land,
with his sisters, his face still
flecked with sea foam.*

The Laindjung Story
*by Biragidji. After being ambushed
by his enemies, Laindjung rested in
the depths of the sacred pool, Gululdji, before emerging at top.*

The Water-Walkers
by Midinari. Supported by water-lily pads, birds appear to walk over the surface of the Mirarmina waterhole.

Serpent and Eggs
by Dawudi. The great Rainbow Snake curls about his eggs in the sacred waterhole at Mirarmina.

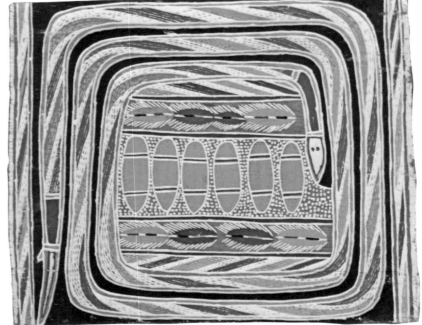

The Mother Protector
*by Nagurridjilmi. Ngalyod, the
Old Mother, in the form of the
Rainbow Snake, protects an orphan boy.*

The Constellation of Scorpio
*by Lardjanga. One of the rare as-
tronomical paintings of the aborigines.*

The Creator Ancestor,
Laindjung,
*by Munggeraui. Laindjung is
shown after his face has been
blackened by the smoke and flames
of a great fire.*

Laindjung
by Mahkarolla.

Banaidja
*by Libundja. Banaidja, the son of
Laindjung, the creator ancestor.*

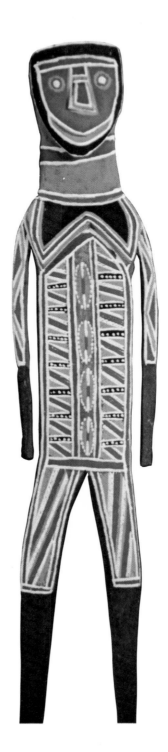

The Younger Sister
*by Dawudi. The sacred caterpillars
on her body lack side strokes, in-
dicating they are immature and,
hence, that this is the younger of
the two Wagilag Sisters.*

The Wind Makers
by Abadjera. Tribesmen chant to encourage the northwest wind to rush out of its home in the bloodwood tree; when it blows, it will bring rain.

The Fire Spirit
by Naridjin. Background design shows the course of a fire from its beginning (diamonds with white dotted lines) through its raging height (diamonds with solid white cross-hatching) to its decline into embers (black diamonds).

The Man-Eater: The Mutjinga Myth, I

Dominance of men over women is everywhere evident in aboriginal life, extending beyond the physical sphere to the domain of ceremony and ritual. The men are the magicians, the *kirman*, or ceremonial leaders. The men possess the most secret totems. The men chant the sacred songs of power.

However, the repeated appearance of myths that justify male ascendancy suggests that at some early period the roles were different. In common with the Wagilag and Djanggawul legends, the Mutjinga story of the Murinbata people of the Port Keats region tells of a woman in the Dreamtime who had more power than the men. Because she misused this power, she lost it—for herself and for all women subsequently—to the male sex.

IN THE DREAMTIME, in the land of the Murinbata people, a great river flowed from the hills through a wide plain to the sea. As it is today, the land then was rich with much fish and game. From the river rose at one place a series of high hills, where lived an old woman named Mutjinga, a woman of power. She it was who called the invisible spirits to her side with secret incantations that none other knew. She was a *kirman*, leader of the ceremonies in which the people sang and danced the exploits of the totemic beings so their spirits would be pleased and would bring food in its season and many children for the people. In those days, all the things in the world had both a physical form that could be touched, seen, and felt, and a spirit form, which was invisible. When living things died, their spirits went to a secret cave where they remained until it was time for them to be born again.

Mutjinga was caretaker of this cave. Only she knew where it was. In the cave, she kept the sacred totems to which the spirits returned.

Mutjinga could speak with the spirits. Because she had this power, she could do many things which the men could not. She could send the spirits to frighten away game, to waylay people at night, or to cause a child to be born without life. The men feared the power of Mutjinga and did not consort with her. They called upon her to lead their dances and teach them songs, but none came to sit by her fire.

Mutjinga became lonely and sent for her young granddaughter to keep her company.

Mutjinga and the girl gathered bulbs and nuts and caught small game, but Mutjinga found no satisfaction in this food, for she craved the flesh of men. Near her camp, she made a large pit in the ground. Over this she laid some branches, which she covered with a layer of earth. In the middle she left a hole, just large enough for a goanna to enter. Cunningly, she smoothed the earth so nothing of her work showed. When a hunter came by searching for game, Mutjinga would change herself into a goanna and run out so the hunter could see her. Then, as he took up the chase, Mutjinga would scurry through the opening into the hole. At the bottom she kept a large stone club, and there she waited. When the hunter dashed up to catch the goanna, he would plunge through the thin earth around the opening and land with a crash at the bottom. Before he could recover, Mutjinga would kill him with her club. Then she would haul him to the fire to cook and eat. What was left over, she placed in the stream to keep. The granddaughter was unhappy at what she saw, but she, too, ate of the meat.

Whenever a hunter did not return, the people would look fearfully at the mountain. "He has displeased the spirits and they have killed him," they would say. "But so long as we obey the spirits when they speak through Mutjinga, we will be protected."

When the men quarreled among themselves or had a problem, they called for Mutjinga. "Tell me what has happened," she would say to them, asking each to speak in turn and listening carefully to his words. When they had finished, she would leave the men and go by herself to the cave where the totems were kept to consult the spirits. On her return, she would tell the men what the spirits had commanded and the men would obey her words. Always the men feared

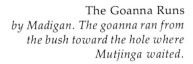

The Goanna Runs
by Madigan. The goanna ran from the bush toward the hole where Mutjinga waited.

and obeyed Mutjinga, for only she could communicate with the totemic spirits.

Early one morning, after all the stars had lived out their short lives and fallen to earth to be born again the next night, Mutjinga blew on her fire stick to start the breakfast fire. Down in the camp, the men moved out to search for game with the first light of dawn. A hunter saw the smoke of Mutjinga's fire rising in the still air. Curious, he came close and saw the granddaughter tending the fire.

"A big goanna just ran past," said the child, pointing to the opening of the hole—for so Mutjinga had taught her. The hunter ran eagerly for the goanna. The thin earth gave way, he crashed through, and Mutjinga killed him.

When the hunter did not return, the people looked fearfully at the mountain. "He has displeased the spirits and they have taken him," they said. "But so long as we obey the spirits when they speak through the words of Mutjinga, we will be protected."

One morning, after the girl had lit the fire, she noticed a tall, young hunter moving up the hillside. She recognized him and hastened to tell Mutjinga. "My brother comes hunting the goanna. You must do him no harm," she pleaded.

But Mutjinga had made up her mind. "He is a man like other men," replied the old woman. "My hunger is like fire inside me. If I do not eat him, I will eat you," and she pinched the child's arm to test it.

As the hunter approached through the bush, Mutjinga muttered the magic that would change her into a goanna. The little girl heard and cried: "What shall I do? Mutjinga will eat my brother!"

In desperation, the granddaughter repeated the magic words of Mutjinga so that she, too, was changed to a goanna. She scurried toward her brother. "He will follow me into the bush and spear me. This will satisfy him and he will return to camp before Mutjinga can kill him," thought the child as she showed herself clearly to the hunter.

But Mutjinga perceived the girl's plan and also ran into the clearing. Now the hunter saw two goanna: one large and plump, the other small and thin. Swiftly he moved toward the larger animal, his spear ready. Mutjinga dashed down her hole and the hunter plunged after her through the thin soil. When he landed, shaken and dazed, the old woman killed him with her club. Some of him she ate, but most she left in the cool stream to keep.

The next morning, the little girl was at her early chores when she saw two men coming up the hillside. As she watched, recognition lit her face and she turned toward Mutjinga.

"It is my father and brother who come. Please do not harm them," she implored.

"I crave their flesh. If you trick me again I shall eat you, as well as your father and brother," Mutjinga warned. "This time I shall wait beside you until the men appear so you cannot deceive me."

The men approached the fire, paid their respects to the old woman, and greeted the child warmly. "Daughter, have you seen your brother who came hunting this way yesterday?" the father asked.

Mutjinga hastened to reply for the child. "No, we have not seen him," she said. "It is too bad, for nearby are many goanna holes. There is a large goanna right there," and she pointed to the hole where she kept the club.

"I thirst. First give me water," said the father.

"There is cold water in the stream," the little girl told him as she pointed down the hill.

The two men walked through the bush to the stream. As the father bent to drink, he saw the leg of his elder son, which Mutjinga had weighted down in the water with a large rock. At once he understood.

"The old woman will kill us unless we kill her first," he said to his younger son, and the two men returned to the fire.

"The goanna went into the tall grass," Mutjinga told them when they appeared. "Leave your spears and light a fire to burn the grass. This will drive the goanna out, and when it runs toward its hole, you can kill it with your spears."

The men went to fire the grass. As soon as they were out of sight, the father said, "Son, climb this tree and watch the old woman closely. She works powerful magic."

This the son did, and he saw Mutjinga speak the magic words. She repeated them twice. He watched as the woman and the girl changed into goannas. From the limb of the tree, he observed the larger goanna chase the smaller one into the bush. Soon great billows of smoke were rising from the burning grass. The small goanna scuttled from the bush, its companion nipping at its heels. They ran past the hunters and disappeared down the hole.

"Get the spears," the father commanded and ran toward the hole. Just as the son returned, spears in hand, the ground beneath the father gave way and he plunged through. Waiting at the bottom was Mutjinga, club raised for the kill. But the son hurled his spear and Mutjinga fell bleeding to the ground.

The father seized her roughly. "Say the magic words that will release my daughter or we shall kill you," he threatened.

Painfully Mutjinga did as she was bidden. The daughter changed into her human form and the two men and the girl climbed from the hole.

"Daughter, show us the secret cave where the spirits are hidden," said the father, "and teach us the magic words you have learned from the old woman. We shall take the spirits to another place, and we shall have the power."

And so it was. The father took the totems from that place and hid them in another cave. He became the *kirman*, the song leader, and he taught the people the sacred dances and ceremonies. To him they brought their problems and he judged between them when they quarreled. And to this day, the men have kept the power.

The Child-Eater: The Mutjinga Myth, II

AFTER MUTJINGA recovered from her wounds, she went to live in the camp of her clanspeople. The men no longer feared her, for now they had the spirit totems. Mutjinga kept only the power to make women pregnant, for this the men had not thought to take from her.

One day a woman of the camp came to Mutjinga. "I am empty, for I have no child," she said. "Tell me how I may cause a spirit child to enter my womb."

"When the moon has just been born, go far down the river with your husband," Mutjinga said. "Camp there with him until the moon dies. You will see a strange sight, a sight you have not seen before. When you return, tell me what you have seen. I shall know if a spirit child has found you."

The woman and her husband departed when the moon was bright and new, and they returned at the appointed time. The woman came to Mutjinga and said, "We found many yams by the river. One night, when our sleep was heavy, small stones fell from the sky and wakened us. Neither I nor my husband have seen such a thing before. See, I have brought some with me," and she held out a handful of pebbles.

Mutjinga placed her hand on the woman's belly. "It was a spirit child that woke you by throwing those stones," she said. "The spirit returned to camp on your husband's shoulders. Lie down and open your legs."

The woman did as she was instructed, and Mutjinga touched her toe, calf, and vagina, all the while muttering magic words.

"The child has now entered your womb. It shall grow within you and shall be born when all is ready," Mutjinga said.

So the woman bore her child. Many other women came to Mutjinga, and soon the sounds of children filled the camp.

Mutjinga still hungered for human flesh, but the men forbade it to her, saying, "We shall kill you if you eat another man."

One day all the women and children spread out near the camp in search of roots and bulbs. One woman who strayed farther returned with good news. "I have found a bee tree full of honey. It grows on the island in the river. Come help me fell the tree and gather the honey," she said.

The other women hesitated. "It is too far," one said.

"The river we must cross is deep in places," said another.

Still they longed for the honey. Finally, Mutjinga spoke. "Go. I will care for the children," she said, and the women were glad to accept.

When they had gone, Mutjinga felt empty, for she craved human flesh. "Let us go bathe in the river," she said to the children. They went to the river and Mutjinga watched as they laughed and splashed and then grew weary. A little boy came from the water to rest on the bank. Mutjinga called to him: "I have made a soft place in the grass. Come and sleep while the sun is hot."

The child followed Mutjinga into the bush. As soon as they were out of sight, the old woman swallowed him in one big gulp. "Ah, how good that tasted," she exclaimed.

She called the other children, one by one, and swallowed them as quickly as she could, for in the distance came the singing of the women as they returned from the honey tree.

Mutjinga lay down by the fire and pretended to sleep, for she did not want the women to see how her belly was swollen with the children she had eaten.

"Where is my child?" the first mother asked, shaking her.

"All the children are bathing in the river," replied Mutjinga.

The mothers put down their honeycomb and hurried to the bank. The sounds of their voices rang upstream and downstream as they called for their children. But the children did not come.

Now the voices of the women rose in anger and Mutjinga became afraid. She rose from her place by the fire to find a place to hide, but one of the women saw her. "Wait," she screamed as she saw Mutjinga's huge belly. Mutjinga ran heavily off into the bush while the women called their husbands to bring spears.

"Here are her tracks!" one woman cried. The men took their spears and began to follow, but at the river the trail ended. The men split into two groups: One went upstream, the other down.

Soon the downstream group saw a cloudiness in the water where the mud at the bottom had been disturbed. Mutjinga, heavy with children, had passed this way. The men quickened their steps and shook their spears. In a place where the banks were steep, the signs disappeared. One man ran forward, another ran back. One man ran into the bush, another searched the bank.

"She has crawled up here!" shouted one, pointing to a place where Mutjinga had climbed from the river and left her finger marks in the clay.

The men quickly scaled the bank and followed Mutjinga's trail to the edge of a deep pool. They ran around, but there were no footprints on the other side.

Mutjinga had submerged herself in a clump of reeds so that all but her eyes and nose were hidden. But her breathing stirred the water, attracting the sharp eyes of one of the men.

"There she is!" he cried.

Now the mothers caught up with their husbands just in time to see them aim their spears to kill Mutjinga.

"Stop! The children are in her belly," screamed one of the women. But one man raised his club and leaped into the water. As Mutjinga rose in alarm, he struck at her neck with all his strength and dragged her body to the bank.

"Her belly moves. The children live," said the woman. They cut Mutjinga open, and the children, though crowded one upon the other in her belly, were still alive. Each was carefully lifted out, washed, and sat by the fire to dry. Then they all returned to camp.

The others had given up the search, and now, when they saw the children, they gave great shouts of joy. To celebrate, the men painted totemic designs on the children, and sang and danced a great ceremony. "Henceforth, we shall initiate our children by conducting this ceremony," they said. And so it has been.

The Singing Woman: The Kukpi Myth

The Snake Woman, Kukpi
by Madigan.

Even today, among the aboriginal people, women have their own ceremonies from which men are excluded, and they will often dispute male rights, especially in marriage, sexual relations, and ceremonial affairs. Clearly, myths such as that of Kukpi, the Singing Woman, reinforce male dominance, because the women still need to be given reasons for it.

IN THE DREAMTIME a black snake came from the sea to the land of the Murinbata people. Drops of cold seawater fell from its scales as it crawled onto the sand. There it assumed the form of a woman called Kukpi, who cut herself a digging stick and set off on a long journey.

As she walked, Kukpi sang an unending song. She sang of the sea: of the great water that heaved and rolled, of her longing for the salt wind, of the driving rain that beat the waters, and of the hot sun that warmed her back when she rested on the surface of the waves. Each evening when she stopped to rest, she thrust her digging stick into the ground. When she removed it, pure cool water gushed forth, forming the billabongs and creeks that survive to this day.

Kukpi reached a place where high cliffs rear up from the river. There, in a snug hollow, she made her camp. For many days her song echoed from the rocks as she searched for bulbs and tubers and hunted wallaby and goanna. One day a hunter appeared, hot in pursuit of a wallaby. His spear was poised for the kill when Kukpi sprang from the bush with her own weapon in hand and with deadly aim impaled the animal.

At once Kukpi called to the startled hunter. "Take the wallaby," she said. "It is yours to roast over your fire."

The man grunted but since he was hungry took out his fire stick and made a fire. Soon he had the wallaby sizzling in the coals. "Do you want some?" he asked Kukpi, who was standing nearby observing him.

She refused but did not depart. When the man had finished eating, Kukpi pointed to a cleft in the cliff. "There is the best way to return," she said. "Take what remains of the meat with you."

He put the wallaby on his shoulder and walked up the path through the cleft. Almost at once he found himself on a steep cliff overlooking the river where the trail seemed to end. As he looked over the edge to find the path, Kukpi approached from behind. She was singing a song of power, a song of magic. When the man heard the words of Kukpi's song, he felt a strong force pushing against him, urging him forward. He resisted, but the power words compelled him

The Snake Woman, Kukpi
by Rock Ngumbe.

toward the sheer drop of the cliff. He shouted and fought frantically to stop himself but could not, and in a moment he slid over the edge and was dashed to his death on the rocks below.

At the foot of the mountain, the hunter's family awaited his return. The moon rose, the night wore on, and the hunter's wife voiced her misgivings. "He had an accident," she said. In the early dawn his brother took up his spears and set out to find the hunter, following the tracks still fresh in the soft earth. Through the trees came the voice of a woman singing. He followed the sound to a hollow near the base of a steep cliff. There sat Kukpi at her camp fire, singing a song of the sea.

The man approached and inquired after the lost hunter. Kukpi pointed to the cleft in the rocks. "He went there," she said. "You will find a steep place where the path leads."

The brother walked in the direction she had indicated, with Kukpi following. When the man reached the edge of the cliff, he stopped to find the path. Behind him rose the words of Kukpi's song. The power words pushed him forward until he, too, fell over the cliff edge and to his death on the rocks below.

In the hunter's camp was an old man named Paduru. His white beard reached to his chest. His eyes were deep and wise. When both hunters failed to return, Paduru set out to find them. He followed their tracks and soon in the distance heard Kukpi's voice as she sang her song. Paduru stopped. "That is where the hunters went," he muttered, advancing silently until he could peer through the bush at Kukpi. "This woman sings a sacred song, a song of magic. It is a song I do not know, but it is only for men to sing, only for the *kirman*, the ceremonial leader, to sing." Quietly he sat and listened until he had learned the words of the song. Then he stole back to camp.

"The two men are dead. They were killed by magic," he told the people. The women began to wail, and they cut their flesh in grief.

The next day Paduru returned to the place where Kukpi dwelt. Again he hid and waited. Kukpi took up her digging stick and spear and went off to hunt, singing her unending song of the sea. When the song had died away in the distance, he entered the hollow and looked carefully about. Near Kukpi's bed, he found two stone *tjurunga*, oval slabs on which sacred designs had been engraved. These Kukpi had brought with her from the sea.

"Only the men may possess *tjurunga*, for they have great power which the women must not come to know. I will carry these back to camp and hide them," Paduru decided.

Fearing that Kukpi, missing the *tjurunga*, would follow his tracks, he formed a plan and ran quickly back to camp.

"Make *tjurunga* exactly like these," he said to two old men whose task it was to make the sacred totems.

"It will take many days," they replied, "for the stone is hard and yields slowly."

Impatiently, Paduru picked up a piece of wood and began to chop at it with his stone ax. When he had cut two pieces in the same shape as the stone *tjurunga,* he called to the men.

"Help me," Paduru directed. Quickly they carved the wood, refining its shape and chiseling designs into its surface until they had achieved perfect duplicates of the original. Then Paduru ran to the hollow where Kukpi made her camp. She had not yet returned. Carefully he replaced the sacred stones and left.

Now Paduru called the men together in a place where the women could not hear. "The woman Kukpi carries sacred *tjurunga,*" he told them. "She sings songs of power. With this forbidden magic she has killed our brothers. She is too powerful for us to overcome, but we have seen her *tjurunga.* We have copied them in wood. We have made designs in the wood that are the same as the designs in the sacred stones. Now our *tjurunga* are like hers. And I have heard her song of magic. I hid in the bushes and listened. I learned the words. Now I will teach you."

The women of the camp were angered. They had not been permitted to hear the secrets of Paduru. The next morning, two of these women crept to Kukpi's camp. They waited until she had gone hunting; then they snatched the stone *tjurunga* and returned triumphantly home.

"We have the sacred stones," they announced, "and these shall be for the women only."

Paduru stroked his beard and said nothing. When the two women went off to hide the *tjurunga,* softly he crept after them and killed them with his ax. He took the *tjurunga* and hid them in a cave.

"But how will I prevent the women from finding the *tjurunga* and using them against the men?" he wondered. He sat down before the cave and pondered this question.

The shadows had begun to lengthen when Paduru stood up and made haste to fetch the wooden replicas. In each he bore a hole, and fastened a long string. He lifted a *tjurunga* by the string and began to whirl it above his head. The movement caused a roaring noise that rose and fell as the *tjurunga* whirled now fast and now slow. For a long time Paduru whirled. For a long time the roar filled the air and echoed through the bush.

When he returned to camp, the people were clustered in groups, whispering of the terrifying noise they had heard, the roar and howl that had come from the bush.

"That is the voice of the Singing Woman searching for her sacred stones. She roars in anger. She has killed two women who stole the stones from her," Paduru said.

The women were greatly frightened and fell silent. When time had passed, Paduru took the initiated men to the cave, where he showed them how to make the roaring voice of Kukpi. Even today, when a man of the Murinbata people whirls a wooden *tjurunga* on a long string, the women tremble at its roaring voice.

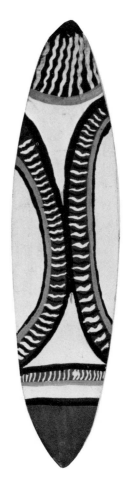

The Bull-Roarer
by unknown artist. The booming noise made by the bull-roarer as it is swung around the head on a string is the voice of Kukpi.

The Unloved One: The *Ubar*-Drum Myth

Women in aboriginal society were expected to yield to the sexual demands of their husbands. The *ubar*-drum myth gives the Dreamtime precedents for female sexual compliance and details the fate of a wife who spurns the marriage bed.

The legend also tells the origin of the *ubar* logs and the ceremony surrounding their use. The *ubar* are logs hollowed by termites; the aborigines cut and trim them. They serve three functions: as fish traps, as containers for the bones of the dead, and as drums. Though the hollow-log drum appears in the sacred rituals of several other areas, it has special significance to the Gunwinggu people of the western region and to their tradition of male dominance.

IN THE DREAMTIME, there lived in the Gunwinggu country of western Arnhem Land a great hunter and magician called Yirrawadbad. None knew his parentage: It was said he had come from the islands beyond the horizon. Though Yirrawadbad had gray in his hair, he was betrothed to a young girl named Gula, and he brought her gifts of food to indicate he was ready to marry her. But Gula found Yirrawadbad old, fierce, and ugly. She preferred Bulugu, a much younger man, and wished to be his wife. So she made no answer to Yirrawadbad's gifts.

Her father was outraged. "Yirrawadbad is first among the hunters," he said. "Always he will bring food to your fire—kangaroo and wallaby and sweet honey from the bee tree. These will he also share with us. You are promised to him, and you will marry him."

The mother disagreed. "Yirrawadbad is ugly and has an evil temper," she said. "He is sure to beat Gula, for she has no experience in caring for a man. Let him take another wife."

The father had his way, and he summoned his sisters to prepare for Gula's marriage. The women made ready the fire and beside it placed a heap of soft bark from the paperbark tree. As night fell, Yirrawadbad brought goose eggs to the new camp, and Gula cooked them. Together they ate, sharing the food with their kin, who had gathered to celebrate the union. Afterward, Yirrawadbad lay down on the bark bed and tried to draw Gula to him. Reluctant, she held back. Yirrawadbad berated her and pulled roughly. Still she refused. The clanspeople heard the commotion from their fires. They smiled and gossiped among themselves.

A few yards from the nuptial bed, Gula's aunts were making ready to lie down, for it was their duty to see that the marriage was properly consummated. They heard Yirrawadbad's rough voice as he spoke fiercely to Gula. But still she refused his advances. The aunts came close and urged her to give in. "No," Gula said.

"The girl is bewitched," Yirrawadbad roared. "I will drive out the spell," and he went to fetch a stick to beat his new wife.

"Yirrawadbad will break your bones," said the aunts, seizing Gula by the shoulders and legs. She struggled, but the aunts forced her into a spread-eagle position and then called to Yirrawadbad. "Come, the girl is ready," they said.

"I will beat her first," he shouted back.

"She waits for you," one aunt cried. "Are you man enough to satisfy her?"

Yirrawadbad roared in anger, but he came and lay with his bride. For several nights the aunts slept close to be sure Gula obeyed her husband. Then Yirrawadbad took the girl on a long walkabout, and the couple was alone for many days. When they returned, he made a shelter of large bark sheets placed over a framework of poles. Then he gathered a great pile of soft paperbark for a bed inside the shelter.

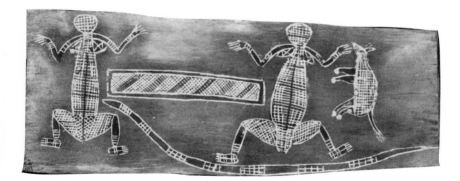

The Ubar Ceremony
by Nonganyari.

"We will sleep here," he told Gula.

But Gula had other ideas. She dug yams and lily bulbs and gathered shellfish for Yirrawadbad's meals. She kept his fire, and she brought water to the camp. But she would not sleep in his bed.

Instead, she made a nest of dry grasses for herself in a deep but tiny cave. After she had prepared the evening meal, she would crawl into the cave to sleep. Though Yirrawadbad tried to follow, the cave was too narrow for him. Many nights Yirrawadbad coaxed Gula to come out. She pretended not to hear. Many nights Yirrawadbad lost his temper and threatened Gula in a voice that all the camp heard. But she would not come to him.

Yirrawadbad appealed to Gula's mother. "Gula is your wife," the woman replied. "I have no power over her."

Gula's father threatened to beat her, but the girl would not bend. "Yirrawadbad is my husband. It is forbidden that any but he shall beat me," she said. "If you touch me," she added, "he will spear you."

The anger of Yirrawadbad grew. Many days he left camp to hunt and fish, and to nurse his rage. Finally, he decided he would kill Gula and her mother. Through magic he would avenge himself so none would know how they died.

First, Yirrawadbad went to the camp of his mother-in-law and stole a woven string she used to tie the dilly bag around her neck. Then he found a net bag in which Gula often carried bulbs. With these in hand, Yirrawadbad sought out a cave high up on a hill some distance from the camp. There he ground earth colors, mixing them with water and orchid juice. On the wall of the cave he painted two figures—a large one representing Gula, and a small one representing her mother. At the feet of each, Yirrawadbad designed a snake in the act of striking, for by this means he planned they should die. He made a fire, and while he passed the string and net bag through its flames, he chanted magic words to call upon the snake to kill the women. Then he returned to camp.

Days passed, but no harm came to Gula and her mother. Yirrawadbad watched and saw that his plans must change.

The next day, Gula and her mother went into the bush to hunt bandicoot. Yirrawadbad knew well the path and quickly went to a place nearby, where he had noticed a hollow tree fallen across the track. Then in the dirt he made bandicoot tracks which led directly to the hollow tree. He sang a magic song to turn himself into a snake, crawled inside the tree, and waited.

The women came by and saw the bandicoot tracks. "Here is a bandicoot. We will follow the tracks to catch it," the mother said. So they followed the tracks to the hollow tree.

Yirrawadbad heard them and began to make scratching noises inside the log. The mother stopped. "The bandicoot hides in this log, daughter," she said. "Guard that end of the tree, while I reach into this end to catch him." She reached in and almost at once felt a prick in her hand. "The bandicoot scratched me," she cried. "It goes to your end, daughter. Catch it!"

Gula put in her hand and felt a scratch also. Her mother rose and waved her hand, but before she could speak, the venom took hold and she fell to the ground. Gula also rose, but the poison quickly spread and she, too, fell down.

Yirrawadbad crawled from the log and turned himself back into a man. He stood over the limp bodies of the women. Only their arms still twitched. When she saw Yirrawadbad standing over her, Gula moved weakly to spread her legs. "Come lie with me, husband," she said. "I will be a good wife to you."

But Yirrawadbad refused, saying, "It is too late. You and your mother have brought this punishment upon yourselves. So it shall happen to a woman who spurns her husband. So it shall happen to the mother who sides with daughter. All men shall learn that such is their power over women. To this end, I shall teach them to make the hollow log in which I hid into a *ubar* drum. They shall beat the drum and tell my story to the young men. It shall be a sacred ceremony. Only the men shall know it, so only they will have the power. It shall not be for the women."

Yirrawadbad took his spear and fire sticks and left that place. For a long time he traveled about the country. Whenever he stopped at night by a fire where people were camped, he sent the women away and told the story of Gula and her mother. He taught the men to sing the songs, and he showed them how to make the *ubar* drum so they could conduct the sacred ceremony. At times Yirrawadbad appeared in the bush as a snake, but only the men who saw him lived to tell of it, for whenever a woman came upon him, Yirrawadbad struck her with his deadly fangs.

The Man-Killer: The Wilintji Myth

Usually in the myths, men triumph over women, either through guile or physical strength. The Wilintji myth reverses this. It tells of a woman who danced her male rivals to death and completed the symbolic act by eating them.

It has been reported that the Aranda tribe of central Australia has a myth, the Alknarinja, which also tells of Dreamtime spirit women who danced in competition with the men.

IN THE TIME OF THE DREAM, when spirit people first came to the earth, a woman named Wilintji lived among the Gunwinggu. She had a camp by herself near the top of the Liverpool River. She was comely and well formed, and when men first saw her they hungered after her. But though she drew men as honey attracts the bee, Wilintji had no love for her admirers. Like the spider that devours the partner with whom it mates, she brought death to the suitors who came to her fire. When the young men cast eyes at Wilintji, the old men warned them: "Do not go to her fire. She will dance you to death, and then she will eat you."

The women knew the truth of the matter, and when they were in the bush gathering yams and grubs far away from the men, they told one another about Wilintji and how she came by her hatred of men.

When Wilintji was a child, they said, she ran naked with the other boys and girls. Sometimes she would see young lovers as they stole to a trysting place in the bush. Wilintji would watch their lovemaking with wide eyes, her thin, flat hips undulating and her mouth imitating the soft, sharp cries she heard. Soon she took one of her playmates aside: "Be my husband and we will lie together," she proposed.

They went to the soft grass by the lagoon, and Wilintji lay back and cajoled the boy. But he could not repeat the pleasurable acts she had seen. Wilintji berated her partner: "You are still a baby. Go suck milk from your mother." Greatly angered, the boy turned upon Wilintji and beat her until she ran screaming to the camp.

Wilintji had been betrothed since birth to her second cousin, Marriki, who already had one wife. When the girl's breasts had barely begun to swell, Marriki came one night and took her to his bed. Wilintji went in anticipation: Now she would know the pleasure the younger boy could not give her. But Wilintji was small and hard to enter, and Marriki could find no satisfaction in her. "Go back to your mother," he told her, and she left humiliated.

At night Wilintji often crept from her bed of paperbark and crawled through the bushes until she came to a clearing where the men conducted sacred ceremonies that women were forbidden to see. For long hours she lay there, absorbing every word of the songs and raptly watching the feet of the dancers. When she was alone, she secretly sang the songs and practiced the dances she had observed.

One day her mother sent her with a gift of food to Marriki: "He will be your husband. You must learn to please him."

"Marriki does not like me," Wilintji objected. Nevertheless, she took the food.

Just before she arrived at Marriki's camp, she decided to make magic that would cause Marriki to like her. And so she began one of the power songs she had learned from watching the men. Unexpectedly, Marriki walked from the bushes. "If the other men hear you sing the sacred songs, they will kill you," he threatened. "You must never sing them again." Then Marriki thrashed her until she cried out in pain.

When the rains began, Wilintji passed her blood for the first time. She became restless and found her way to the camp of Anba, an older man who came from a distant clan and lived by himself in the bush. Anba was kind to her and Wilintji returned often to his camp fire. Soon she was sleeping with him every night, and in his bed learned the ways of love.

Marriki heard of their relationship and berated Wilintji. "You are my wife. Stay away from Anba. He is not of our people."

But Wilintji refused: "I am not yet your wife. Anba is kind to me, and I shall go to him."

Marriki and his brother and several of their kinfolk stole to Anba's camp one night soon after and speared him. When Wilintji arrived later, she found the older man dead. Grief-stricken and enraged, she confronted Marriki: "You killed Anba," she accused. "Now you and the other men must conduct the hollow-log ceremony so his spirit will return to the Sky World."

But Marriki refused: "We will not dance the sacred ceremonies, the *mareiin*. That we do only for our own people."

"His spirit will wander about and cause much trouble," Wilintji warned. But Marriki was obdurate, and when Wilintji continued to insist, he beat her with his spear-thrower until she ran screaming to her mother's fire.

That night, after the fires had burned low and the camp was still, a familiar sound drifted on the night air, disturbing the sleep of Marriki. At once he recognized the tapping of singing sticks beating the refrain from the sacred burial ceremony, and he knew that Wilintji had decided to bury Anba herself.

Quickly he awakened the other men. They gathered their spears and made their way to Anba's camp. The glow of a large fire lit the clearing. Wilintji, her body painted with the ritual designs, had sung the sacred chants and was now dancing the ceremony that only the men were allowed to conduct.

In great anger, Marriki and his companions advanced toward Wilintji. They brandished their spears and ordered her to stop. "Many of

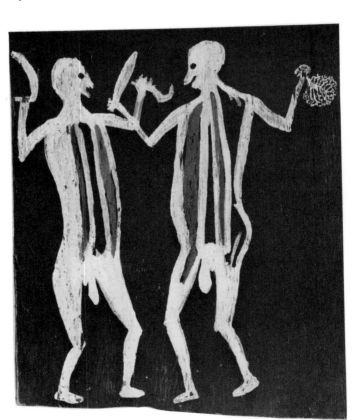

The Dancers
*by Yirrawala. Two men dance to
death with Wilintji.*

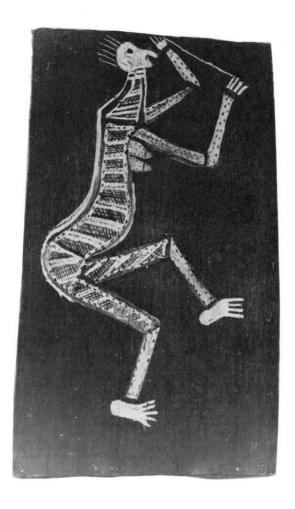

The Man-Killer
by Nabadbara. Wilintji, the man-hating woman, dances the men to death.

you came to kill Anba," she cried. "You were brave, for he was only one. Spear me also, so you may again prove your courage."

Marriki and his friends drew aside. "Anba's spirit will return and cause us harm. We must make stronger magic than Wilintji's."

So the men put down their spears and began to dance. They called out the power song of their totem. Wilintji taunted them. "My dancing is more powerful than yours. I will dance until Anba's spirit returns and causes you to lose your desire for women."

"I call fire," Wilintji sang loudly.

"I call goanna," each of the men sang.

"I call the scorpion's bite," sang Wilintji.

"I call the catfish," roared the men.

Wilintji danced powerfully. Her eyes were bright; her breasts swung from side to side. Sweat ran down her face and body. The men also danced, singing and uttering defiant cries. The Moon Man climbed high in the sky, sank to the horizon, and disappeared in his home beneath the earth. Still Wilintji and the men danced. The Sun Woman cast powdered ocher in the eastern sky to mark her coming, and her bright beams took the place of the smoldering fire.

Still the dance continued. But now the arms of the men dropped to their sides; their heads fell to their chests; their eyes glazed. Only their legs moved, up and down. The more the men weakened, the stronger Wilintji became. As the heat of the day mounted, the men began to stagger. They moved in little jumps like speared kangaroos. But Wilintji appeared fresh and strong. She lashed them with mockery. She tugged at the belts they wore about their waists until they loosened and fell to the earth. Then she slapped the men on their buttocks and reviled their weakness.

One by one, the men dropped to the ground until only Marriki remained, lurching from side to side as if he had been bitten by a brown snake.

Wilintji danced close and seized his testicles. "Come to my bed," she taunted. Marriki struck at her weakly, moaned, and fell in a heap to the ground.

And so it was that Anba's assassins all died. Wilintji rested for a time. She took a drink of water, then felt the pangs in her stomach. She was hungry after her great exertion. As she gathered her aching limbs to search for food, she saw the men lying on the ground like speared kangaroo.

"I killed them, so I will eat them," Wilintji muttered. So she cut up one of the men and roasted the meat for her meal. She made her camp at this place and has stayed there ever since.

On some nights the women hear the tapping of the singing sticks far off on the wind. They hear the voice of Wilintji singing the sacred songs, the songs that belong only to the men. They exchange pleased glances, but to the men they say nothing.

The Wife-Killer: The Malamu Myth

There is no need to explain the moral of this story, which tells of two wives who quarreled so often that their husband in desperation finally left them to die in a cave isolated by flood waters. Here, again, the details vary according to the locality, the age-grade, and the special circumstances of the telling.

IN THE DREAMTIME, in the rocky hills of the Gunwinggu country, lived a man called Malamu who could make rain. He was highly respected, for when the dry season lengthened to drought, Malamu would call upon the Great Rainbow Snake. He would take a pearl shell from his medicine bag and scrape off a little powder. This he would mix with a special herb and bury in the ground to the accompaniment of sacred chants. Sometimes several days might pass, but inevitably Malamu would point to a small cloud on the horizon and announce that the Great Rainbow Snake had appeared and rain was on its way. And always his words came true.

Malamu had a wife, Lamanga, and three grown children with families of their own. Recently Malamu had taken a younger wife, Milimili, who had not yet conceived. At first both women took pride in Malamu's reputation; together they shared with pleasure the respect he earned. From dawn to dark the women ranged the countryside, searching for tidbits that would please Malamu.

But after a time jealousy sprang up between the wives. Soon there was no peace between them. On everything they disagreed, and the noise of their arguing accompanied them wherever they went. Malamu tried to make peace. "Be silent," he would say and then try to discover the cause of their dispute. But both wives would turn on him and berate him until their scolding drove him away in disgust.

The other men saw, and they taunted Malamu: "You are no better than a dog at your own camp fire; the women scold you when they wish," they would say, laughing among themselves.

This ridicule angered Malamu, and he decided to end the bickering between his wives. The next time they began to argue, he stepped between them. "Hold your tongues," he shouted, "or I shall beat you until the blood flows."

But his threats failed to impress them. "Who will lie with you by the camp fire at night if you beat us?" they asked. Malamu fell silent, for he knew how hot his blood ran when the camp fires died and the shadows fell.

The next day the three set out to cut down a bee tree for the honey it held. As usual, the women began to argue. Soon they were shouting and screaming. Malamu felled the tree, scooped out the honey, and dropped it in bark containers. Still the bickering continued. Exasperated, Malamu roared, "Be silent or I will make magic that will turn you both to stone!"

Milimili laughed at him. She dropped her waistband and pressed her loins against Malamu. "Will you be satisfied with a stone for your wife?" she asked. Malamu returned her embrace, for he hungered especially for his younger wife. Lamanga smiled mockingly.

As the quarreling continued day after day, Malamu became desperate. Finally he decided what to do: He untied his little string-bag and took out the pearl shell. He made the rain ceremony and soon a great storm arose. Day and night the rain fell, swelling the streams and flooding the land. Before long, the camp fire of Malamu had been doused and the bark shelter washed away. Now the two wives bitterly berated each other for causing the storm.

"We will go higher into the hills. I know a cave in which we will be warm and dry," Malamu suggested.

The women followed as he led the way through ravines and tumbled rocks. So rough was the path that they fell silent. Finally, they came to a chasm over which a fallen tree formed a bridge. Malamu led his wives across, and soon they reached the cave. As they made a fire and prepared to cook their meal, Milimili and Lamanga again took up their perpetual quarrel. Angry voices beat the air as they waved their hands and stamped back and forth.

Malamu had been waiting for this moment. Silent and unobserved, he left the cave and made his way down the hill. He crossed the chasm on the fallen tree, then stopped on the other side and sang the rain song. Within a few moments torrents of water fell heavily from the sky, weakening the bank on which the fallen tree rested. Too heavy now for the crumbling bank, the tree broke loose and crashed to the bottom.

The Quarreling Women
by Mijaumijau. Malamu's two
wives drive him to desperation
with their quarreling, so he plans
to kill them.

"Now I shall silence the women forever," Malamu said, and made a magic that would turn them to stone.

That night Malamu slept peacefully and awoke refreshed. But when he had eaten, the hot blood once more rose in him. Now he thought regretfully of his wives in the cave. The noise of their quarreling grew dim in his mind as he imagined the rounded thighs of Milimili and the soft fullness of her breast. For several days he remained at the camp, his desire growing stronger each day. When he could stand the craving no longer, he ran to the chasm, replaced the fallen tree with his magic, and then made his way toward the cave where he had left his wives. His magic had worked, for on the brow of the hill stood two round rocks, each shaped like a breast. Malamu recognized the larger one as Lamanga, the smaller as Milimili. The women had turned to stone.

Malamu summoned all his powers to transform the rocks back into women. But no matter what charms he used, he failed. In grief

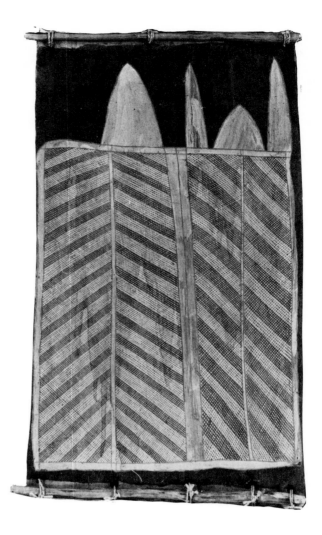

The Wife-Killer
*by Anchor Barlbuwa. Malamu and
his quarreling wives are turned to
stone. The rounded shapes are the
breasts of the wives, the elongated
stones represent the penis of
Malamu.*

and despair, he embraced the stone that had been his young wife. It did not respond. Then Malamu clasped the larger stone in his arms. It, too, remained cold and inert. In desperation Malamu made magic for the last time and turned himself into stone so that he could ever be close to the women he desired.

Today, when the Gunwinggu people come to the hill called Obirri, they see two stones on its crest that are rounded like the breasts of women. They point to the larger and say, "Here waits Lamanga," and to the smaller, "This is Milimili." Near each is a long projecting stone, standing erect like the male member. This, the people say, is Malamu, who turned himself into two stones so he could satisfy himself with both his women.

PART V
MYTHS OF
EVERYDAY LIFE

THE ABORIGINAL learned much about his everyday life from the myths. Following the example of his Dreamtime ancestors, he learned how to straighten his spears, how to catch fish, and what to do when game vanished before the drought. The myths told him how to soak nuts and tubers in water to leach out poison, how to fish below the waterfall and not above it, and how to make a fish trap or a bark basket. He repeated the stories in order to become expert in these skills that were so necessary to his survival.

The myths also told him to be brave, to be generous and share his food, to settle quarrels amicably. They explained things that puzzled him: Why spiders live in dark caves, why his skin is black, and why he must follow the prescribed rules in conducting the ceremonies.

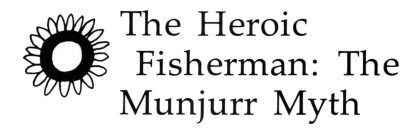

The Heroic Fisherman: The Munjurr Myth

The aborigines faced hardship and danger daily, so it is no wonder that courage was instilled in the youths by example and precept. The myth of the brave fisherman is typical of those told around the camp fires to show the young the kind of behavior they should try to emulate.

IN THE DREAMTIME, in the country of the *Manggalilji* people of northeast Arnhem Land, lived a great fisherman called Munjurr. In his bark canoe he ventured far out to sea, spearing kingfish and dugong for the people of his camp. Wise in the ways of wind and tide was Munjurr. When the waves rolled high, of all the men, he alone skillfully steered his canoe between the combers. When others feared to fish even in the surf, Munjurr calmly paddled through the white-capped breakers to the fishing grounds beyond.

One morning, Munjurr strode to the camp fire of his friend, Nurru, the best drone piper in the camp. Nurru was practicing power notes on his *didjeridu* in preparation for a ceremony to be held before the moon died.

"Come fish with me," invited Munjurr.

Nurru objected. "The waves are high today. Surely the canoe will be overturned."

"This is a fine time to catch the big fish, for when the surf runs high they come close to shore," Munjurr pointed out.

"Today let us stalk the wallaby," said Nurru, trying to divert him. "Tomorrow, when the wind dies, we can fish."

But Munjurr would not be put off, and now he tried a new approach. "You are known as a brave man, Nurru. You and I will bring back a great catch today, and our friends will be proud that only we dared brave such rough waters. If we meet difficulty, you can sound a power song on your *didjeridu* to help us."

Nurru was still reluctant, but his pride was touched. He followed Munjurr to the beach and helped pull the canoe from the bushes. Carefully, the two friends checked the strands of woven fiber that bound the bark sheets to the frame and to each other. Satisfied the canoe was watertight, they stowed the fishing gear and the drone pipe aboard, splashed into the surf, and quickly began to paddle.

Almost at once a great wave caught them. It took all Munjurr's skill to regain control and steer a course through the mountainous surf. But slowly he drew away from the treacherous shore to the relative calm that lay beyond the reef. There the two men navigated easily and turned their attention to the fish.

Walu, the Sun Woman, had barely moved across the sky when Nurru suddenly grasped Munjurr's arm, leaned close, and pointed past the stern of the canoe. "A whale!" he hissed. "It comes this way."

Munjurr looked. Some distance away, a large humpbacked whale had surfaced and was moving toward them. Water ran in rivulets from its sides and flowed in curves from its snout as it cut through the sea. The story of *deimiri,* the whale spirit, was often repeated around the camp fires of the *Manggalilji* people. Remembering the vivid descriptions of *deimiri's* three mouths—two of which were in its tail—and how the whale seized and capsized the canoes of fishermen, Munjurr turned and gave the command.

"Paddle hard!" he shouted to Nurru.

Desperately they paddled as the great whale plowed toward them,

The Fishermen
by Madaman. The two fishermen paddle out beyond the breakers.

bearing down faster than they could pull away. When the small eyes and blowhole were clearly visible, Nurru picked up his drone pipe and began a power song that he blew with all his might. Almost upon them, the whale unexpectedly raised its snout and plunged beneath the surface of the sea. In its place, the water heaved with tremendous force, seizing the canoe and sucking it toward the vortex in a dizzying spin. The two fishermen fought for balance, but the canoe capsized and hurled them into the sea. Dazed and confused, they struggled in the swirling water.

Munjurr recovered first. Seeing his spears pop to the surface, he swam toward them. Quick as he was, they floated beyond his reach. Now Nurru revived and snatched futilely at his drone pipe as it bobbed off. Meanwhile, Munjurr had laid hold of a paddle. "This way," he shouted at Nurru, gesturing toward the distant shore. He began to swim, pushing the paddle before him so he could rest when he grew tired.

Nurru swam also, but with less strength and speed. As they approached the shore, the surf grew rough, the currents unpredictable. Munjurr was a strong swimmer and had drawn well ahead of his companion. But now even he had to stop occasionally to rest on his paddle. Nurru, the weaker of the two, could not rest. As he struggled through the waves, his arms grew heavy and slow, his legs barely moved. He began to sink.

Munjurr turned, saw his friend's difficulty, and swam toward him. "Take hold of the paddle!" he cried, thrusting one end at Nurru while he held fast to the other. Nurru caught hold, but the paddle proved too light to buoy them both, and again Nurru sank. Munjurr released his end and the paddle rose to the surface, pulling Nurru up with it.

"Hold onto it!" called Munjurr again, and then he swam off.

The last rays of Walu were streaming along the horizon when the incoming tide cast Nurru onto the beach. As he lay there, barely breathing and limp from exhaustion, he still clutched the paddle in his hands.

But Munjurr did not return. Not that day, or the next, or even the day after that, though his people combed the beaches for him. The waves had claimed his body, carrying it far out to sea. And his spirit had gone to the Sky World, where Barama, the powerful creator ancestor, waited to greet him.

"You saved your friend," said Barama, "but you lost your family, your friends, and the land of your birth. So that you need not grieve, I make you my messenger. You are to carry my words to the people on earth and bring back their messages to me. In this way you will be content."

Munjurr made his camp beside the Milky Way, the great river that flows across the Sky World. He fashioned a canoe like the one he had used on earth, launched it in the river, and continued to fish as hap-

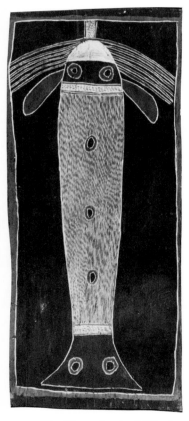

The Humpbacked Whale *by Gungujuma. The humpbacked whale with two mouths in his tail with which he overturns fishermen's canoes.*

pily as before. From time to time, Barama sent him to earth with messages, as he had promised, and from these journeys Munjurr always returned refreshed.

Below, in the land of the *Manggalilji*, wet season followed dry and was succeeded by wet, until Nurru's eyes grew dim, his shoulders stooped, and his feet no longer shuffled far from the camp fire. One morning, when the surf ran high and the winds blew strong, his spirit joined the spirit of Munjurr beside the Milky Way to fish forever in the great river and sometimes stalk the turtle and water birds that make their homes along its banks.

The Spirit Messenger: The Opossum-Tree Myth

For thousands of years the aborigines preserved a way of life well adapted to their exacting environment. In spite of constant hostility among the clans over women and territorial rights, the social structure offered stability and continuity. The myths were a strong force in cementing the fragile structure of human relationships, for they told of the great lawgivers in the Dreamtime who laid down the rules for living peacefully together.

The clans of the *jiridja* moiety tell of three closely related lawgivers: Barama, the "big man," is the most powerful; associated with him are Laindjung and his son, Banaidja.

The link between the people of earth and Barama is a sacred tree that grows at a place called Djeragbi, on Cape Shield. Towering into the sky, this great tree is the home of Marngu the opossum, who serves as messenger between Barama and the clanspeople.

A magic tree is commonly found in other mythologies. Some early peoples of Europe believed that the earth revolved around the axis of a great tree whose roots were anchored in the underworld and whose branches reached into the Sky World. This tree, which appears also in Asian, Polynesian, and other mythologies, is subject to a range of meanings, from the phallus to the tree of life. Whatever its specific context, the tree is always a focus of action and attention about which significant events revolve.

Although it is difficult to ascertain the real meaning of the opossum tree to the aborigines, it does play a central role in some of their myths. To develop this version, I have pieced together a number of loosely related episodes told by the *jiridja* moiety clans. The primary myth relates the incident of Guwarg the night bird's search for Marngu the opossum. To introduce this theme, I have added an instance of adultery—a typical

The Thunder Man's Wife
by Lardjanga. Djambuwal's wife holds the clubs she strikes together to cause the thunder.

Tortoises Mating
by Libundja. Minala the tortoise and his wife copulate beside the river.

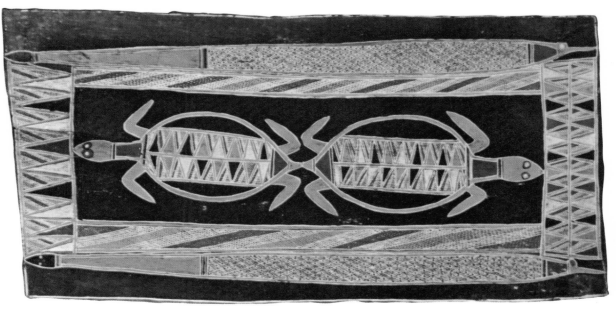

Macassan Praus
by Biragidji.

The Shark
by Mini-Mini. The tiger shark, depicted by one of Groote Eylandt's outstanding painters.

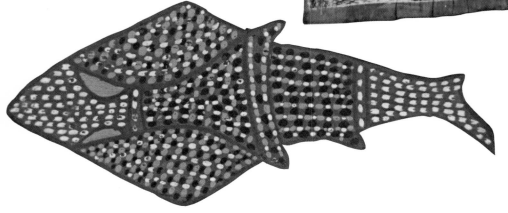

Two Funeral Skulls
by Yirrillil. The spirits of the deceased remain in the skulls until they leave for the Island of the Dead.

The Water Carrier
by Naridjin. Napilingu carries a bark container similar to the ones she taught the women to make.

The Night Bird
by Naridjin. The night bird, Gu-
warg, perches on the sacred tree in
which the opossum, Marngu,
lives.

Skulls and Bones
by Djadjiwui. Skulls and bones,
with totemic designs of the de-
ceased.

The Adultress
by Aurangnamirri. Bima faces her husband, Purukapali, after learning that their son had died while she tarried away from camp to commit adultery.

Purukapali and His Dead Son
by Mandarbarni. Purukapali holds his dead child, wrapped in a paperbark shroud.

The Evil Tree Spirit
by Malangi. The black shape in the center of the painting is the evil tree spirit; the diagonal lines represent the grass; here lurks the poisonous snake that killed the great hunter, Gurramingu.

The Rainbow Snake
by Indji Tharwul. The creator father, Kunmanggur, in the form of the Rainbow Snake.

The Kangaroo and the Snake
by Malangi. *The kangaroo that
Gurramingu killed and, in the
lower left corner, the snake that
killed the hunter.*

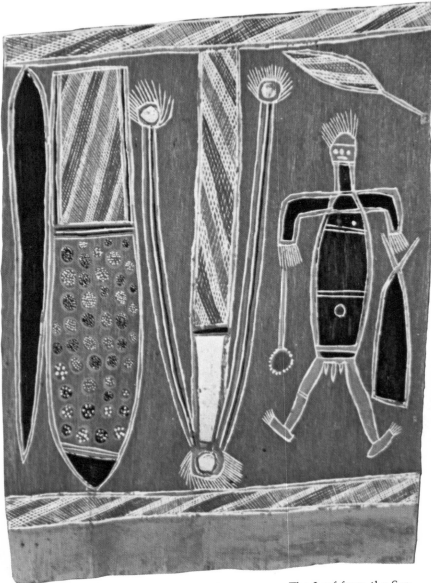

The Leaf from the Sea
by Libundja. Yalngura learned
about Bralgu, the Island of the
Dead, from a yam leaf that blew
over the water to Arnhem Land.

Murajana, The Cheerful Spirit
by Libundja. After the funeral ceremony, Murajana comes with a
happy smile and laughter to help
the mourners forget their sorrow.

cause of dispute—that incites fighting and requires the intervention of Barama, through his messenger, Guwarg. The subject of Barama's communication is a peace ceremony, the *garada*.

Today the aborigines say that the sacred tree still towers into the Sky World at Djeragbi, but that it is visible only to fully initiated men after they have chanted the proper invocations.

LONG AGO the *Manggalilji* people of northeast Arnhem Land lived peacefully together. One day a visitor from another tribe arrived. His name was Borok and he sang gossip songs at the camp fire and became popular with the unmarried girls. Soon he noticed Kulta, a married woman, and she returned his glances. One evening she left the camp fire and walked off by herself. A few minutes later Borok also took leave.

Kulta's husband accosted her angrily the next morning. "You went to lie with the stranger, Borok," he accused.

"I did not!" his wife stormed. "You are jealous. You invent tales."

Her husband refused to believe her, and Kulta appealed to her kinfolk for support. The quarrel raged for many days. Soon the shouting reached the ears of Borok. Both sides came to him with threats and hard words, and Borok had to leave the camp. The next morning Kulta also disappeared.

Fighting broke out among the antagonists. Spears flew and blood spilled. A vengeance party set out in pursuit of the departed visitor. They came upon him that night, camping alone. "He has had his satisfaction with the woman and has sent her away," they concluded, and then they killed him. The party tracked Kulta and found her digging yams for her meal. "You have done wrong and must die," they cried, and they speared her to death.

When the assassins returned to camp, Kulta's relatives were outraged and lost no time in planning revenge. They set up a new camp by themselves. Then they lay in ambush and speared Kulta's assassins to death, one by one.

Soon a murderous feud was in progress which the creator spirit, Barama, sadly observed from his camp in the Sky World. He shared his sorrow with Munjurr, a spirit being who was his companion. "The people forget my words," said Barama. "They are unhappy because they quarrel among themselves. Go, Munjurr, to the earth below and find Marngu the opossum. Tell him he is to remind the people of my teachings. Let him say that those who quarrel shall declare their grievances before all the people. The people shall judge who is at fault, and they shall spear the guilty one so that he bleeds but does not die. The blood that falls to the ground shall atone for the wrongdoing, and the people once more shall be at peace."

Munjurr agreed to undertake the journey. The next morning he took the form of Guwarg, a bird with black feathers and red eyes, and set out. He flew up and down the coast seeking Marngu the opossum.

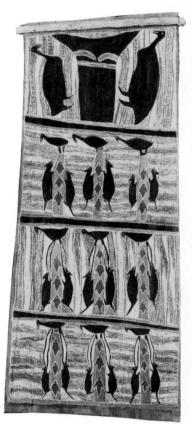

Night Birds and Opossums *by Nanjin. Nanjin had the right to paint these multiple versions of the myth, which have added power.*

Marngu was not there. He turned inland and combed the forests and the swamps. Marngu was not there. Wherever Guwarg went, below him he heard shouts and screams of fighting women. He saw men lurking in ambush, their spears leaving pools of blood on the ground. Even the children quarreled and threw stones.

Greatly troubled by what he saw, Guwarg redoubled his search.

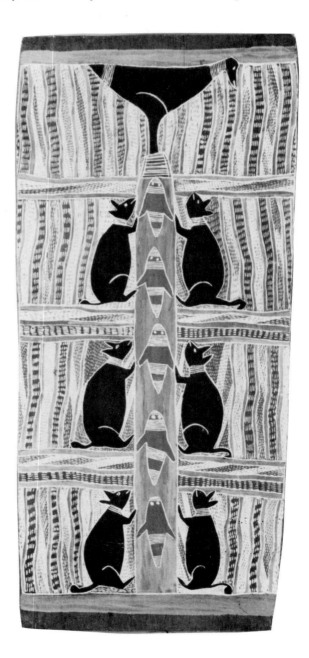

Possum and Night Bird
by Naridjin.

But the opossum could not be found. The next day, when the sun had become hot and bright, Guwarg finally caught sight of Marngu as he climbed a tree. By the time he had swooped down, the opossum had vanished without a trace.

The Sun Woman began to walk down the sky toward the horizon. The shadows grew long. Exhausted and discouraged, Guwarg alighted on a sacred tree, Waligul, which grows beside the beach at Djeragbi. It is a giant tree; its roots anchor in the sand and its trunk grows straight up until its topmost branches reach the Sky World. As Guwarg rested on a branch of this tree and brooded over his failed mission, a flock of cicadas began to fly around him. Guwarg looked up and called to them: "Help me find Marngu the opossum. I come from the Sky World with important words for him."

"We will help," they responded, and flew off in every direction. But their search also went unrewarded.

As night fell, Guwarg heard a movement inside the tree, a sound of scratching and scrambling. An opossum soon pushed his nose from an opening in the trunk that led to his lair. Guwarg looked. Perhaps, he thought, it was Marngu. "Is that you, Marngu? Come talk with me. I am Guwarg, from the Sky World," he called loudly.

Marngu studied the bird, then scurried toward him and sat quietly by his side. "I have been looking everywhere for you. I come with a message from Barama. Where have you been?" asked Guwarg with some annoyance.

"I sleep all day. I come out only at night," replied the opossum.

Appeased by the opossum's reply, Guwarg hopped closer to him and told him everything Barama said he must teach the *Manggalilji* people. Many hours passed as they talked. The moon came to life, illuminating the beach and the sea urchins lying on it. Crabs crawled from their burrows and left their paths in long lines on the white sand.

The next morning, Marngu changed himself into a man and went among the camps of the *Manggalilji*. He called the quarreling people together and told them Barama's words. But since they could not agree who was at fault, each side selected three representatives who would let themselves be speared in the thigh as a peace offering. The people danced and sang as the blood flowed, joyful that the hostilities were over.

So it was that the people learned to live peacefully with one another. To this day they settle their quarrels as Barama taught them. To this day Guwarg flies only at night so he can meet his friend Marngu. To this day the sacred tree at Djeragbi grows tall and straight. The opossum still has his den in the tree, and the cicadas still fly about carrying messages to the people. The patterns left in the sand by the crabs have become sacred totemic designs that the *Manggalilji* paint on their bodies and on bark to commemorate the story of the opossum tree.

The Night Bird
by Naridjin.

The Opossum
by Naridjin. Marngu the opossum looks up at Guwarg, the messenger bird who had come to find him.

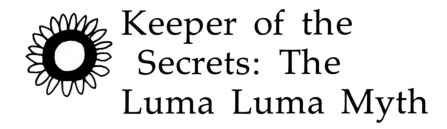

Keeper of the Secrets: The Luma Luma Myth

At intervals, often years apart, aborigines from many different groups gather at well-marked locations to conduct sacred ceremonies that celebrate the lives and deeds of their ancestral heroes. Often the bodies of the men are painted in distinctive designs to represent mythical figures.

The Luma Luma myth is one of the most important ceremonial cycles of the Gunwinggu tribe in western Arnhem Land. It is a feature of the age-grading rites that are conducted to initiate the boys into manhood. As the myth is sung and danced, it emphasizes the lesson all must remember: that adultery brings evil in its train.

LUMA LUMA was a giant who came long ago from the place of the mists, bringing with him many wives and children.

When the sun burns hot overhead the people sit in the shade of the palm trees and speak of Luma Luma. They tell of the long spears he carried and the knobbed club which he kept always close to hand, ready to break the heads of those who opposed him. They say that he belonged also to the sea and that at times his huge body could be seen surging through the waves in the form of a whale, accompanied by the barramundi fish, who was his constant companion.

At night, when the camp-fire embers die down and the shadows hide their faces, the people retell the tales they have heard from their fathers: of the children Luma Luma lured from their mothers, then killed with his club and roasted over his camp fire; of the women he took from their husbands and lay with openly in camp. They tell also of the great snake that made its way through the bush after Luma Luma, and at night shared his bed. And here the voices of the people die and they stare into the fire, for some things must not be spoken.

When Luma Luma first came to the Gunwinggu country long, long ago, in the Dreamtime, none knew from what land he came, or whether from the sea. He came through the heat haze, his massive form clearing a path through the grass for his wives and children, who walked in a file behind him.

The people accosted the strangers but when the giant with the great club showed he had no fear of them they let him pass. They saw that he carried a spear-thrower and many long spears as well as his club and that over his shoulder hung a net bag in which were many sacred totems—carved figures of the barramundi fish, the mackerel, and the goanna.

Luma Luma and his family camped at a place where there were many Gunwinggu people. At once, Luma Luma went to the men and made known his special powers. "I shall teach you songs and dances that will bring favor from the totemic spirits," he told them. "If you perform the ceremonies as I show you, the game shall increase. You

Body Designs
by Yirrawala. First-year body design (left) and second-year body design (right). Patterns are used as guides for painting the bodies of initiates in the age-grading rites, as directed by Luma Luma.

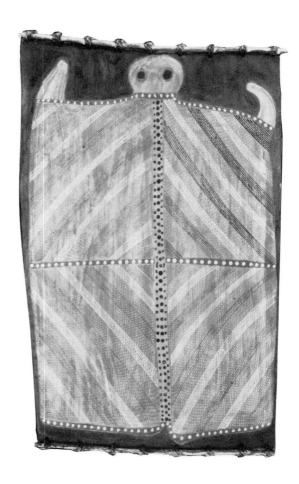

The Whale Who Became a Man
*by Ginilgini. Luma Luma changes
from his whale form into a man.*

shall have many children; sickness shall not visit you and you shall be happy."

The people learned the songs and dances and performed them faithfully. Luma Luma always led the singing and dancing and he guarded the totemic figures jealously. "If you sing the songs without the *mareiin,* the sacred totems that I have brought, the spirits will be angry," he told them. "Your bones will ache and your flesh will rot and you will die." So the people obeyed Luma Luma and sang and danced only when he was present with the totems to lead them.

Time passed and Luma Luma became interested in the wife of one of the men. "Come to the grassy place by the lagoon and lie with me," he urged her. But the woman repulsed him and this angered him greatly. "You shall yet do as I bid," Luma Luma told her. He took her net bag that she had hung on a tree and carried it to his fire. There he held it in the smoke and sang a magic song. The wife watched and she feared greatly, for Luma Luma's powers were well known. That evening she found the giant's footprints where he had walked in the soft ground from the camp to the lagoon. Luma Luma's magic reached out to her; she placed her feet in his prints, stretching to match his giant stride as she followed his path. When Luma Luma returned he saw the footprints and knew the woman had given in. That night her husband slept alone; the people heard as he beat his fist on the ground in his rage and fear.

Now each time the men went fishing or hunting, Luma Luma would seduce one of their wives. When the men returned, Luma Luma brought out the sacred totems and danced and sang the power ceremonies. So the men were afraid to confront him.

Soon some of the men began to plot against Luma Luma. "We will go to a secret place, where we will call upon the spirits to help us get rid of Luma Luma," they said. So the men went to a distant water hole and made a camp fire. They carved totemic figures and began to sing power songs, calling upon the spirits of the mackerel, the barramundi, and the goanna to help them overcome Luma Luma.

The giant was hunting when he saw smoke rising. He was surprised, for it was the middle of the day when camp fires were rarely lit. Luma Luma walked cautiously through the heavy grass until he

The Jealous Leader
by Bardjaray. Luma Luma and the net bag in which he carried his powerful totems.

The Barramundi
*by Mijaumijau. Western Arnhem
Land features the X-ray style. The
heart, lungs, and backbone of this
barramundi fish are shown.*

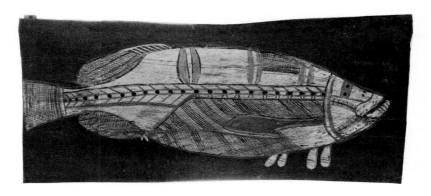

came to the clearing from which the smoke rose. Here several men
were conducting a sacred ceremony. Luma Luma watched. They were
dancing his dances and singing his songs, holding totemic figures
they had carved themselves. Shouting with anger, Luma Luma leaped
out of the bush, waving his spears. "You are not performing the dance
properly," he roared. "The spirits will be angered and will destroy us
all."

Surprised and frightened, the men tried to run away, carrying
with them the sacred totems. But on one side Luma Luma and his
spears blocked their way, on the other side was impassable bush. In
their fright, the men jumped into the water hole and began to swim
across. The sacred totems broke free and floated on the water. Luma
Luma saw the men were now beyond his reach. He was determined
they should not keep the totems, so he threw a spear at the nearest object, a wooden mackerel totem, and called out its secret name as he did
so. The totem turned into a mackerel and swam off. Luma Luma threw
his two remaining spears at the barramundi and the goanna totems,
and they, too, came to life and disappeared. Seeing this, the men
feared Luma Luma's power even more. They climbed out of the pool
and ran back to the camp to tell what had happened.

Now some of the men still plotted together and they laid a trap for
Luma Luma. They chose an open space by the sea, where Luma Luma
could come upon them only from one direction. Here they lit a fire and
placed green twigs on the blaze so a light smoke would be visible.
Then they covered their spears with sand and began to dance on the
beach, each man dancing back and forth over his spears.

Luma Luma saw the smoke and soon came storming into the
clearing. But the men were ready. At once, each grasped his spear between his toes and lifted it to his hand. The spears flew. *Thunk.
Thunk. Thunk.* Again and again they threw. The stone points drove
home until the green parrot feathers at their bases disappeared into
the giant's flesh. The spears pierced his shoulders. They lodged in his
belly. They stuck out from his arms.

Luma Luma tried to fight back, but he was weakened from the
blood that gushed to the sand. "Don't throw any more spears," he

said. "Let me live a little longer and I will give you the sacred totems. I will teach you the secret power words so that you will be able to call upon the spirits to help you. Then, when I am gone, you will remember my name with honor."

So they let Luma Luma live and he showed them the most secret mysteries. He taught them invocations and sacred names they had never heard before. From its hiding place in the bush he brought forth a carved figure of the Rainbow Snake, wrapped in paperbark. He poured water on the fire so that a cloud of steam arose. Then he held the sacred object in the steam and told them: "I purify this totem, for it is the strongest and most sacred. It will watch over you and cause your numbers to increase and prosper."

The Sun Woman was drawing close to the horizon when the end of the ceremonies neared. Across the water her beams made a path of light. "This is the last ceremony," said Luma Luma. "When I am gone, you shall dance it to commemorate my death. Both men and women shall dance it."

After he had shown them the final dance, Luma Luma walked down the sand and into the water. When they saw this, the people gathered on the beach. As they watched, a barramundi leaped from the sun path and fell back into the water with a splash. Luma Luma walked far out. The water reached his chin. It reached his eyes. It covered his head. Where he disappeared, a whale surfaced. It spouted water into the air, then swam down the sun path and followed the barramundi toward the deep waters.

"Luma Luma has become the whale," the people said. "The barramundi swims with him in the sun path and is his companion. Both shall always be sacred totems to us." And so it has been.

Luma Luma As a Whale
by Nguleingulei. Luma Luma in his whale form swims down the sun path with his friend, the barramundi.

The Greedy Boy: The Djert Myth

The aborigines usually divided food so that each person received a share depending upon sex, age and kinship.

Since weaker members of the tribe, both children and old people, had to look to the stronger for food to keep them alive, the rules for sharing were strongly enforced. Children learned the rules from their earliest years and here the myths served both to entertain and instruct. The story of Djert, who became a sea hawk, is a typical example, recounting the fate of a youngster who refused to share.

A BOY NAMED Djert lived in the *Manggalilji* country. He was of the sea hawk totem, as was his father and his father's father. "Your spirit is the spirit of the sea hawk," his father told him. "Remember well that your first ancestor took his food by force from the other birds, but then they would have nothing to do with him. Even today the sea hawk lives alone." But Djert was young, and his father's words meant little to him.

Djert had two brothers and three sisters who were generous in sharing the berries they picked and the shellfish they caught. Djert, however, was not like them. When he found crayfish in the shadowy places beside the lagoon, he grabbed it and ran into the deep shade of the mangrove trees to eat the tasty flesh by himself. If he came upon the nest of an emu with a clutch of eggs in the tall grass, instead of calling the others, he would walk by as though nothing were there. As soon as he was alone he would sneak back and sit in the grass beside the nest, cracking and relishing each egg until he had gorged himself.

One day their father decided to take Djert and his brothers fishing. They gathered their long, three-pronged fish spears and went to the beach, where the canoe had been hauled up on the sand. On the shore several sea gulls fought over a dead fish that had been left by the incoming tide. Far up in the blue sky a sea hawk soared in narrowing circles. Suddenly its wings folded and it dropped like a stone to the beach. The boys watched as it burst upon the gulls, scattering them right and left. In a moment, the sea hawk flapped slowly aloft, clutching the fish in its talons.

"Stop!" shouted the younger brother. He picked up a stone to throw at the bird, but Djert slapped aside his hand:

"He is stronger. Let him have the fish."

The younger boy held his smarting arm. "I wish you were a sea hawk. You act just like one." Djert nodded his head and smiled. Then he raised his arms and flapped them like the wings of the sea hawk.

The father and sons carried the canoe to the water and launched it. They went out beyond the breakers where the waves swept the canoe to great heights and the boys could see the long strings of clouds on the horizon.

Soon the father saw a mullet in the water and cocked his pronged fish spear. Far up in the sky, the sea hawk, too, saw the mullet. Suddenly, it folded its wings and plummeted downward. The father yelled to frighten it off. Djert watched, his eyes bright, as the bird seized the fish in its talons and flapped toward its nest in the high cliffs. "I shall be a sea hawk," he announced to his brothers, flapping his arms and rising. The canoe rocked. The father glanced back angrily, but Djert continued to wave his arms like wings.

The Fishermen
by Munggeraui. The boys go out to fish with their father.

"Sit down," commanded the father. Djert scowled but slowly complied.

Now Djert picked up one of the three-pronged fish spears and hefted it into his hand. Carefully, he stood up, drew back his spear, and riveted his eyes on the heaving water. The father observed his son, and now he grunted his approval. The younger boys steadied the canoe with their paddles. Through the water flashed a sleek barramundi, the rays of the sun glancing off its scales like small fires. Djert continued to watch intently as it approached, his arm cocked just the way his father had taught him. The spear flew. It hit. The fish leaped and thrashed. In his excitement, Djert plunged overboard and threw himself directly on the struggling fish. The canoe gave a great lunge. Without a moment's hesitation, the father dove in after him. In a few minutes he was back in the canoe with Djert and the flopping fish.

As darkness neared, they returned to shore. The barramundi was their only catch that day. While his father and brothers busied themselves beaching the canoe, Djert snatched the barramundi and ran off into the dense mangrove thicket at the water's edge. He returned empty-handed.

"Where is the fish?" the father asked. Djert raised his arms from his shoulders like the wings of the sea hawk. Defiance hardened his mouth.

"I caught the fish. It is mine. Only I shall eat it," said Djert.

"Food is shared. Everybody in the family has a right to eat of the fish," the father responded. "Bring it out and we will return to camp and cook it."

Djert was stubborn. "The fish is mine. Only I shall eat it," he insisted. His brothers moved closer to their father and looked sidelong at Djert. One put his fingers in his mouth.

"Long ago the Mother told us always to share," declared the father. "Evil comes to those who forget her words. Bring the fish to camp."

He turned and walked away, followed by the two smaller boys. Djert looked briefly toward the mangroves where he had hidden the fish. "No," he said. For supper the family ate lily bulbs and mangrove worms, and they chewed on water peanuts until their hunger dulled. No one mentioned the fat barramundi hidden in the mangroves.

Each day thereafter, while the younger boys searched for crabs among the rocks, Djert and his father went out in the canoe to fish. Offshore winds and rough seas worked against them. Several times the sea hawk returned. Djert watched the bird as it soared above them. "I shall be a sea hawk," he said to the wind that tossed the salt spray aloft.

Suddenly, the sea became generous. The wind died and the waves rolled smoothly. Sea gulls landed on the surface in groups to visit with one another and watch the minnows play in the clear water.

The father's spear struck time after time, and soon a half dozen fish twitched in the bottom of the canoe. Within a few hours the canoe was full, and they paddled triumphantly back to shore. The sun had not yet reached the zenith, but Djert was hungry.

"I will make a fire on the beach and we can eat one of the fish we caught," he suggested. The father said nothing. Djert turned to his brothers. "Help me gather wood," he snapped. Soon the coals were glowing, ready to cook a fish.

In the shade of a large boulder, the father dug a hole in the sand, piled in the catch of fish, and covered it with wet seaweed. He kept out only one large, fat barramundi. Silently and carefully, the father scooped aside the coals, laid down the barramundi, and heaped the embers over it. "The fish smells good," commented Djert loudly. His father did not reply.

Djert hugged his stomach. His nose quivered as he sniffed the tantalizing odors coming from the fish. He licked his lips. Soon the father rose. He took a stick and dug the fish from the coals. With his stone knife, he cut it apart. Djert watched as his father cut a generous portion for each of the younger boys, then carefully picked up a piece of the fish and placed it in his mouth.

"Where is my share?" Djert asked. The father said nothing. "I want to eat, too," complained Djert. He moved to help himself of the fish. The father rapped his reaching fingers with the back of his stone knife.

"You did not wish to share your fish. There is none for you now."

Djert's face screwed up. His mouth worked. His eyes watered. Dejectedly he turned and slouched to the shade of the pandanus tree, where he watched the others eat. Saliva filled his mouth.

Then a sea hawk flew into view from the cliff. Its broad wings curved out over the water, and it began the long arcs of its patrol. When it came close, Djert could see the lordly bearing of its head. His own arms felt the pull of the hawk's muscles as it thrust itself through the air. The bird stretched its head to search for prey in the tossing water. Djert's eyes tightened in the sharp wind. "Take me with you, brother," he called. His voice was carried away by the breeze. Djert's arms rose. He stretched his head as far as it would reach. His voice was thin and high as he called again: "Let me go with you, brother."

The father had finished eating. He wiped his hands and glanced along the beach to see what had become of Djert. The boy was nowhere to be seen. The father's eyes searched the foreshore and came to rest on the pandanus tree. There stood Djert, his arms outstretched, his body taut. Feathers covered his arms, his torso, and his legs. His arms had become wings; his mouth had narrowed to a sharp beak. With a shrill cry he thrust himself into the air. The father and brothers watched as the sea hawk beat its way into the blue sky, then turned and soared in long arcs over the shining sea.

The Bitter Fruit: The *Lala* Myth

Drought sometimes set in during the long dry season, when the wind blew steadily off the arid deserts to the southeast. The sun burned the land, the water holes contracted, food and game became scarce. The *lala* myth tells of a prolonged drought during which a man discovered how to use *lala,* a fruit with a hard shell that grows in profusion but is so bitter ordinarily that it cannot be eaten. The fruit of the zamia bush, *lala,* is a member of the Cycadaceae family.

IN THE MARINGAR COUNTRY, which is near that of the Murinbata people, there lived a spirit man named Rairem. The dry season had set in and there was little food. The birds and game scattered to find the water holes; the land was hot and dusty; the fruit and berries became tough and bitter. Rairem searched far and wide for food, but each day the search became more difficult. "My belly is empty," Rairem said. "If I do not find food, I shall dry up and die."

Far and wide he searched until finally he came upon a flat plain on which grew many clumps of bushes. Here was a water hole and near it Rairem made his camp. Then he set out to search for food. On the bushes, he saw many berries growing. These were called *lala,* but they had a hard shell and when he cracked them the fruit was so bitter he spat it out. "Here is food, but I cannot eat it," Rairem said. "Perhaps I can soak out the bitter taste."

He picked a great many *lala* berries from the bushes, placed them in his net bag, and carried them to the water hole. "I will leave them in the water," he said. Each day he tasted the berries and on the third day the bad taste was gone. Rairem broke open the *lala* berries to eat them, but the water had made them so soft that shell and fruit were crushed together. "This is too hard to eat," Rairem said. So he made a bag of a piece of paperbark and placed the *lala* berries in it. Then he roasted the berries in his fire until they were firm. Now it was easy to crack the shell, and when he ate the berries they were more tasty than ever. "This is good," said Rairem.

He continued his travels and at each place where he camped, he searched for the *lala* growing on the bushes. Finally, he came to the end of the country in which the berries grew. There he changed into a bird and flew back and forth over the territory through which he had traveled. To this day the people hold this flat country sacred to him and when they are hungry and soak the *lala* and roast it as Rairem did, they remember his exploits and commemorate them in dance and song.

The Berry Picker
by Majindi. Rairem made a paper-bark bag and put the berries in it, then placed them in the water to soak out the bitter taste.

When the Rains Came: The Napilingu Myth

The aborigines' nomadic life required them to carry all their possessions with them as they moved from place to place. Consequently, they developed temporary shelters only, and their tools and utensils were lightweight. During the wet season, families could camp in some comfort where caves or other natural shelters were available. In regions where this was not possible, the people learned to construct lean-tos out of sheets of bark stripped from the paperbark trees. From the bark also they fashioned containers for carrying fruits, other foods, and even water.

Paperbark has a special significance to clans of the *jiridja* moiety of northeastern Arnhem Land. The great leader, Banaidja, son of Laindjung, turned himself into a paperbark tree on the banks of the sacred water hole, Gululdji. When the people strip off this bark, they see on its undersurface raised lines similar to the honeycomb design that Banaidja painted on his chest as a sacred totem. Sometimes they also say that the thin bark represents the skin of Banaidja. Because it can be peeled in sheets and is pliant, the bark is one of the most versatile and useful materials the aborigines have.

The following myth tells of the paperbark and how the people learned to use it. The central character is Napilingu, a spirit being who came from Groote Eylandt with her husband in the Dreamtime. The paperbark tree, *Melaleuca leucadendra* and the stringybark, *Eucalyptus tetrodonta,* both provide pliable bark sheets that are folded and tied with fiber twine at the ends to form containers.

IN THE DREAMTIME, the woman Napilingu came to the *Manggalilji* country of northeast Arnhem Land. She was tall and strong and well formed. Her mind was quick, her hand deft, and she could hurl a spear as skillfully as she could dig yams. Napilingu came from beyond the horizon where the clouds hide Bralgu, the Island of the Dead. She came paddling her canoe through the mists made bright by Walu, the Sun Woman. With her came her husband, Burlung, a kindly man, long and thin. Together they paddled, driving the canoe on the long swells to the shore. They made camp and ate of the food they had brought. After resting, they took up their spears and dilly bags and walked inland.

Napilingu carried a long, pointed yam stick. It was decorated with sacred designs that gave it power. Never did she let the yam stick from her sight, keeping it even from Burlung. The power of the yam stick belonged to Napilingu alone.

As they traveled, Napilingu swelled with child. One day she stopped and said to Burlung, "We will camp here, for there are many children in my womb ready for life. Some I will leave at this place, for this is to be their land forever."

The Bearer of Water
by Nanjin. Napilingu carrying on her head the bark container she taught the women to make.

So it was that Napilingu gave birth to three boys and three girls, who grew so quickly that, before the moon had died once more, they were adults and had made camps of their own. Napilingu and Burlung continued their travels, stopping at all the places we know in the *Manggalilji* country, and at each place they left camps of the *jiridja* moiety.

One day the clouds lowered before the northwest wind, and thunderheads began to scud across the sky. Soon spears of lightning flashed through the clouds and glanced in jagged flames off the rocky cliffs. Rain poured in sheets from the black clouds, filling the dry watercourses. Day after day the rains continued until the rivers overflowed and the country was flooded. The people suffered by their fires under the trees, for they had no shelters. One by one the camp fires went out, and the men, women, and children huddled miserably together. Napilingu and Burlung traveled among them to bring cheer, but the children fell sick, the limbs of the men grew heavy, and the women searched vainly for food.

"What can we do, husband?" asked Napilingu. "Our people cannot find shelter or warmth. They cough. There is no game. The fruit and berries are moldy."

Burlung thought long. Then he sighed and said, "The great snake sends the rain and we cannot stop it. Surely the people will die."

As Napilingu thought how to help her children, the rain ran into her eyes and down her neck. Discouraged, she took her digging stick and walked among the trees. There she saw two tortoises that had pulled their heads inside their shells and paid no heed to the rain.

"The tortoise does not suffer from the rain," thought Napilingu, "for it carries its own shelter."

As she walked on, turning over leaves and bark with her yam stick, she saw on the ground a large piece of bark that had fallen from a paperbark tree. Under the bark huddled a mouse, snug and dry.

"The mouse also finds shelter," said Napilingu to herself. She looked up at the long pieces of bark that hung from the tree and flapped in the rain. Her thoughts were interrupted by a young woman who carried a baby in her arms.

"My child sickens from the rain and cold. Help me, Napilingu," she begged.

Napilingu looked about. Again she glanced at the long pieces of bark hanging from the tree. Suddenly she seized a strip and tore it free. "Here," she cried, placing it over the baby.

The woman held the bark in place with her hand. "Good! Good!" she exclaimed, for the child was protected from the rain.

Again Napilingu pulled at the bark on the tree, but in its sodden condition it broke off in small pieces. Impatiently, she took her yam stick and thrust it into a split in the bark to pry loose a larger piece. The stick slid easily behind the bark and separated it from the trunk.

"Aha!" Napilingu said and continued to force the bark with her stick until she was able to free a large piece. She lifted the sheet carefully and draped it over the head of the woman to ward off the rain. The mother exclaimed in pleasure and held tightly to the bark.

Now Napilingu pried off several more bark sheets and placed them against a fallen log. "They will form a shelter like the shell of Minala the tortoise," she said to the mother. While the woman huddled with her child in the lean-to, Napilingu seized a tree that had been hollowed by termites. She dragged it toward the shelter, dug dry wood from its core, and with this built a fire under the lean-to. Soon the woman and child were dry and warm. Napilingu was greatly pleased.

"Now you and the child need food," Napilingu remarked, looking at the soggy berries hanging on a bush nearby. She took a piece of paperbark, folded it and tied the ends with fiber string she took from her dilly bag. "I will fill this with berries," she told the woman, "and they will dry out in the warmth of the fire so you and the child may eat." Napilingu filled the bark container with berries and placed it beside the fire. She then folded another piece of bark, allowed it to fill with rainwater, and left it beside the container of berries for the mother to drink. "Now you and your child will remain warm and safe until the rain ceases," said Napilingu.

Napilingu went to Burlung and showed him what she had discovered. Together they made a bark shelter for themselves and bark containers for food and water. Then Napilingu went among her people and taught them how to shed rain and make vessels with the bark.

When the rains ceased, Napilingu called her people together and announced, "The spirit of the paperbark tree has been good to us. The tree and the yam stick that pried off the bark shall be sacred to our people. They shall be our totems, and we shall tell of them to our children and remember them in our ceremonies." And so it has been.

Bark Water Container
by Naridjin. A bark water container, with Napilingu portrayed on the front.

The Spear-Maker: The Jirukupai Myth, I

Since the aborigines did not invent the bow and arrow, the spear remained their chief weapon. The mainland tribes used spears with stone or bone spearheads, which they hurled at enemies and game. The spear was placed on a spear-thrower, a flat stick with a hook at one end which acted as an extension of the throwing arm. The Tiwi of Melville and Bathurst islands differed from mainland aborigines on two counts in their use of the spear. First, they did not employ the spear-thrower; second, they made spears with beautifully carved barbs that are not duplicated elsewhere. These were of two types: those barbed on one side only, called male spears and used exclusively by the men, and those with barbs on both sides, the female spears, which were used by both men and women.

A Tiwi myth tells of the man, Jirukupai, who originated the barbed spears and later turned into a crocodile. The spears he devised were used in the *pukamani,* or sacred, ceremonies and were taken on revenge forays to execute a man who had stolen a woman or had committed some other grave crime.

LONG AGO in the land of the Tiwi, the people had no spears. They used clubs and stones to hunt the wallaby and kangaroo, but the animals were quick and alert; even though the hunters went out every day, often there was no meat in the camp. When a hunter returned with game, the women smiled at him.

At that time there lived among the Tiwi a spirit man named Jirukupai. One day long ago he had walked through the sea to the shore; that was all anyone knew about him. At first he spoke a different tongue, but quickly he learned the language of the Tiwi. Soon the people discovered he was a magician. When the sky was bright and clear, Jirukupai would sometimes say to the children, "I will soon make rain. Run to find shelter."

At first the children taunted him and refused to run. But each time, black clouds formed on the horizon, lightning flashed across the sky, and rain poured down.

"Jirukupai is a magician. He makes rain," said the children to their parents.

One day Jirukupai was speaking to the wife of Abomara. He became so engrossed in her words that he forgot himself and touched her in a too-friendly manner. Abomara saw and his anger rose. He came forward, pushed his wife away, and reproached Jirukupai.

Jirukupai returned to his own camp fire. With a sharp stick he drew a human figure on the ground. He thrust the point of the stick into the figure and said, "This is Abomara. Thus Abomara shall die." Loudly he repeated the words, again and again, until all the camp knew.

Two mornings later when Abomara awoke he felt a slight pain in his back near the kidneys. He rubbed the place and found a sharp piece of wood embedded in his flesh. That day, Abomara's strength passed from his body. He could not eat, nor could he rest. His eyes grew dull, his muscles twitched. Soon after the first camp fires were lit, he died.

"Jirukupai makes powerful magic," the people said, and they feared him.

Far from the camp rose some hills. The ground there was rough, with many boulders scattered about. Hidden among the rocks was a small glade. Here Jirukupai had a secret place where he practiced magic. Every few days the people saw him leave the camp and walk toward the hills. "Jirukupai goes to cast his spells," they said, and they stayed away from the rocky place and its secrets.

Much time passed. The hair of Jirukupai turned gray. His two wives had borne many children who now lived in their own camps. Although Jirukupai's arm was no longer strong and his pace slowed early when he hunted, the people saw that Jirukupai always had meat. When others returned empty-handed, saying, "The kangaroo have gone far away to search for water," Jirukupai was sure to return with a kangaroo over his shoulder. When the hunters said, "We saw wallaby, but they ran so swiftly we could not catch them," wallaby would be roasting at Jirukupai's camp fire. When the others saw Jirukupai and his women eating meat while they had only yams and berries, it was hard to say which was greater—their wonder or their envy.

"Jirukupai is an old man. His ear is dull. His sight is clouded. He grows weak. Yet he kills the kangaroo when we cannot. It must be that Jirukupai makes magic," the men remarked. Whenever Jirukupai returned to camp, they examined his catch. Always it showed a deep

The Crocodile Dance
by Ali. The rectangles represent the skin of the crocodile, which Jirukupai became.

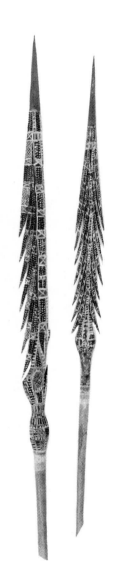

Male and Female Spears
*by Wombiaudimirra. Spears made
by the Tiwi; male spears have
barbs on one side, female on both.*

wound from which blood had flowed. "Jirukupai uses magic to approach the kangaroo," they muttered. "His magic makes it unafraid so he can kill it with his knife." For in no other way could they account for the wounds.

Finally, the men decided to stalk Jirukupai and see him work his magic. They watched and saw that before he set out to search for game, he went to a secret place in the bush. There he uncovered several long, straight poles, each with a row of backward-pointing teeth along one side, near the sharp tip: These were spears, which the men had never before seen.

With these strange weapons in hand, Jirukupai scouted about until he came to the feeding grounds of the kangaroo. The midday heat had passed, and the animals were coming out to feed. Jirukupai broke off a bush large enough to conceal his form. He held this before him and began to move toward the kangaroo. As it stooped to feed, he moved swiftly forward. The kangaroo looked up. It looked around. It saw only bushes. It lowered its head to feed, and once more Jirukupai advanced. Soon he was within a stone's throw of the kangaroo.

The men strained to see Jirukupai. His arm drew back, then flashed forward. *Whoosh* sang the spear through the air. *Thunk*. It struck the kangaroo hard enough for the men to hear. The kangaroo bounded once, then its legs collapsed and it fell to the ground. The men watched intently as Jirukupai lifted it and started back to camp. On the way he stopped at the secret place and once more hid his spears. Then he returned with his game.

The men debated. "We cannot take the sticks he throws, for then he will see us use them and will have the right to seek revenge. Let us make our own sticks and hunt as he does."

So they cut long, slender poles, and carved the backward-pointing barb near the top. Then they crept upon the kangaroo just as Jirukupai had done. A spear flew—and fell short. Another spear flew—and missed. The kangaroo bounded away unharmed. All day the men stalked the kangaroo. Again and again, spears sang through the air, but they failed to find their mark.

"We will go to Jirukupai and ask him to tell us his secret," the men agreed. "Perhaps he will show us how he makes his sticks so straight that they fly true." So they approached Jirukupai and asked.

"If I tell you, you will soon kill all the game," said Jirukupai. "Then I must go farther and farther to find kangaroo. I grow old. I will need to carry the game a long distance to my camp fire. This will be difficult. So it will not go well for me if I tell you the secret."

The men thought long on this. Then they returned to Jirukupai. "Tell us, old man, and we will share our game with you. Of everything we kill, we will bring a portion to your camp fire. Only tell us how to make pointed sticks that fly straight and true."

"Ho!" said Jirukupai. "If I tell you the secret, then I will be at your pleasure. If the game grows scarce or if you become angry with me, you may not keep your promise. I will suffer because I have helped you."

"What would you have us do?" the men asked. "It is not right that you refuse to share your secret."

Jirukupai thought a long time. At last he spoke. "I myself will make you the spears. I will make them straight and true so you will kill much game. But the first portion of each kangaroo you kill must be brought to me. After I have taken my portion, you can divide the remainder among yourselves. So long as you do this, I will keep you supplied with the spears you need."

So it was that Jirukupai made spears for the men. Whenever the weapons were broken or lost, Jirukupai made new ones and brought them to the camp. Now the men speared kangaroo and wallaby each day. When they returned from the hunt, they stopped at Jirukupai's camp fire so he could cut the first portion. Jirukupai sat by his camp fire and was content. To this day, the hunters still bring the first portion of the meat to the old men.

The Crocodile Man: The Jirukupai Myth, II

SOON JIRUKUPAI had more food than he could eat. If I give this food to others, they will be obligated to bring me many gifts, he thought. So he called the hunters to his camp fire. Choosing a fine kangaroo, to this man he gave a choice cut, to that one a shoulder, to another a leg.

The men felt indebted to Jirukupai. One brought him a stone knife, well fashioned and sharp of edge. Another offered him a carrying bag, knotted from the rolled fiber of banyan roots. Still others left at his fire fine belts, fighting clubs, and forehead bands.

Each day Jirukupai took the finest gifts and went alone to the secret glade in the hills. None dared follow, for they knew he carried his gifts to the spirit people. Any intruder would surely die. "He calls upon the spirit of the First Mother, and the Old Woman answers. He offers her gifts, and she helps him. Jirukupai has much power," the people said.

The men feared Jirukupai, but many of the women looked upon him with admiration. He came to them while their husbands were away on long hunting trips, and they did not resist him. In the camp the bolder women openly cast their eyes at him, and some even found excuses to visit his fire. The wrinkled wives of Jirukupai found no lack of young women wanting to befriend them.

Although his hair was white and his face lined, Jirukupai blossomed. His eyes became sharper, his step again firm. When he spoke at the camp fires of the other men, they listened attentively. But secretly they envied his success.

Jirukupai was especially attracted to a comely young woman called Ringga. Though she had taken up with a young hunter, Yodi, she lost interest and began to appear at Jirukupai's camp fire. Before long, the old man took Ringga as his third wife.

Now Yodi spoke angrily against Jirukupai. "He will take your wives," he warned the men, "for he has much food that we bring him. He has belts and opossum fur coverings and bark water-carriers that we give him. Your daughters will go to his camp fire, and your wives will steal into the bush with him."

The men muttered and tried to discover how Jirukupai made the spear shafts fly straight and true. But Jirukupai was cunning and protected his secret.

Yodi determined to follow Jirukupai to the spirit place in the hills and there learn the secret of the old man's power. First he made magic to protect himself. When everybody had gone into the bush to gather food, he stole to Jirukupai's sleeping place and took some of the soft paperbark from the old man's bed. With banyan strings, twigs, and bark, he fashioned a human figure and painted eyes and mouth with white clay. Then he cut a long, thin splinter of wood and sharpened it at one end. When this was done, he began the power song of his totem, the goanna. Over and over, he called upon the ancestor spirit for help. At the end of each song, he thrust the splinter into the figure and murmured, "So shall Jirukupai die."

When he had finished, Yodi put the bark figure in the dilly bag that hung from his neck and set out to find Jirukupai at his magic rites. Soon he was in the hills. Jumbled piles of boulders, their pitted sides stained with splotches of yellow and orange, blocked his way. A goanna scuttled across his path, its tongue darting in sham menace. Yodi felt his breath come hard, his blood pound more than the steepness of the trail warranted. He licked his lips. A twig cracked underfoot. A bronze pigeon froze in his path, then suddenly flew into the bush with a loud whirr of wings. Yodi stopped. He took the dilly bag between his teeth to give him courage, clenched his jaws, and moved ahead with extreme caution.

Then he saw a thin stream of smoke rising from the rocks ahead. In a few minutes Yodi had made his way through a line of eucalyptus and stood in sight of Jirukupai as he bent over a fire. Yodi crept behind a thick screen of bushes to observe.

Jirukupai was singing the song of the Old Woman. Carefully he placed his gifts of food and clothes in the fire and watched until they were consumed. The spear shafts were stacked beside the fire. Each he passed back and forth through the flames until it smoked; then he worked the softened wood against the hard ground so that the spear shaft became straight and true. This was his secret! As silently as he had come, Yodi stole back to camp.

The next day Yodi and a group of men lay in wait for Jirukupai near the place in the bush where he hid his spears. They watched him gather up the spears and start back along the river toward the camp. Many spears he carried, and they were long and straight.

One of the men balanced a spear. It sang through the air and struck Jirukupai in the back. The old man let out a cry of pain and began to run. More spears flew from the bush. They flew straight and true, and they struck Jirukupai. He dropped his bundle of spears, fled screaming to the river, and plunged in. The hunters raced to the bank and cocked their spears expectantly. But Jirukupai had disappeared.

The next day the men returned to the river, saying, "We must find the body and conduct the burial ceremonies lest his spirit cause us harm." Everywhere they searched: along the banks, among the rocks, and around the gravel spit that ran into the river. Jirukupai's body had vanished.

One of the men waded into the river and began to walk upstream. His head turned left and right as he watched the shoreline for Jirukupai's body. Suddenly he saw a strange animal lying in the sun on a sandbank. It had a long snout and a long mouth; long, too, was its tail. Its dark, leathery body was marked with ridges.

The man called to his companions, who came to observe the strange creature. They looked at its long snout. One of the men felt the welted scars on his body that marked old spear wounds, and then he pointed to the ridges on the hide of the animal. The men looked at one another and nodded their heads. Yes, they agreed, this was Jirukupai; he had turned into a crocodile.

To this day Jirukupai the crocodile lives in the river. The Tiwi people carve barbs on their long spears to resemble the barbs of his back and tail so that their spears will fly straight and true when they hunt him. Jirukupai's long jaw is ready to seek revenge on the men whenever he comes upon them. The women, too, he waylays and devours, for he has not lost his longing for them.

The First Crocodile by Uringi. After his enemies speared him, Jirukupai turned into the first crocodile.

The Bold Woman: The Spider Myth

Spiders have a special significance for many of the aboriginal groups. Some believe the spider's web catches the spirit of the newly deceased if it attempts to wander before the funeral ceremonies are completed and the spirit is escorted to Bralgu, the Island of the Dead. This myth tells how the spiders were first created and why they are found in dark caves.

IN THE COUNTRY of the Kalwayiin near that of the Murinbata people, there lived in the Dreamtime the ancestral spirits called Wandi who shared the same country. There was a woman among them named Jitai, who attracted men as the beehive draws honeybees. Jitai's husband had been killed in a fight and she had not married again. But she hungered for men and was bold and immodest with the husbands in the camp. The other women wore pubic coverings and sat correctly, with the heel of one foot drawn up to cover their private parts. Jitai often let her shield hang loosely, or forgot to wear it, and when she sat, her legs were parted. Other women looked at the ground demurely and never spoke when strange men appeared in the camp. Jitai not only looked at them boldly; she talked and laughed with them. If the stranger appealed to her, she might even lay her hand carelessly on his arm or shoulder—something the other women would never do.

Jitai slept with some of the men and pleased them greatly, but others she rejected. "You are ugly," she said, or "Your arms are too short," or "Your eyes are squinted." The rejected men began to murmur among themselves. "It is not Jitai speaking, for the other men are

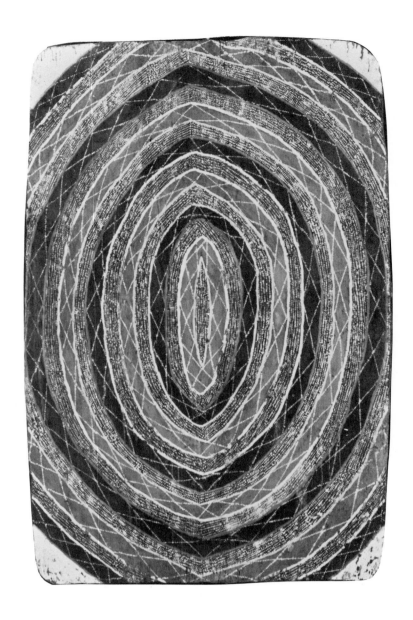

The Soul-Catcher Spider Web
by Ali

telling her these things about us. That is why she will not sleep with us,'' they said. So they went to the others and protested to them.

The wives began to talk among themselves. They complained to their husbands, for they knew that Jitai lay with men who were in an improper kin relationship to her. ''The ancestral spirits will be angered and will destroy us,'' they warned. The men who had relations with Jitai spoke in her favor; those she rejected complained angrily. Soon quarrels broke out. A spear flew and then another, and blood began to flow. Finally the men who favored Jitai drove off the unsuccessful ones and forced them to leave the camp with their families.

From that time the groups traveled about the country in two bands. Whenever they encountered one another, they fought fiercely. During the day, each band would send out scouts. If they caught sight of their enemies, they would lie in wait to ambush them. At night, when one band of the Wandi camped, another would creep upon them in the dark and try to kill them where they slept.

The men who had allied themselves with Jitai suffered most and soon over half their number were killed. "We must use our magic powers to protect ourselves," they said, "or soon we shall all be dead and then Jitai will fall into the hands of our enemies."

So they sang magic songs and called up snakes with poison in their fangs to kill their opponents. But the other group made magic also and killed the snakes as soon as they appeared. Then they called up a great cloud of stinging hornets, but the other men changed themselves temporarily into rocks and the hornets did them no harm.

Then the men with Jitai used their magic to pile up great hills of earth and stone, and on the sides of the hills they dug caves where they could camp in safety. However, the other band of Wandi climbed the hills and attacked them in their caves. Ever higher they piled the mountains, but still they were attacked.

Finally the men with Jitai made a mountain higher than any ever seen in that country. Its top reached into the Sky World and its sides were hidden by clouds. In a deep cave on the side of the mountain they camped with Jitai. One morning the men caught a goanna and cooked it; as they ate, they caught sight of their enemies far below, climbing slowly toward them.

"Let us climb to the top of the mountain and stay forever in the Sky World, where our enemies cannot find us," the men said. So, with Jitai accompanying them, they began to climb. Over great boulders, past cliffs and chasms they toiled. After a time the air became thin and cold. The mist swirled about them. The higher they climbed, the more they gasped and struggled for breath and the thicker the mist became.

Jitai suffered most of all. Soon she fell to the ground. "I cannot go on. You must leave me," she said. But the men picked her up and carried her back down the mountain. Through the clouds they carried her, past the towering rocks and the deep ravines. Finally they came to the cave they had left. "Our enemies will find and kill us," Jitai said. "We must hide from them."

So they changed themselves into spiders. They crawled into the crevices in the rock and hid themselves in the darkness. When their enemies appeared, they found nothing. The spiders and their descendants spread to the other caves and made their homes on the riverbanks and among the rocks and there they are found to this day.

The Spider
by Djinu Tjeemaree. The spiders hide in crevices in the rocks—a symbolic representation.

The Man Who Became Black: The Ship-Totem Myth

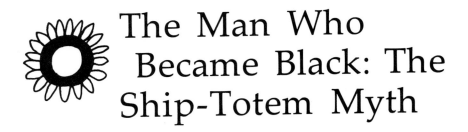

We do not know whether the aborigines gave thought to the color of their skins until the coming of the Makasans, but they undoubtedly noted that the seafarers from the north were a lighter brown. The advent of white Europeans brought even greater contrast. In their myths, the aborigines explain why these differences in skin color arose. The ship-totem myth is told on Groote Eylandt and would appear to be relatively modern; certainly no older than the Makasan visits in the early seventeenth century.

LONG, LONG AGO the Ingura people of Groote Eylandt had many camps. They spent much of their time in the open bush and on the hills, stalking the kangaroo and wallaby. The stretch of water that separated them from the mainland kept trespassers away and made it easy to detect and repel enemies, so the people hunted and fished and lived together in peace.

In those days, the Ingura people were different, for their skins were white, unlike the people on nearby Bickerton Island and the mainland, who were a rich, dark brown color.

Among the Ingura lived a young man named Bajima. He had been circumcised and the first scar had been cut on his chest. Soon he would bring to his camp fire the girl Tageea, to whom he had been betrothed before her birth. When Bajima killed a kangaroo, often he would take a haunch to Tageea's parents. "Eat and give a choice portion to the girl who will be my wife," he would tell them. But his heart was not in his words; he said them only because that was the custom. Tageea was short and fat. She giggled when Bajima came near. So his eye remained cool and there was no stirring of his blood toward her.

However, Tageea was deeply smitten with her prospective husband. She found excuses often to visit his fire; there she stood at a distance, gazing with admiration at every move Bajima made, but responding only with giggles and a shy retreat into the bushes if he so much as turned to speak to her.

This exasperated Bajima. "How can I take such a child to my bed?" he asked his mother. "She has as much appeal as Inigia, the goose." His mother tried to reassure him. She spoke to Tageea, encouraging her to bring food to Bajima and to sit and talk with him. But nothing came of it.

To the west of the land of the Ingura lay Bickerton Island, inhabited by the brown-skinned Wuramura clan. They were a fierce people and proud. Because of the difference in their skins, the Ingura mixed little with them, although at times the men would meet together for the great *arawalta* ceremony that celebrated their common descent from the creator ancestors. Among the Wuramura lived a medicine man named Mungada. He had come long ago from the mainland and brought with him secret lore he had learned from the old men of his tribe. Mungada did only good with his magic; he healed the sick, settled quarrels, and brought peace to those who fought with one another.

The fame of Mungada spread far, and Bajima knew of his powers. He determined he would go to the camp of Mungada and ask him to cast a spell so that the ardor of Tageea would cool and he might find a wife more to his liking. So one day Bajima paddled to Bickerton Island. About his neck he carried the spirit bag which he had worn during the *arawalta* ceremony, where it had acquired the power to protect him. In it, he had placed a bit of Tageea's hair, which had caught on a thorny branch when she left his camp.

As the island came into view, Bajima gradually made out a large object floating on the water near it. He could see a number of figures on the shore. Coming closer, he saw it was one of the great canoes with sails that brought the Makasans on the northwest monsoon to trade for trepang. He knew the Makasans came in peace, but he approached the overhanging stern of the boat with caution. His eyes took in the tall tripod mast as he paddled quickly to shore. Several Makasans were eating around a fire. They looked up and stared at his white skin. One called out in his own tongue, but Bajima did not understand and hurried quickly past.

Soon Bajima came to the camp of Mungada. The medicine man was tall and broad of shoulder. Cicatrices scarred his body, and a sacred design was painted on his torso. Around his neck he carried a bag which contained the magic substances he used in casting spells. As Bajima approached, Mungada saw his white skin and knew him for one of the Ingura people. "What brings you across the water to my camp?" he asked. Bajima explained his mission: "I am betrothed to the girl Tageea. She causes my stomach to become sour and my eyes to

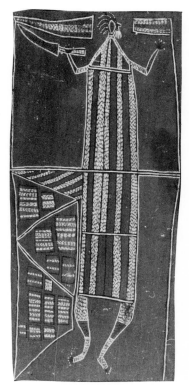

The Medicine Man, Mungada *by Mandaga. The medicine man helped people with his magic.*

The Malay Prau
by Bukunda. The Makasan prau
was anchored to the beach.

dull, yet she loves me with all her heart. Make me a spell that will turn
her to another man. Let me be free of her.''

Mungada thought on this. ''She is betrothed to you and her people will be angry. It is better that you marry her,'' he said. But Bajima
would not change his mind. ''I will give many gifts to my mother's
brother and his wife. You have strong magic. Turn the girl Tageea to
another. I cannot make her happy,'' he said.

Mungada smoothed a place on the ground. There he drew a figure
with breasts. On the head he carefully placed the scrap of hair. This
was Tageea. Then he drew another figure, that of a man with his back
turned to the woman. Mungada cupped his hand beneath Bajima's
armpit and scooped it back, covered with sweat. He let several drops
of the sweat fall on the male figure. This was Bajima. Now he began to
sing in a high, droning monotone. Slowly, with his hands, he
smoothed the figure of the woman until it disappeared. Twice he
redrew the woman and each time he smoothed it away. ''Now you are
free,'' Mungada said. ''But be careful, for your heart is empty, and you
will try to fill it with the first woman you see.''

Bajima gave Mungada the gifts he had brought and thanked him
profusely. He turned to leave, only to find a tall, lithe woman swinging easily down the path toward him. Her breasts were high and firm,
and her smooth brown skin gleamed in the sunlight. Bajima gazed at
her with pleasure. He moved to greet her, but Mungada took him
gently by the elbow. ''I will go with you, for the Makasan men on the
beach may cause you trouble because of your white skin,'' he said.

But Bajima was not to be put off. ''Who is the girl?'' he asked.

Mungada nudged his elbow again. "She is Dablian, the daughter of my sister," he said. Bajima's face showed his pleasure, for the girl was of the opposite moiety and not forbidden to him. In spite of Mungada's gentle tugging, he turned to the girl and greeted her warmly. She looked curiously at his white skin, but his strong build and frank, open gaze pleased her, and she responded with warmth. Bajima stayed for a short time and talked with the girl. As he began to leave, he took the spirit bag from his neck and placed it in the girl's hand. The bag was Bajima's most prized possession; in offering it to Dablian, he was asking her to marry him. The girl looked at the bag, then at Bajima. She saw the look of disapproval on her uncle's face and tossed her head. Her hand closed on the small leather bag, and she tied it around her neck. Then, with a backward look at Bajima, she ran off down the trail.

Mungada rose. "Your skin is white; she cannot be your wife," he said.

Bajima was silent. "You can make magic; change my skin so I also shall be brown," he begged after a few moments. But Mungada shook his head. "I do not have the power."

From the beach came the sound of singing and the creaking of masts as the mainsail was raised on the Makasan *prau*. "The Makasans are preparing to return to their country," Mungada remarked. He thought a moment. "It is said that the Makasan man, Bapa Jago, can make powerful magic. I will talk to him." He searched in his spirit bag for two pearls that glowed in the sun as he showed them to Bajima. "The Makasans value these. I will give them to Bapa Jago, and he will help you before he leaves."

So it was that Bajima stood before Bapa Jago, a small and gentle man who wore trousers of batik. Bapa Jago took charcoal from the fire pit, mixed it to a paste with water, then plastered it over Bajima's white skin. In his strange tongue, he repeated an incantation three times. "Bathe in the water," he directed. Bajima splashed in the tidal pool. But when he stood on the sand, his skin was as white as ever. Twice more Bapa Jago repeated the spell. Twice more Bajima bathed and his skin remained white.

Bapa Jago appeared nonplussed. Finally he went aboard the boat and came back with a handful of black powder, which he placed in a small pile. He positioned Bajima so that the wind was blowing in his direction. "Don't move," he directed. Then he dropped a lighted coal on the black powder. A great blaze and a cloud of smoke shot up. All the sailors left their tasks and drew near. The smoke poured over Bajima, all but suffocating him, but he did not move.

When the smoke had cleared, Bapa Jago again inspected him. His skin was smudged, but it was still white beneath the grime. Bapa Jago grunted. He thought awhile, then talked to several of the men. With their help, he lit a great fire on the beach on which he placed green wood. Then he bade Bajima stand in the smoke that poured forth.

Bajima suffered more grievously than before. But he endured, for his longing for the girl was great.

The ship's gong sounded. Its great sail bellied out in the freshening wind. It strained against the anchor rope that held it. Bapa Jago looked carefully at Bajima. "Your skin begins to darken," he said. "But I must leave, for the wind carries our ship back to our country."

Bajima looked at his skin. His hands and arms were darkening, as were his legs and chest. Hope lighted his face: the spell was working. "Stay until the spell is finished," he begged Bapa Jago. But the sailors were tugging at the old man. The last canoe was ready to leave for the ship. Bapa Jago patted Bajima's shoulder. "I must leave, but at every camp I will make a great fire. I will repeat the magic spell so the smoke will reach you and your skin will become brown."

So it was that each day a great pall of smoke rose on the horizon and was blown by the wind until it reached Groote Eylandt. As the Makasan ship moved north day by day, the smoke originated farther away. But always it reached the island of the Ingura people, to which Bajima had returned. Each day Bajima saw his skin darken to a deeper tone. And he saw, too, that the skin of all the Ingura people became brown. When the Makasan *prau* reached Melville Island, the sailors stayed a long time, boiling their trepang before they set off for their home. Each day the long streams of smoke flowed across the sea, and steadily the skin of Bajima and his people became darker, until they were as dark as everybody else. Because they were closest to the fire, the Tiwi people of Melville Island became even blacker than those of the other tribes.

One day Mungada led a group of people to the beach. Bajima had come to claim Dablian. Amid singing and happy shouts, the two pushed off in a canoe. Bajima placed his foot against that of his bride. In the sunlight both their skins shone warm and brown.

PART VI

THE COMING OF DEATH: FUNERAL MYTHS

Pukamani Grave Poles
and Baskets
*Grave poles surround the body of
the deceased.*

WHEN DEATH COMES to an aboriginal, it brings both sorrow and fear, as it has to humans from earliest days. To the living, death is both a mystery and a threat: The living look at the corpse and wonder where the life they knew has gone; they look again and fear grips them that one day their own bodies shall also be as cold and empty.

Most of the clans believe death is caused by sorcery, so the bereaved take great care to limit the effect of the magic. A number of obligations must be fulfilled. First is the need to persuade the spirit of the dead person to return to the sacred water hole from which it came before birth, so that it will not wander and bring harm to the living. The few belongings of the deceased—man or woman—must also be distributed. If the deceased is a man, his rights to sacred designs and secret knowledge must be assumed by the proper recipients and arrangements must be made for his wives to remarry or enter a new household.

A variety of ceremonies accompanies these events. Rituals begin when death appears to be at hand. After death, kinfolk gather and sing totemic songs. Wives and relatives lament; the wives cutting themselves until blood flows to convey proper grief to the spirit that is hovering nearby. Songs are sung while the totemic design of the departed is painted for the last time on his body. The ceremonies continue as the corpse is placed on a tree platform or buried in the ground until the flesh is decomposed.

Several months later, further rituals mark the exhumation of the bones, which are painted with ocher, broken with a stone, and buried in a hollow log. Grave figures or posts are carved and placed by the

Pukamani Grave Pole,
Melville Island

grave so the spirit will know where to return and will not haunt the living. The senior wife may carry the skull of the deceased around her neck on a cord for a time to show the depth of her sorrow. Some of the small bones are given to near kin, either to use in sorcery or to pass on the power or *mana* of the departed.

The ceremonies, evolving over millennia, serve many purposes. They help ease sorrow and relieve fear. At the same time, they draw the survivors together in bonds of shared grief, sympathy and support. And, finally, they reaffirm for all that the laws, values and customs that were decreed by the totemic beings in the Dreamtime are still alive and in force.

Burying the Dead
by Madaman. The body of the deceased is laid out. Fires keep the spirit away.

How Death Came: The Purukapali Myth

The Tiwi of Bathurst and Melville islands have their own version of the coming of death, which they tell in the myth of Purukapali. Tiwi funeral ceremonies are called *pukamani,* which means sacred or taboo, and are quite similar to those of other regions, except for the use of the unique *pukamani* poles.

The poles, frequently six to fifteen feet high, are carved and decorated between the time of death and final burial. They are made in only a few basic designs, which are thought by some researchers to be derived from similar grave posts used by coastal tribes of central Papua, New Guinea. At the conclusion of the funeral ceremony, large empty bark food baskets are upended on top of the poles to show that all is over. The strongly sculptured, dramatic posts, made from ironwood, remain at the grave site to decompose slowly over the years.

The primary theme of the Purukapali myth is told in fairly uniform fashion among most of the Tiwi groups; however, there are many variations in the details. I have tried to maintain the basic story while reconciling minor differences.

Bones and Skulls
by Djadjiwui. The bones and skulls are painted with totemic designs.

IN THE PLEASANT LAND of the Tiwi people, Purukapali lived with his wife, Bima, and their infant son, Djinini. This was in the earliest days when spirits became men and death had not yet come to the earth. In their camp also lived Purukapali's younger brother, Tjapara, strong and handsome. Many times the brothers stalked wallaby together, but most often it was Purukapali who carried game into the camp and received the women's praise.

Tjapara had no wife and he hungered for Bima. One morning after the brothers had returned from the hunt, Bima rose and placed

Pukamani Grave Pole and
Baskets
*The baskets are split and placed on
the prongs of the grave pole to
show all is finished.*

the sleeping Djinini beside her husband, who was skinning a slain wallaby.

"I go find yams," she said. "Guard the child. He will sleep now and will have my milk when I return."

She picked up a net bag and walked off into the bush. Tjapara watched her swinging hips and said, "I saw shellfish at the shore. I will go gather them," and he strode off toward the beach, leaving Purukapali with the sleeping child.

As soon as he was well out of sight, Tjapara quickly circled back through the bush and came upon Bima as she bent over her digging stick. Softly he crept upon her and clasped her from behind.

"Lie with me," he urged.

Only a moment did the wife of Purukapali resist. Then the long hours slipped quickly by. In the camp the child cried for his mother's milk. Still the couple tarried. From the camp came the faint voice of Purukapali calling his wife. Bima started to rise, but Tjapara was still eager. "Soon," he said and pulled her toward him.

Now the Sun Woman carried her torch to the horizon and the shadows grew long. Again the voice of Purukapali sounded, angry and stricken. Bima rose to answer, but Tjapara placed his hand over her mouth.

Preparing the Bones
by Madaman. The bones are painted with ocher and laid out for final ceremonies.

The Entreaty of Tjapara
*by Mani-luki. Tjapara asks that he
be given the dead baby for three
days so he can restore it to life.*

Purukapali and His Dead Son
*by Mandarbarni. Purukapali holds
his dead son in his arms.*

"We must go bathe, or Purukapali will know we have lain together," he said.

The two went to a hidden cove and entered the water. They played together in the coolness and ate some crabs they found near the shore. This was Tjapara's favorite food. But Purukapali's angry voice again reached their hearing. The frightened Bima took her net bag and hurried to camp. She found Djinini on the grass, cold and still. Death had come to him in the early darkness. Bima lifted the child and pressed him to her breast.

Now Purukapali turned on his wife. "He was hungry. He cried for you and you did not come. Now he is gone from us and will not return," said the father, and he wrested the dead infant from Bima's arms.

Bima began to moan and beat her breast. "I am a bad woman, for I let my son die," she cried.

Hearing this, great anger came to Purukapali. Still holding his dead son, he turned on Bima and began to beat her with his free hand. As she bent before his blows, Tjapara stepped from the bush and thrust himself between the couple.

"Give the child to me, brother, and I will bring him back to life in three days," he said.

But Bima lashed out at Tjapara in despair. "You killed him!" she accused, "for you would not let me go!"

Now did Purukapali understand. Still holding fast to the child, he picked up a forked fighting stick and attacked. "You, too, shall die!" he screamed at his brother.

Tjapara refused to run and begged again for the child. But Purukapali threw the stick in response and struck his brother in the eye. "You will die as the baby died," he shouted. In his excitement, Purukapali dropped the lifeless body of Djinini.

Half blinded, Tjapara fought back. Soon the two men were locked in combat. Blood gushed from Tjapara's gouged eye and from the gashes on his face. He began to weaken.

Now Bima picked up Djinini and held him out to her husband. "Take the child you loved so dearly," she pleaded. "Do not kill your brother."

Her plea went unheard as Purukapali again hurled his killing stick. Tjapara fled to a tall tree and frantically began to climb. When he reached the top limb, he let out a great shout and leaped into the sky, rising higher and higher until he reached the moon.

Purukapali returned to camp and took Djinini's body in his arms. "I shall die with my son," he announced to the Tiwi people. "And all who now live also shall die."

Then he danced the first ceremony of death and sang of the events that led to it. "This shall be your *pukamani* ceremony," he decreed, "and you shall dance it to remember those who die." Purukapali wrapped his son in paperbark, walked backward into the sea, and disappeared. As he sank beneath the surface, a whirlpool formed which marks the spot to this day.

Bima lived on, but grief soon made her haggard and old. She wandered about the camp, complaining in a shrill voice until she, too, died. Her spirit lived on as the curlew bird, which still flits and cries mournfully about the beaches.

Tjapara became the Moon Man. He can be seen in the night sky, his face marked by the bruises and wounds that Purukapali inflicted. He still feels Purukapali at his heels, for he never ceases his restless journey. Hungry from his travels, he gorges on crabmeat, growing rounder and fatter each day until he has feasted so much he falls sick. His wasting body is the waning moon. Each month he dies, but after three days he comes back to life and begins his journey once again. His loneliness is over, for he has found many wives, the planets, who accompany him on his journey across the sky.

So death comes to the people of earth, the Tiwi say, but always life returns.

The Grief of Bima
by Djulabiyanna. Bima in sorrow after she neglected her baby son to commit adultery and he died.

The Killer Snake: The Gurramuringu Myth

The aborigines usually attributed death to the work of magic or an evil spirit. Myths sung and mimed during funeral ceremonies often described how death came about, and warned the living of dangerous conditions to be avoided. In their mortuary rites the people of the Urgigandjar clan, who speak the *Djinang* tongue, tell the story of Gurramuringu, the great hunter, who sat under a tree one day to cook his food. A snake came from the grass and killed him. Another myth tells of the evil spirit that lived in the tree. I have combined the two and have added local color.

IN THE DREAMTIME, the Djanggawul sisters and their brother thrust their sacred *rangga* sticks into the ground at the places where they stopped to rest. When they withdrew the sticks, the holes filled with water and are today the sacred water holes of the aboriginal people. The water hole of the Urgiganjdjar clan is at Milmindjal to the east beyond the Woolen River. It is a deep well, surrounded by wooded banks and fed by creeks and springs so it is always full.

In those *wongar* times many spirit beings came to live at the water hole. The catfish spirit came and lurked in the deep holes at the bottom of the pool. The spirit of the harmless file snake came also, to make its home in the bushes beside the pool. The spirit of the emu came, of the diver bird, and of the hawk, and they turned themselves into the creatures that we see today.

One day the water-lily spirit came to the pool. It saw where the water overflowed among the mangroves and where the sun shone warmly on the shallow water. "This is a good place for me," the spirit said, and settled into the shallow water. Down into the rich mud it sent its roots. And on the surface of the dark water it spread rich green leaves to catch the sunlight. Soon the blue and white petals of its flowers nodded in the bright air.

The waters of the pool were quiet and peaceful. Bees droned among the flowers; emu chicks ran from the bushes behind their mother. Here was a place of warmth and contentment.

Near the pool lived Gurramuringu, the mighty hunter. He was known throughout the country for his skill in tracking game, and for the number of kangaroos and wallabies he brought back to camp and shared with others of his clan. Gurramuringu had a wife, Durandur, and several grown children. Durandur was of the water-lily totem, and she took delight in sitting on the grassy bank of the pool and talking to the lilies. They swayed and nodded in response to her words. When the diver duck swooped from its perch by the water hole, Durandur would watch its swift flight and smile. When the duck's eggs hatched and the ducklings swam close to the shore like yellow balls of fluff, Durandur caught flies for them and laughed as they snatched them up in their tiny bills.

As Durandur's devotion to these friends grew, many times she told Gurramuringu, "Hunt where you will, but do not take your spear to the pool at Milmindjal; there the spirits come, and I would protect them."

Gurramuringu nodded and stayed far from the pool. And so the seasons passed. Then, one day when the rain poured down and the spear of the Lightning Man pierced the sky, an evil spirit, black and many limbed, found his way to Milmindjal. Seeing the pool was a pleasant place, he turned himself into a great tree, thrust roots deep into the bank, and spread long, dark branches over the water. Then the tree spirit called to the deadly brown snake. "Come live with me by the Milmindjal pool," he said, "for here there is food in plenty." So the snake came and made its home in the deep bush by the pool.

That year heavy rains flooded the land. Gurramuringu ranged far and wide with his spear, but game became scarcer and scarcer. One day, in discouragement he spoke to his wife, Durandur. "The game has fled. For many days now my spear finds no target. We hunger. At the pool is much food. The duck and the emu are there, the goanna and file snake. I will hunt there."

"The spirits who live at the pool are my friends," protested Durandur. "Do not kill them." And she had her way.

Soon after, the rain ceased and the sun shone once again. Durandur went to the pool and took her place on the grassy bank. Somehow, it seemed, a great tree had grown where no tree had been, a tree whose dark arms loomed out over the water. Durandur was puzzled.

Just then, her attention was diverted by a diver duck swimming from the reeds into the warm sunshine. Four ducklings paddled be-

Wife of the Mighty Hunter *by Malangi. Durandur, who cared for the creatures of the water hole.*

hind her. Durandur smiled. "You have a fine family," she called. The diver duck fluttered its wings and turned its bright eyes toward her.

Unnoticed by its mother, one of the ducklings veered off toward the bank after a juicy bug that had floated by. Suddenly a brown snake whipped from the bushes by the water's edge, fastened its fangs around the duckling, and retreated into the foliage. Durandur screamed, picked up a rock, and threw it into the shrubs. But snake and duckling vanished. Death had come to the peaceful pool.

Now, as the days passed, the rays of the sun grew strong. Once again the game fled and the spear of Gurramuringu remained at his

The Evil Tree Spirit
by Malangi. *The evil spirit turned itself into a tree and lay in wait for Gurramuringu.*

Kangaroo and Snake
*by Malangi. The kangaroo caught
by Gurramuringu, the great
hunter, with the deadly snake.*

side. The evil tree spirit noticed that Gurramuringu never approached the pool. "I will entice the mighty hunter," said the tree to the brown snake, "and when he is near, you can kill him."

The next time Gurramuringu set out to hunt, the evil spirit was prepared. As Gurramuringu crept through the bushes, a kangaroo sprang into the open. The mighty spear flew: the kangaroo stumbled, recovered, and bounded away. The hunter set off in pursuit as the kangaroo fled toward the pool. Again Gurramuringu took aim and this time the kangaroo fell to the ground and lay still. As the hunter ran

The Hunter Rests
*by Malangi. Gurramuringu stops
to cook his food by the water hole
after a successful day's hunting.*

forward, a goanna scuttled across his path. The club of Gurramuringu
flashed through the air and caught the goanna behind its head. It, too,
fell dead. Soon Gurramuringu killed an emu, then he noticed the surrounding bushes were heavy with berries, so he paused long enough
to fill his dilly bag with them.

Laden with meat and fruit, Gurramuringu turned toward camp.
Just then he caught sight through the trees of the grassy bank and
bright waters of the pool. "I will stop and make a fire and cook some
food to refresh myself," thought the weary hunter.

He set down his catch beneath the spreading limbs of the tree and went off to gather wood. When the fire was blazing, he cut up the kangaroo and put a haunch on the flames. Then he settled back to rest. Suddenly a sharp pain shot through his leg. With a shout, Gurramuringu lunged for the brown snake that had fastened its deadly jaws into his calf muscle. The earth shook; the bushes quivered and bent. But the venom crept through the veins of the mighty hunter and his struggle was quickly over.

As the Sun Woman walked toward the horizon and the shadows lengthened, Durandur came to the pool to fetch the evening water. There, at the foot of the dark tree, she found Gurramuringu, cold and still.

So it is that the people commemorate the life and death of the mighty hunter, Gurramuringu. They tell of the evil tree spirit and of the poison fangs of the brown snake. Whenever death comes to the Urgigandjar camps, this tale is repeated so all will know.

Gurramuringu,
The Mighty Hunter
by Malangi. When the great hunter stopped to cook his meal after a day's hunting, the snake bit and killed him.

Death of the Great Hunter
by Malangi. Gurramuringu's corpse is shown in the center as the mortuary rites take place after he was killed by a poisonous snake.

How Mutjinga Lived Again: The Crab and Crow Myth

According to some threads of Murinbata tradition, the people did not really want to kill Mutjinga, the child-eater, after she swallowed the children but were forced to since she had willfully violated their laws.

The Murinbata people know that crabs, if left alone during molting, do not die, but rejuvenate themselves by shedding their old shells and growing new ones. Mutjinga's spirit retained its life by assuming the form of a crab. The crow, meanwhile, symbolizes man; it is impatient and vindictive, demanding that the old woman die.

In some versions of this myth, the crab offers the option of renewed life to the crow, if only he will follow her example of shedding and replacing an outer covering. However, the crow is disbelieving and reaps the consequences.

THE OLD WOMAN, Mutjinga, was speared because she had eaten the children of her clanspeople. The men had cut her open and taken the children from her belly. Mutjinga lay in her blood, but her spirit did not leave her body; her spirit still lived.

"We will not conduct a proper burial for the old woman, for she wronged us," the ceremonial leader said, "but we do not want her spirit to haunt us, so we will bury her body in the ground." Mutjinga heard these words, but her eyes did not move. Her mouth did not move. "They may bury me, but I shall not die," Mutjinga thought.

The men dug a hole. There they placed Mutjinga with her face down, so her spirit would not leave the body to cause them trouble. Then all the people returned to the camp with their children.

Birds came and scratched in the fresh earth on Mutjinga's grave. The Sun Woman traveled far in her journey across the sky. Shadows lengthened and small animals came from the bush. An opossum came to Mutjinga's grave, searching for bulbs, and the birds flew away. In the ground Mutjinga's spirit rested and waited, for it had not died.

In the trees a crow spirit sat on a branch. He watched then flew from the branch and alighted on Mutjinga's grave. He knew her spirit still lived beneath the earth. The black bird cocked his head and spoke to Mutjinga in his loud, harsh voice. "It is proper that you should die, for you have done wrong," the bird called. "You should die now!"

Mutjinga's spirit heard; her spirit spoke: "Aiyee, I shall not die. I was hungry and I ate. For this I shall not die."

"It is proper that you should die," said the crow spirit. "The men cut you open and you shall die. When you come out of the hole I shall kill you myself."

"Aiyee," said Mutjinga. "When I come out of the hole you shall not kill me." So Mutjinga stayed in the hole for five days. While she was there in the darkness, she changed herself into a crab. She grew a hard shell that covered her everywhere, so the crow spirit could not kill her. Only the long slit where the men had cut her open remained. This she closed tightly by pressing the two halves of the shell together.

On the fifth day, Mutjinga threw the earth aside and crawled out of her hole. The crow spirit was waiting for her. With his bright eyes he looked at her hard shell as she came slowly out of the ground. He lifted his beak. "That is not the right way to die; it takes too long," he said. "I will show you how."

Then the crow spirit reached forward quickly with his sharp bill and plucked out the crab's eyes. Mutjinga, the crab, struggled out of the hole. She searched about blindly with her strong claws for her assailant. The crow spirit cocked his head to strike again.

The Mutjinga Myth
by Nanjin. With his sharp beak the crow pecked at Mutjinga, the crab.

Mutjinga drew her claws about her and became quiet, calling up powerful magic. She then waved her claws and her magic reached to kill the crow spirit. The black bird felt it coming. His harsh voice called out; his wings beat the air; he fell to the ground. The crow spirit lay still—he was dead.

Thus the Murinbata believe that crabs do not die, but that when they grow old they go into a dark place to renew their shells and become young and strong again. But men die just as the crow spirit died.

The Morning Star: The Barnumbir Myth

The pale light of the morning star glancing from treetop to ocean or lagoon was a familiar sight to the aborigines, who usually stirred and awakened to kindle their fires in the early dawn. Stars, like other heavenly bodies, were personified in the myths. Some clans say that the home of the morning star is Bralgu, the Island of the Dead. When the spirit leaves the body, they believe, the morning star lights its way to the last home.

The Barnumbir, or morning star, ceremony plays a part in many Arnhem Land mortuary rites. Here, the morning star is represented by a totem made of a stick closely wound with banyan string that incorporates white feathers or down. A tuft of white feathers at the top symbolizes the star itself, and either feather extensions or long strings that culminate in further tufts of feathers are added to indicate the rays of the star.

In those versions of the myth that give Bralgu as the morning star's home, two old women play a prominent part as caretakers of a large basket in which the star is held. Each morning they let the star out on a long string and, as the sun rises, draw it back to the basket.

The myth is told in various parts of Arnhem Land, but primarily in the northeast and central regions. Here also the bark paintings, carved figures, and feathered poles are most frequently found. On Groote Eylandt another variation exists, for there the morning star is said to dance above the treetops as it brings fire to the earth, to be used anew each day.

Since it is impossible to establish a consistent theme for this myth, I have made a composite that begins with Barnumbir as a companion of the Djanggawul on Bralgu, and have carried the story forward as she attempts to be helpful to them on their journey to the mainland.

IN THE DREAMTIME, a spirit woman named Barnumbir lived on Bralgu, the Island of the Dead. Young and joyous, she glowed with a bright light like a star in the Sky World. All day she went about her tasks in song. Barnumbir loved the open, rolling country, the trees and bushes, the flowers and birds of her native country. She liked to climb the gentle hills and enjoy the breeze and sunshine.

Sometimes she looked out over the sea that rolled toward the far horizon. "The sea is empty and cold. Never shall I go upon its waters," she said. While other girls went fishing with the men in their

The Morning-Star Totem
by Bininjuwi.

bark canoes, Barnumbir stayed on the land. While her bolder friends swam out to the breakers, she bathed only in the warm, clear waters close to shore.

"I am afraid," she told them, "for I once dreamed that my spirit would be lost if ever I ventured upon the waters. My spirit would wander far, finding no home. That is why I fear the deep waters."

Among Barnumbir's many friends, her closest were the two Djanggawul sisters. Each day the three girls dug yams and picked berries together. Many secrets they shared.

One day the Djanggawul sisters told Barnumbir they were about to embark on a sea voyage with their brother. "We must go with him, for he is in trouble and must leave Bralgu. He has need of us and we must go," they said.

Barnumbir was distraught. "You must not leave! You are my closest friends. What shall I do without you?" she begged.

"We do not wish to leave," they sadly replied, "but our brother is of our blood. We must help him cross the sea and make a home in the strange land to which he goes."

"Even though I fear the sea," said Barnumbir, "I would go with you."

But the sisters refused, saying, "Our canoe can hold only three. We must leave you behind."

With a heavy heart Barnumbir sought the counsel of friends. Was there a larger canoe? No, she was told, the Djanggawul had the largest. Could she paddle a second canoe? The strength of one girl was not enough, they advised. Could Djanlin the magician make magic so Barnumbir could travel through the air as a star above the canoe of the Djanggawul? one man asked. Her glowing light would brighten their way over the sea at night.

And so Barnumbir, reluctant with fear, approached Djanlin and said, "I would accompany the Djanggawul in their journey across the sea. I would go as a star to light their path. Can you sing a magic song to transform me into a star?"

Djanlin reflected, then said, "This I can do. But know that when you pass from sight of Bralgu my magic power will wane and disappear. I cannot call you back and you will remain forever a star traveling above the tops of the waves. Think well on the matter before you decide."

More disturbed than ever, Barnumbir sought out Dunjun and Malumbu, the sisters of her mother. She found them rolling fibers of pandanus root between hand and thigh to make string which they coiled in a large basket placed between them.

"Help me," Barnumbir begged. "I would go as a star with my friends the Djanggawul to guide them over the sea. The magician has said that he can make magic for me but that when I pass from sight of Bralgu his power disappears and he cannot bring me back. What shall I do?"

The Barnumbir Totem
by Gakupa.

For a long time the aunts rolled pandanus fiber. The coils of string grew high in the basket. Finally Malumbu replied. "Leave us to think on the matter. Tomorrow we will speak."

The next morning Barnumbir returned to the camp of her aunts. "We can help you," Malumbu told her. "Walu, wife of the Djangga-wul brother, will light the way of the canoe by day. By night they will follow the stars. But in the early morning, when the stars have fallen and Walu still sleeps, the Djanggawul will have need of you. In these dark hours harm may come. In the blackness will they be glad for one small light to follow in safety."

Then Dunjun added, "Djanlin will make magic so that you will float as a star above the canoe of the Djanggawul. We will tie our string to you and then you will travel over the water, casting your beams for the Djanggawul. A small light will it be, but light enough to follow."

"But how shall I return to my home?" asked Barnumbir in alarm.

"When Walu rises above the horizon, we shall tug on the string and pull you back to Bralgu," explained Malumbu. "We shall pull you back to our basket. All day you shall stay with your people and all night. But early each morning we shall let you out on the string. Your light shall dance on the treetops as we let you out. It shall dance on the water. It shall light the way of the Djanggawul, and they shall not be lost in the darkness of the sea."

And so it is that each day just before dawn, Barnumbir, the morning star, appears in the sky. The other stars have fallen, so her small light shines brightly. She dances on the treetops, then she twinkles briefly on the black waters. When her task is done, she returns to her home on the Island of the Dead.

Bark Coffin,
Morning Star Ceremony
by Djadjiwui.

The Happy Spirit: The Murayana Myth

Death, among the aborigines, evokes displays of intense emotion. Grief at the loss of a loved one is given free rein. Mourning is a public event. However, the pain of loss is not unmixed with fear and suspicion. Since the aborigines usually attribute death to sorcery, no death is "natural," and the spirit of the deceased must be placated: Revenge must be taken against the evildoer; the proper ceremonies must be conducted. Only then will the spirit return to the sacred water hole.

The story of how death first came varies according to linguistic group and clan. Many versions related by the people of the central and northeast regions describe the journey of the dead person's spirit to the Island of Bralgu, home of the spirits of the dead that lies in the ocean beyond the rising sun. Associated with these myths is a spirit being, called both Murayana and Gunbulabula, who appears to the people after the completion of the funeral ceremonies, singing and dancing to drive away grief.

The sources from which I constructed the Murayana myth include statements of artists that accompany their bark paintings on this theme, material culled from conversations with other informants, and the writings of W. H. Warner.

LONG AGO, in the time of the Dream, at first there was no death. People lived in happiness upon the earth; food was plentiful and the soft wind was sweet in the baobab trees. But death came and the Dream ended.

Death came in darkness, when the land lay swollen with the first rains of the wet season. To Yalngura death first came; it came like the great ax that falls to the ground from the hands of the Lightning Man.

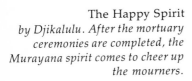

The Happy Spirit
*by Djikalulu. After the mortuary
ceremonies are completed, the
Murayana spirit comes to cheer up
the mourners.*

Death came from a land lost in the mists of the sea and it came first to
Yalngura.

This was the manner of its coming. Yalngura was a Gubabingu
man, and one morning when the wind blew strong from the water, he
stood watching storm clouds, deciding whether to venture beyond the
breakers to fish. As he stood there, a large leaf whirled through the
air. Yalngura looked in surprise, for the leaf blew from the water.

"There is no land in the sea from which the leaf could come," he
thought. "What magic is this?"

The leaf whirled and twisted through the air. Then it landed on
Yalngura's shoulder. He saw it was a yam leaf. "From what land do
you come?" he asked.

"I come from a land of peace and happiness, the Island of Bralgu,"
replied the yam leaf. "It lies beyond the mists. There is much game.
Yams and berries, geese and fish—all are plentiful. Spirit beings live
on Bralgu. Their women are comely and loving, eager for new men
with whom to lie."

"I will go to Bralgu," said Yalngura, "and if it is as you say, I shall
come back and take also my wives and children."

Yalngura took the yam leaf in his hand and hurried to tell his wives and friends what he had learned. But of the soft-limbed, comely women who waited on Bralgu, he said nothing.

"I will need food and water, for the trip is long," Yalngura told his wives. "Help me."

They demurred, for they did not wish him to leave. "We have all we need here," they said. "Stay and be content."

But Yalngura insisted. He thought of the tender arms of the Bralgu women and said, "I must go. There is much good for all of us on the Island of Bralgu."

So he pushed off in his canoe and paddled steadily in the direction from which the yam leaf had come. His eldest wife was reluctant to see him go. After a few days, she went to Murayana, the spirit man, who lived by himself in a grove of trees. The people liked Murayana and respected him, for he was a happy spirit, smiling often and giving good counsel in times of sadness and trouble.

The Leaf from the Sea
by Libundja. A yam leaf floats in from the sea, alerting Yalngura to the Island of the Dead hidden beyond the horizon.

The Spirit Dances
*by Burunday. The happy spirit,
Murayana, dances to cheer up the
mourners after the mortuary
ceremonies.*

"My husband has gone to the Island of Bralgu," she said. "Already I long for him. Make magic so he will return quickly."

Murayana secured a hair belt Yalngura had left with his eldest wife and chanted a magic song over it. "Your husband has already reached the island, but the magic will cause him to return," he told her.

In the deep night, when the camp fires sputter and wink in the darkness, the old men huddle in the warmth of the flames and whisper of the fate that befell Yalngura. They tell of the comely maiden he found on the Island of Bralgu; their voices linger on the words as they tell of her soft breasts and eager arms and the delight she found in Yalngura, the man who came to her from the sea.

But Yalngura soon left her, they say, for the magic of Murayana was powerful. Even as Yalngura was finding pleasure with the maiden of Bralgu, the thought of his own camp fire and his wives and children tugged at him. In the chill of morning, when Barnumbir, the morning star, rose above the treetops, he left his tender companion deep in sleep and paddled into the darkness that shrouded the sea. After many days he returned, and his wives and children greeted him with delight.

That night Yalngura slept with his eldest wife. When the stars had
fallen from the sky and night was black, his wife heard Yalngura cry
out. But then the night fell silent again. The morning star winked
above the treetops. All was as it should be. She yawned and returned
to sleep.

When morning came Yalngura's wives and children stirred,
stretched their limbs, and rubbed the sleep from their eyes. Yalngura
did not stir. Empty and fixed were his eyes; his limbs were cold and
still.

The voices of the old men fall to whispers as they end the story.
The comely maiden on Bralgu longed for Yalngura, they say. She came
with Barnumbir, the morning star, to find him. In the darkness she
came and took the spirit of Yalngura from his body. To the Island of
Bralgu she took Yalngura, that he might bring the pleasures of love to
her once more.

So it was that death came. Today, when the funeral ceremonies
are conducted, the people tell of Yalngura. When the ceremony is over
and the grief of the people is exhausted, Murayana comes and helps
ease their sorrow. He smiles and dances, and the people find happiness once again.

# Notes on the Text

The notes below are in the same sequence as the text pages. The last names of authors are given. Numbers in parentheses refer to the work cited in the bibliography; numbers following the colon are page numbers.

Foreword

Do the Australian aborigines still live in a Stone Age culture? Today this is true only of those who remain in the bush and avoid the settlements. Most have adopted some features of modern Australian society and are in transition. Processed food and beer in pop-top cans are indispensable, but periodically men, women, and children go "walkabout" in the bush to recapture the life their forefathers knew. It is not unusual to see a man playing the age-old songs on the *didjeridu* with the mouth of the drone pipe resting in a plastic bucket to increase resonance; and when he is finished, the musician may ride off on a shiny new motorcycle.

The emu (*Dromaius novae hollandiae*) is the largest bird found in Australia, often reaching six feet in height. The male bird incubates the eggs. The aborigines hunt them for food and relish the eggs, which weigh one to two pounds.

PART I: ART AND MYTHS OF THE ABORIGINES
The People and Their Myths

Scientists from the Australian National University under D. J. Mulvaney have unearthed heaths and shell middens at Lake Mungo in New South Wales that PAGE 9 are carbon-dated at 32,000 years old; further discoveries during 1974 push this back to 40,000 years.

General information on the history and culture of the prehistoric period will be found in McCarthy (43). There is a discussion of alien influence on the Arnhem Land clans, ranging from the visits of the Dreamtime spirits to post–World War II in Berndt and Berndt (5). An excellent selection of writings that describes voyages around the northern coast and early visits by Europeans is contained in MacKnight (44).

PAGE 17 Totemism is based on the idea that there is a unique relationship between a group of people and specific creatures or things, which they regard as their totems. They believe these totemic beings played a special role in their creation and well-being. Since people are usually prohibited from marrying within their own totemic group, totemism is associated with exogamy.

The totemic beliefs of the Australian aborigines are similar to those of other primitive peoples; however, since the aborigines are among the earliest of living peoples, the remnants of their traditional beliefs are especially interesting.

Further information on the sources of religious belief will be found in the following works: Durkheim (16) discusses the conscious and unconscious influences in developing religions; Lowie (42) gives an early and landmark analysis of the development of religious thought; Radin (56) treats of the socioeconomic forces that influenced religious expression, as well as the nature of the religious experience; Watts (70) explains the impact of primitive beliefs on Christianity; Campbell (10) contains a spiritual history of human religion.

Background on totemism can be found in: Frazer (21, 22, 23), Goldenweiser (25: 179–293), Kroeber (35: 48 ff.), Lang (37), Leach (38), and Levi-Strauss (40, 41).

More specific data on Australian aboriginal totemism appears in: Berndt and Berndt (9), Roheim (59, 60), Strehlow (67), and Warner (69).

Discussions of totemism as practiced in specific regions of Arnhem Land include:

Northeast and Central Regions (the Murngin people): Warner (69: esp. 244–450).

Western Region (the Gunwinggu people): Berndt and Berndt (6: esp. 112–148).

Tiwi (Tunuvivi) People: Mountford (49).

Port Keats Region: Falkenberg (20).

Groote Eylandt Region: Worsley (73: 851–860).

PAGE 18 At birth, the Australian aboriginal becomes a member of a number of social groupings such as tribe, clan, and moiety. Most important of these is the group made up of descendants of his totemic ancestor. The men complete prescribed rituals known as the *Dua Narra* and *jiridja narra* ceremonies, to advance through progressive age groupings.

General social organization of the Australian aborigines is described in Berndt and Berndt (9: esp. 26–91), Elkin (17), Hiatt (29: 267–286), Meggitt (46: 211–217), and Radcliffe-Brown (55).

Tindale (67a) has published the results of his lifetime of research in a definitive work on the ecology, nomenclature and structure of the aboriginal tribes.

The social organization of the aboriginal peoples of northern Australia is discussed in: Berndt and Berndt (9), Davidson (14: 614–631), Hiatt (29: 268–281) and (30), Spencer and Gillen (64), and Spencer (63).

Descriptions of social organization in specific regions can be found in the following:

Northeast and Central Regions: Elkin (18), Warner (69: 15–137), Webb (71: 406–411). Hiatt (28) deals with social organization and the stresses of conflict within it among clans in the general area of Maningrida, northern Australia.

Western Region: Elkin, Berndt and Berndt (19: 254–301).

Tiwi People: Goodale (26), Osborne (53).

Groote Eylandt: Rose (61); Turner (68) provides a detailed study of the social and language groupings of Groote Eylandt and adjacent islands. Tindale (67b) did pioneering research.

PAGE 23

There is an extensive literature on mythology, of which I found the following of pertinent interest: Campbell (11), Kellett (33), Kluckhohn (34), Kupka (36), Levi-Strauss (39) and (41), and Murray (52).

Collections of myths from north Australia, presented by region, appear in:

Northeast and Central Regions: Berndt (2), Kupka (36), Mountford (48: 267–455), Mountford and Roberts (50) and (51), Chaseling (12: 157–166), and Robinson (57).

Western Region: Berndt and Berndt (6: 117–125), Holmes (31), and Mountford (48).

Groote Eylandt Region: Mountford (48: 19–106), Rose (61: 215–218), and Stokes (66: parts 1 and 2).

Tiwi People: Mountford (48) and (51), Goodale (26), and Morris (47).

Port Keats Region: Falkenberg (20: 86–99) and Robinson (57).

PAGE 25

The aboriginal people are now leaving what Margaret Mead calls their *postfigurative* phase of cultural development, in which the elders teach the children almost everything they know and in doing so perpetuate the past. Such is the pressure for change that they are almost simultaneously entering stages Mead terms the *cofigurative,* in which grown-ups and children both learn from their peers and *prefigurative,* in which adults learn a great deal from their children. I was forcefully reminded of the aptness of Margaret Mead's classification when, at Oenpelli, I saw a young man who had been to school in Sydney teaching an older man to drive a truck and, in the sparkling new "supermarket" at Groote Eylandt, a girl from the settlement school showing her grandmother where to find the tinned bully beef she wanted and how to carry it through the checkout counter.

As Margaret Mead points out, all societies now face the same challenges as the aborigines. While we and our children must learn lessons of the past, our paramount need is to set young people free so they can learn from their own experience. Mead (45).

Regions and Art Styles

Little work has been done on the geographical regions and their varying artistic styles. Most useful are the following: Berndt (4: 26–43), Cole (13), Mountford (48), and data collected by Professor Edward L. Ruhe, University of Kansas and James Davidson, Melbourne.

The Artists and Their Work

There is evidence that aboriginals from many areas of Australia and Tasmania have painted figures and designs on the bark sheets that formed the walls of their shelters; however, only the work of the Arnhem Land artists has been preserved in significant amounts. At first almost all of this was for ritual or other purposes and was sold only incidentally; for the past thirty years or so, however, paintings have been made expressly for commercial purposes. Some of this work, done by initiated old men who paint only in the traditional style, is virtually the same as that made for ceremonial use; but an increasing volume of the painting is made simply to be sold, and this work tends to follow European patterns. Efforts are being made by the Australian government, through various agencies, to preserve the traditional designs and materials. One hopes that these efforts will be successful.

Information on the Veddas and their painting will be found in Seligman and Seligman (62). A discussion of aboriginal art styles appears in Berndt (4: 26–43).

PART II: CREATION MYTHS

Many of the aboriginal clans tell of a fertility mother who gave birth to the first children. Known variously as Gunabibi, Kadjari, Kalwadi, and Karwadi, she is discussed in several publications. These include Berndt (8: 12–17), Falkenberg (20: 86–94) and Stanner (65: 4–5, 81–84).

Sisters of the Sun: The Djanggawul Myth, I

In my retelling, I have carried the myth back to its beginnings, piecing together fragments of information from many sources, both published and firsthand. I have attempted to establish a linear sequence for the events and to provide some rationale for occurrences, such as the journey of the morning star, that are often given as episodes apparently unrelated to the main theme of the myth. I have also avoided, as wearying to the reader, a plethora of detail.

Fragments of the Djanggawul myth come from many sources. Warner (69: 335, 336) describes the myth in the context of the *Dua Narra* age-grading rituals. Berndt (2) provides the most comprehensive statement and analysis of the myth, together with a translation of the Djanggawul song cycle as it is sung during the ceremonies. Chaseling (12) and Wells (72) have given firsthand accounts of the myths as they learned them from the old men who visited the mission stations. D. S. Davidson (15) discusses the question of the origin of the first Australians; he also cites a useful bibliography. I have also secured data from Geoff Spence, Byron Bay; James A. Davidson, Melbourne; and Alan Fidock, Darwin. Explanatory notes for their paintings by Mawulan, Madaman, and Wandjuk were very helpful. Some of these bark paintings were collected by Dr. Stuart Scougall and given preservative treatment as early as 1959—and thus are among the oldest still intact.

The names given the Djanggawul brother and his sisters vary at different locations, as do details of the story. I have found versions at Yirrkala, Elcho Island, and Milingimbi. The Gunwinggu people near Oenpelli tell of Maraladj, a female creator spirit who came to their country from the plains south of Milingimbi, and carried two dilly bags from which she emptied out the first people of the tribe.

The *djuda* tree is the casuarina, *Casuarina equisetifolia*, also known as the she- PAGE 51
oak.

The Lost Power: The Djanggawul Myth, II

The *ngainmara* mats are woven from the bark of the paperbark tree, *Melaleuca*   PAGE 53
leucadendra.

The trepang, *Holothuria edulis*, is also known as sea slug, sea cucumber, and   PAGE 55
bêche-de-mer. The aborigines dove for it in twenty feet or more of water and exchanged it with the Makasans for cloth, axes, fish hooks, pipes and tobacco, as well as other items. The visiting traders set up depots on shore, where they boiled the trepang in iron kettles, dried it in the sun and the smoke of their fires, and carried it back to Makasar, where they sold it to the Chinese.

Batik cloth is made by covering the cloth to be printed with hot wax except for   PAGE 57
the desired pattern. The fabric is then dipped in dye vats containing the desired colors; the uncoated surface accepts the dye; the waxed portions resist it. Some of the aboriginal designs which are the property of the clans of the northeast and central regions are probably derived from batik patterns.

The Good Man: The Laindjung Myth

There are many different versions of this myth, documented from different informants at different time periods. Some versions add a third person, Barama, and some interchange the identities of Laindjung and Banaidja.

I have selected from my notes portions of differing versions that I have heard or read, consolidating them to provide one coherent story and filling out the narrative with cultural information that should be helpful to the reader.

The information on which the myth is based came mainly from Biragidji at Yirrkala and Djawa of Milingimbi. Helpful publications include Berndt and Berndt (7: 302–326), and Mountford (48), Wells (72), Warner (69).

The aborigines believe that a person's spirit continues to exist after his death;   PAGE 60
however, their ideas differ as to the nature and destination of the spirit. Most believe that it divides into at least two parts: one returns to the sacred water hole, there to wait to be reborn into another human body, while the second spirit goes to the Island of the Dead, there to enjoy the pleasures of the afterlife. Some clans believe that the spirit divides into a third part, the *mogwoi* or *mokoi*, a mischievous or trickster spirit that wanders about, playing tricks or even bringing harm to the living.

PAGE 61   The aborigines are very fond of the honey made by the stingless honeybee and search out its hive in hollow trees. The honeycomb is shown in the bark paintings by a diamond design.

PAGE 66   The people wrap paperbark with pandanus fiber and color it with red ocher to make the bundles, called banaidja, which are beaten on the ground to imitate the sound of the leaping fish falling back in the water.

The Sisters and the Snake: The Wagilag Myth

The Wagilag is probably the best known of the Australian aboriginal myths; comprehensive accounts appear in several publications. Warner (69) gives it in detail, with an outline of the ritual and an analysis of its symbolism. Berndt relates the myth to the Kunapipi cult (3). Mountford (48) provides extensive information. Robinson (57) gives a firsthand report of the myths he collected at Milingimbi.

The version I have developed includes original information from informants at Milingimbi; especially Djawa, Dawudi, and Alan Fidock.

Although these versions of the myth conflict at numerous points, there is substantial agreement on the broad, general theme. This I have tried to preserve by combining elements derived from both the central and northeast clans, and then adding cultural and geographic material to maintain a continuous narrative.

PAGE 70   The aborigines have many devices for attracting the opposite sex. Both men and women sing songs which are designed to notify the other person that he is desired and to excite his interest. Formalized ceremonies are conducted for the same purpose, in which a prescribed sequence of songs and dances is completed. Charms are also used. One of the most popular charms is a carved sea-gull head to which a feathered string is attached. White feathers are used by the *jiridja* moiety, red by the *dua*. The sea-gull is selected because it is believed that it will capture the desired one's love just as the sea gull seizes food in its beak. The sea-gull charm may be hidden in a woman's paperbark bed or in her dilly bag; sometimes the head is placed on the ground in front of the woman, while the man walks into the bush pulling the feathered string so the charm trails behind him. The woman is supposed to follow the charm into the bush.

PAGE 70   Aboriginal women usually give birth without disrupting their daily activities. Female relatives help the woman in labor by chanting magic songs, massaging her neck and shoulders, and kneading her muscles. The umbilical cord and afterbirth are believed to have special powers and are usually buried so enemies cannot find and use them for magic.

PAGE 72   The sacred pool at Mirarmina is several days' travel from the settlement at Milingimbi. There are contradictory reports about it; some say it is small, some large. My informants at Milingimbi, who have visited the pool many times for ceremonial purposes, were reluctant to discuss it, but did say that although it is relatively small in area, it is very deep. All say they approach Mirarmina with respect and sing prescribed songs to notify the great snake of their presence.

The Snake Woman: The Ngalyod Myth

The creator Rainbow Snake appears in Gunwinggu mythology in various guises. She is the primal mother, the Old Woman; she also appears in human form as Waramurungundji with her husband Wuragog. Berndt and Berndt (6: 20–27 and 117–128) and Mountford (48: 210–212) are especially helpful. PAGE 76

Besides being incestuous, the old man's conduct was objectionable in that young boys, rather than girls, had first right to honey when it was found. Ngalyod, who taught people their rituals and dances, was particularly observant of the proprieties. PAGE 77

The round yam, *Dioscorea sativa*, var. *rotunda*, is cut into small slices with a shell. The yam slices are soaked in water for several hours to remove the poison. PAGE 80

The Death of the Father: The Kunmanggur Myth

In the country of the Murinbata people, each clan has its own totemic site, usually a water hole, which is sacred because it was created by the ancestral spirits in the Dreamtime. The initiated men live in the stretch of country surrounding the totemic site; here they bring their wives and raise their families. Kunmanggur, who is also the Rainbow Snake, sends spirit children to the sacred water holes, from which they enter the wombs of the women and are born as children.

Information about Kunmanggur is sparse. The best native informants were Harry Palada and Christopher Parumba at Port Keats. Harry Palada checked an oral rendition of the version given here. Most comprehensive published sources are Falkenberg (20: 192–193, 238–243), Robinson (57: 5–12), and Stanner (65: IV).

The flying fox is one of several varieties of large fruit bats, *Pteropus alecto*, which feed upon fruit and honey. They often congregate in large numbers during the day in mangrove forests. They are knocked down with clubs when roosting and eaten by the aborigines. PAGE 82

The kookaburra, *Dacelo leachii cervina*, is a type of kingfisher, known popularly as the laughing jackass. It feeds on insects but also catches small fish and frogs. The birds make a great clamor in the early morning, starting before dawn, and again as night falls. PAGE 83

Each tribe has the exclusive right to make certain valued objects, such as fishing nets, spears and spear-throwers, and ochers. These goods can be acquired by other tribes only through exchange. Men from each tribe travel periodically to well-known trading stations, where the exchange takes place. A messenger is first sent ahead to notify the other party. The traders then meet, display their goods, and the trade is accomplished. PAGE 83

The Old Woman: The Mudungkala Myth

The aborigines are concerned about the creation of the world only to the extent that it helps explain and support what they are doing today. They have no PAGE 89 interest in theory or philosophical explanations. For this reason, the creation stories tell of things that occurred so early they are beyond memory yet are present today and directly influence the welfare of the people.

The Mudungkala myth of the Tiwi explains how the earth was formed and how the physical characteristics that exist today were created. The Tiwi readily point out the water hole that was formed when Mudungkala urinated, the large stone that was once her ax and the circle of rocks that once enclosed her camp fire.

My chief sources of information for the myth were Goodale (26: 3–4, 293), Mountford (51: 24–30) and Black Joe (Wombiaudimirra).

PAGE 90 Meteors are the single eye of the one-eyed spirit men, the Papinjuwari, who steal bodies and suck the blood of their victims. Their eyes are seen blazing as they streak across the sky on their ghoulish errand. Mountford (49: 144–146) gives a detailed description.

PAGE 91 The aborigines in general believe that conception takes place when a spirit being enters a woman's womb. The Tiwi call these spirits the piti piti and say that they live in the father's tribal territory and that the mother conceives when the father dreams that a piti piti enters her vagina. Goodale (26: 136–146) discusses the piti piti in detail.

PART III: MYTHS OF NATURAL FORCES

PAGE 95 As Berndt and Berndt point out in their *The World of the First Australians* (9), the aborigines reflected their close dependence on natural forces in their totemic and religious beliefs. Not only were rituals and ceremonies developed to encourage and appease the forces of nature, but bark paintings were made and wood figures carved to provide a temporary home for the spirits of the sky and stream.

How the Milky Way Was Created: The Catfish and Crow Myth

Mountford has a helpful discussion of aboriginal astronomy in his report (48: esp. 479–504). In most cases, the Milky Way is believed to be a river which is the scene of various adventures of Dreamtime spirit people. This version draws most heavily on notes for bark paintings by Mawulan and Naridjin and on the Mountford data.

PAGE 97 The Dreamtime spirits were able to change into different forms; for example, the crow spirit might appear as a human or as a crow. After the Dreamtime ended, the crow spirit was continually reborn in the form of the people of the crow totem. Together they constituted the crow clan and recognized the crow totem as their sacred emblem.

PAGE 98 During the age-grading and other ceremonies, the flesh is cut in ritual designs. The scars, or cicatrices, which form become a distinctive identifying mark which may indicate the clan and moiety as well as the age group of the individual. Sometimes ashes or clay are rubbed into the cuts so that the cicatrices will form distinct ridges.

The flying fox is a large bat, *Pteropus alecto gouldii*. It sleeps in the mangrove PAGE 98 trees by day, feeding on fruit and insects at night. It flies long distances, often uttering a shrill whistle while in flight.

Brothers and their wives have a special relationship. All the sons of a paternal PAGE 98 grandfather, for example, are called by a special term meaning "brother" and they regard themselves as brothers. When one brother dies, the next in age marries his wives and takes his children. Brothers have special duties in finding wives for each other and each other's children. Brothers ordinarily have common rights to all the property they own. Except in certain ceremonies, or while on extended journeys, one brother is generally forbidden to have intercourse with the wife of another.

Magic is practiced widely. Black magic, designed to bring harm, often in- PAGE 100 volves drawing, painting, or carving a figure, placing hair, excreta, or a personal possession of the victim on it and then chanting or singing the magic song that will cause the desired event to take place. Warner has a detailed description of beliefs and methods and a sociological interpretation of magical rites (69: chaps. 7 and 8).

An aggrieved person could look to his clansmen for help in seeking revenge. PAGE 101 Since men were dominant, women who injured or insulted men were particularly subject to retaliation. See Warner (69: chap. 6) for a detailed discussion.

The Wind Tree: The Barra Myth

Myths which tell of the origin of the winds are most common on Groote Eylandt, perhaps because its situation in the Gulf of Carpentaria makes it especially vulnerable to the influence of the prevailing winds.

I have incorporated incidents from several myths in this version. Much of the information I was able to gather firsthand came from Abadjera and Jabarr-gwa, commonly called Kneepad, both of whom own rights to the Barra, or northwest wind, totem. Nandjiwarra Amagula also provided data as did Judith Stokes.

On my visit to Groote Eylandt in 1974, I found that Abadjera had recently died. Seeking out Kneepad, I came upon him sitting in the shade of his cabin. He greeted me warmly, but it was clear that his productive days were over. Now too old to paint, he sits patiently, knees crossed, casually brushing away the flies. Still alert, the old man observes everything with interest: the woman striding by with a rake balanced on her head, the children from the mission school, the boy roaring past on a new motorbike. But his hearing is poor and his voice is thin and reedy. Soon he, too, will join his Dreamtime ancestors.

Versions of this myth may be found in Mountford (48: 94–97), Rose (61: 214–217), and Worsley (73: 855).

Wurramugwa, the evil night spirit, is feared by the Groote Eylandt people. PAGE 105 They say he comes at night and tries to steal a dead person's spirit before it can go to Bralgu, the Island of the Dead. To prevent Wurramugwa from stealing the soul, the people smooth the ground surrounding the area where the dead body is resting so they can see the night spirit's tracks. They then light a circle of fires and pile on green branches and tufts of grass to make a dense smoke, which, they believe, will drive Wurramugwa away.

PAGE 105　The bloodwood tree, *Eucalyptus polycarpa,* grows near water and often reaches considerable size. The heartwood is dense and tough and is used to make spears, paddles, and drone pipes.

The Coming of Fire: The Goorda Myth

PAGE 109　My data for this myth comes from Naridjin, who has the right to paint the Murriri version of the story, and from Munggeraui, who "owns" and paints several episodes known as the Bush-Fire myths. *Goorda* or *Gurda* means "fire."

Versions of this myth in the literature include Mountford (48: 293–294 and 404) and Mountford and Roberts (51: 22).

PAGE 111　Circumcision is practiced in many Australian tribes, usually during an early age-grading, or *narra,* rite. The candidates for the operation are gathered together and circumcised as the concluding act of the ceremony. Removal of the foreskin is a visible sign of the young man's new status. He learns the first of the *mareiin,* or sacred songs, totems, and ceremonies, and further secrets are revealed to him at successive *narra* rites throughout his lifetime. In his *The Australian Aborigines* (17: chap. 7), Elkin describes and explains this and other rites.

PAGE 113　Bush fires are set by the aborigines during the dry season and the great clouds of smoke that arise are a common sight to the airplane traveler. I had long assumed that the purpose was to drive out the game so it could be speared by the waiting hunters; however, Kaliowa of Groote Eylandt told me that the real reason was to lure the game to feed on the fresh green shoots; the animals can be seen with relative ease against the background of black ashes and speared.

The Thunder Man: The Djambuwal Myth

The myth of Djambuwal, also known as Bolngo, is told by the *dua* moiety clans of northeastern and central Arnhem Land. My data have come from Lardjanga and Mau, painters of the northeastern region who have the right to this myth. Published sources include Mountford (48: 282–289 and 419–423) and Wells (72: 12–15).

PAGE 114　The Makasans came to the coast of Australia in their square-rigged *praus* from the Celebes as early as the sixteenth century. They sailed in on the northwest winds during October or November and returned with the southeast winds about April. Old Bill Wuramura of Groote Eylandt is one of the few aborigines still alive who had firsthand contact with the Makasans. He told me that they stopped on a regular route, trading for trepang with rice, cartons of tobacco, and a cloth called tapiri, probably batik.

Problems with aboriginal women were avoided because the aborigines forbade their women to mix with the sailors and the *prau* captains ordered their men aboard ship each night. The visitors came ashore in canoes that they carried on their ships. The aboriginal bark canoes were copies of these. During the day the sailors worked ashore, boiling and smoking the trepang.

According to Old Bill, the Makasans, when ready to leave, held a brief ceremony during which they prayed and sang. He remembers helping to pull up the wooden anchors which were sunk in the sand of the beach and tied to the *praus* by long ropes.

The Lightning Man: The Namarragon Myth

This is a myth of the Gunwinggu and other tribes of the western region. Among the artists who have the right to paint Namarragon are Jimmy Mijaumijau, Sam Manggudja, Anchor Barlbuwa and Balirlbalirl. Much of my data comes from them and notes on paintings they have made, together with translations from the Gunwinggu by Peter Carroll.

Other renditions of this myth may be found in Mountford (48: 208–210), Robinson (58: 58–60), and Spencer (63: 334–338).

Medicine men or clever men are of two types: the black magician who brings harm to his victims and the white magician who neutralizes the spell or helps the victim in other ways. Some of the cave paintings found on the Arnhem Land plateau apparently were made for love magic. The figure of the loved one first was painted on the cave wall, then a spell was made to cause the desired event to occur. Berndt and Berndt (6) discuss sorcery and magic as practiced by the Gunwinggu people, while Elkin (17), Berndt and Berndt (9), and Warner (69) contain detailed discussions of magic in general.

PAGE 118

PART IV: MYTHS OF MEN AND WOMEN

Women are generally subordinate to men in aboriginal society. The secret totems and other ceremonial paraphernalia of the men are forbidden to women; in fact, until quite recently, a woman who unknowingly passed close to a hidden *mareiin* object might be severely punished or even killed. The women have their own ceremonies from which men are excluded, but the restrictions for men are not as severe.

Some myths, however, reveal a distant period in which women were supreme. They had exclusive ownership of the powerful totems and led the secret ceremonies that were conducted to appease and entreat the spirits. The myths relate various reasons why these relationships changed and men gained the upper hand; we can only assume that the stories preserve tribal memories of a time when such a reversal of roles actually did occur.

Several useful publications are available which discuss the relationships between men and women in aboriginal life. These include Berndt and Berndt (8), which deals with the Gunwinggu and related tribes; Goodale (26) covers the Tiwi of Melville and Bathurst islands. A useful collection is Gale (24). A general treatment will be found in Kaberry (32).

The Lost Love: The Balada Myth

Aboriginal bark paintings often have layers of meaning, which can be unpeeled only by going directly to the painter. In some cases the hidden information is related to ceremonial life and added details consist of secret names or meanings for totems or other objects. For example, the Rainbow Snake, Julunggul, may be shown in his snake form; however, we also learn that a certain long, narrow rectangular shape with prescribed markings represents Julunggul, as do other figures which are revealed only to those who pass the appropriate age-grading rites. Julunggul, in common with other spirit beings, also has several secret names.

One of the most interesting types of disclosure occurs in the nonrepresentational paintings found among the Tiwi and such western-region tribes as the Gunwinggu. I discovered early that the patterns on the Tiwi bark paintings were much more than nicely rendered designs. After several visits to Snake Bay and continued conversations with Mani-luki (Harry Carpenter) and Black Joe, I discovered that virtually every line had a specific meaning that only the painter understood. I also had acquired several puzzling barks from the Gunwinggu region that showed seemingly meaningless designs. With the help of Peter Carroll and Madelon Hickin and the showing of photographs to some of the artists, I was able to uncover parts of several myths which I had not found elsewhere. The Balada myth is one of these. It is recounted on two bark paintings done by Balirlbalirl Dirdi, also known as Old Bob, who was born in 1905 and still paints in the old symbolic style.

PAGE 126   The Gunwinggu differ from most other tribes in tracing matrilineal descent. This brings the mother's side of the family into a special relationship.

PAGE 126   As we have seen, brothers act as surrogate fathers for one another's children; this also extends to the Dreamtime spirits: if a man is descended from a Dreamtime spirit that became a tree, the tree and its descendants are now surrogate fathers to him.

PAGE 126   The *ubar* ceremony is one of the most important in Gunwinggu ceremonial life; the *ubar*-drum myth, which appears later, will deal with the origin of this ceremony in more detail. The rites are centered on an *ubar* drum which has been cut from a hollow log and brought to the dance ground. It represents the Mother, Ngalyod, and also the log in which Yirrawadbad hid in his snake form and killed his erring wife and her mother. Boys are brought to the *ubar* ceremonies to be initiated. Berndt and Berndt (6) have a detailed explanation of the Gunwinggu rites.

PAGE 127   Violations of the specified kinship patterns in marriage are dealt with severely because they threaten the intricate web of relationships that hold aboriginal society together. Since marriages are arranged, the relatives who have primary responsibility for seeing that the proper union takes place are also most aggrieved if either of the proposed partners breaks the rules.

The First Wife: The Dolphin Myth

This is one of the primary myths of the Groote Eylandt people. It is usually found in episodic form, with the detail varying with the narrator. Published versions include Mountford (48: 82, 88), Rose (61: 216), and Stokes (66, part 2: 15).

The dolphin, *Delphinus tursiops,* has a beaklike snout and is black above, white below. Graceful in the water and gregarious, dolphins congregate in schools, often as large as several hundred in each. Dolphins are intelligent and can communicate with one another, both through recognizable sounds and supersonic pulsations.

PAGE 131

The bailer shell, *Melo diadema,* is a mollusk with a brownish or orange-colored shell. It fastens itself in the sand near coral beds with its large, strong crawling foot. Over a foot long, the empty shells are used by the aborigines to carry water, to bail canoes, and as cooking pots.

PAGE 131

The tiger shark, *Galeocerdo cuvier,* is much feared by the aborigines because of its propensity to attack people when they are swimming or fishing.

PAGE 132

The Faithful Wife: The Tortoise Myth

The Tortoise Myth is based on fragments from the northeast- and central-region clans. Near Milingimbi, in the central region, both the Djambarbingu and the Gubabingu clans tell of the tortoise, Minala, in connection with their circumcision and mortuary rites, while at Yirrkala, in the northeast region, the tortoise is regarded as a Dreamtime ancestor by the *Duwala* linguistic group. Bininjuwi and Libundja at Milingimbi and Djergudjergu at Yirrkala provided information to accompany their bark paintings. Alan Fidock, James A. Davidson, and Dorothy Bennett furnished background data.

    While only fragments of the myth remain, I have developed the plot and added some background information to hold the episodes together. Other versions of the myth will be found in Mountford (48: 321, 385, 391–393).

The aborigines believe a woman conceives when a spirit from the sacred water hole enters her uterus, usually when she is bathing or dipping water from the water hole. Conception takes place in the clan territory of the father, for the child traces its descent from him. A tortoise crawling up a married woman's leg would be a manifestation of the ancestral spirit of the father; the wife would tell her husband of the event so he would know that the child was properly conceived.

PAGE 134

The tortoise is featured in the circumcision ceremony because the neck and head represent the penis of the boy who will be circumcised. According to Yuwati of Milingimbi, when the men cut off the foreskin, they are cutting the neck around the head of the tortoise.

PAGE 135

The marriage is usually prearranged and the union of husband and wife long anticipated. The wife goes to the camp fire of her husband, where her relatives prepare a paperbark bed for the couple. One or more female relatives may sleep nearby to ensure that consummation takes place.

    A man may take as many as twenty or thirty wives in some regions. Since a new wife tends to displace an older one, at least for a time, the established wives may make life hard for the newcomer until the husband tires of the novelty.

PAGE 136

The Tempted One: The Mimi Myth

Mimi figures are common in the cave paintings, so it appears that the aborigines of the Arnhem Land plateau have believed in these thin, sticklike spirits since prehistoric times. The Gunwinggu tell of different types of Mimi—some beneficial, some harmful. Many stories are told about their habits and adventures.

The basic story of this myth was told to me by Sam Manggudja of Oenpelli. Peter Carroll also provided helpful notes in direct translation from the Gunwinggu. Other Mimi information and myths may be found in Mountford (48: 181–199).

PAGE 143   The Mimi kept kangaroos as pets. If strangers happened upon the Mimi encampment, the kangaroos immediately set up a warning by slapping their tails on the ground.

The Man-Eater *and* The Child-Eater:
The Mutjinga Myth, I and II

I secured firsthand information about this myth at Port Keats from Christopher and Djinu Tjeemaree. The myth has been reported by W. E. H. Stanner (65: 40–42) and Robinson (58: 19–22).

PAGE 145   The *kirman* is the person who leads the ceremonies. To do this, he must know all the songs, dances, and myths. Because of this special knowledge and position, the *kirman* also has special status in social and leadership activities.

PAGE 146   The goanna is a species of monitor lizard, *Varanus gouldii*, which reaches several feet in length. Different varieties live on land, in freshwater marshes, and near the sea. The aborigines hunt them for food.

The Singing Woman: The Kukpi Myth

The Murinbata believe that Kukpi made the land: she created the hills and rivers, springs and waterfalls. And she named all these places. However, she did not create people; Kunmanggur did this. Kukpi was also the *kirman* or ceremonial leader. She knew all the songs and taught them to the people.

Accounts of this myth will be found in Falkenberg (20: 90), Robinson (58: 29), and Stanner (65: 125–132). Information on this version was provided for me at Port Keats by Harry Palada.

PAGE 154   *Tjurunga* (often written *djuringa* or *tjuringa*) is a term applied by the Aranda tribe of central Australia to sacred ceremonial objects. It is used by the Port Keats–region tribes for an oval stone or wooden symbol on which sacred designs have been pierced or carved. These are believed to have great power because they have been handed down generation by generation from the Dreamtime spirits.

Bull-roarers are *tjurunga* that are pierced by a cord and then are whirled around the head. This causes a distinctive booming noise which is given various interpretations, such as that it represents the voice of the great snake. The *tjurunga* or bull-roarers are kept in secret caves or stone houses and are brought out with great secrecy for ceremonies. They are rubbed periodically with fat or armpit sweat and kept wrapped in paperbark coverings.

The Unloved One: The *Ubar*-Drum Myth

The great snake reappears in the *ubar*-drum myth as Yirrawadbad, the spurned husband. While it is difficult to trace this to Julunggul, the Rainbow Snake, we have here the common elements of the snake, a phallic symbol; the hollow-log drum, representing the vagina; and the killing of two women. A detailed discussion of the myth will be found in Berndt and Berndt (8: 109–138). Further information will be found in Berndt and Berndt (6: 119–131) and in Spencer (64: 133–134, 218–227). In addition to drawing upon these interpretations, I have used information from Sam Manggudja and Peter Carroll at Oenpelli.

The bandicoot, *Perameles macroura,* is a marsupial that makes its nest of leaves PAGE 158 and grass in the bush or hollow logs. It feeds on insects and small rodents.

The Man-Killer: The Wilintji Myth

The information on which this myth is based came largely from the artists, Nabadbara and Nonganyari. The story of the woman who danced men to death is also known to several of the other painters, although they do not have the right to paint it. Another account of the myth will be found in Mountford (48: 210).

In aboriginal terms, Marriki was Wilintji's mother's mother's brother's daughter's daughter. "Second cousin," the English approximation, does not differentiate, of course, between matrilineal and patrilineal descent.

When differences with their wives arose, aboriginal men felt they had a right PAGE 162 to beat them if they proved too stubborn. A man would often cut and trim a special club, his "wife-beater," and keep it handy for the purpose.

Men invariably conducted the funeral ceremonies, carrying out their as- PAGE 162 signed roles of wrapping the corpse in paperbark, exposing it on a burial platform and arranging for the burial ceremonies.

The Wife-Killer: The Malamu Myth

Men sought to punish their wives for many reasons. Both the reasons and the methods of punishment vary in the myths, but this account is quite typical. In some cases the wives commit adultery or refuse to bring their husbands food; they are then stranded in a deep cavern or on top of an unscalable cliff. In each case the lesson is self-evident.

In this version of the myth I have attempted to build the narrative around the most constant features of the versions I have collected.

The rainmaker is an important magician to the aborigines. The Rainbow PAGE 165 Snake is associated with rain and the magic rites often relate the two. Pearl shell, because it comes from the water, is often used in the ceremony to bring about rain.

PART V: MYTHS OF EVERYDAY LIFE
The Heroic Fisherman: The Munjurr Myth

PAGE 172   This myth is secular. Several linguistic groups tell various parts of it. Accordingly, I have pieced together those parts I have been able to record, and provided a story line to hold them together. Bark paintings by Nanjin and Naridjin of the *Manggalilji* clan, northeastern Arnhem Land, have provided much of the information. Mountford (48: 360–362, 496–498) provides fragments of the myth.

PAGE 173   The whale, which appears frequently in aboriginal myths, was said to have a number of mouths, or, alternatively, suckers on its tail, with which it seized the fishermen's boats and drowned the men.

PAGE 174   Barama is a creator ancestor linked with Laindjung and Banaidja by some of the people of the clans of the *jiridja* moiety.

The Spirit Messenger: The Opossum-Tree Myth

PAGE 177   The aborigines gather around their camp fires every night to sing and recount the myths and legends. Songs also tell about current happenings: the amorous escapades of men and women, and feats of courage. Gossip thus is often rendered in song.

PAGE 179   Peacemaking ceremonies are held to bring an end to armed conflict between individuals or groups. In most cases the antagonists stand before their assembled tribespeople and each in turn becomes a target for the spears of his opponent's group. The drawing of blood on both sides is enough to satisfy the aggrieved ones and to bring the hostilities to a close. The ceremony is called *magarada* by the *dua* moiety clans and *garada* by those of the *jiridja* moiety.

Keeper of the Secrets: The Luma Luma Myth

A complex of myth and ceremony relates to the Luma Luma story. The barramundi is a central feature, together with the whale and the cult hero himself. Before the ceremony is held, the dancers have the barramundi totem painted on their bodies, together with a crisscross design called *rarrk*. Different forms of the design are used as the men advance through the first, second, and successive years of the age-grading *mareiin* rites.

     I have secured some of the Luma Luma data from bark paintings by Mijaumijau and Yirrawala, two of the great old painters of the Gunwinggu tribe and also from Nguleingulei and Ginilgini, outstanding younger painters. Peter Carroll has provided helpful information; the Berndts (6) offer useful background data on the myth.

PAGE 181   A woman who wished to make her amorous interest known to a man would match his footprints with her own. Since the aborigines were superb trackers, the man would either see this quickly himself or would be informed by his friends.

The Greedy Boy: The Djert Myth

The fate of a greedy person is spelled out in a number of myths. The *Riradjingu* clanspeople, who now occupy territories adjacent to the *Manggalilji,* tell of two fishermen who refused to share their catch and were turned to stone as a result. I have put this account together from data provided by the painter who "owns" the myth, Naridjin, and miscellaneous fragments I have gathered based on bark paintings by Madaman and Mawulan.

The Bitter Fruit: The *Lala* Myth

The *lala* myth is the property of the Maringar tribe of the Port Keats region, whose country is inland from that of the Murinbata tribe. Majindi, the painter, "sings" *lala;* that is, this is one of his totems.

 The *lala* berries can be poisonous as well as bitter at certain times of the year. The natives then soak them for a week or more. The meal is used to make small cakes that are carried for food.

When the Rains Came: The Napilingu Myth

The information on which this myth is based comes largely from Naridjin and several of his bark paintings. Napilingu is an important Dreamtime ancestress of the *jiridja* moiety, but her specific role is difficult to define.

The *Manggalilji* believe they are descended from the children born to Napilingu.

PAGE 193

The paperbark tree, *Melaleuca leucadendra,* grows in several varieties in Arnhem Land. The bark and wood are valuable. The bark is used for containers, to make shelters and sleeping pads, to start fires and also is woven to form fish traps. The wood is used to make dugout canoes.

PAGE 194

The Spear-Maker: The Jirukupai Myth, I

The Tiwi make exceptional barbed spears which are features of many of their ceremonies. The spears were first made by a mythical hero, Jirukupai. Information on which I have based this myth comes from Uringi, known as Harry Womba, who has the right to paint the story, and Black Joe.

The Crocodile Man: The Jirukupai Myth, II

Ordinarily, food is distributed immediately after it is secured, each person receiving a portion as a right. However, when a gift is offered and accepted, it sets up a reciprocal obligation. In violating the first custom and taking advantage of the second, Jirukupai further incensed the tribespeople.

The Bold Woman: The Spider Myth

The spider and its web are the subjects of myths in several Arnhem Land regions. This story from the Port Keats region is built from several bare episodes that are recounted by the tribesmen. I have personalized the story by adding names and local color.

PAGE 203　Aboriginal women ordinarily behaved with considerable decorum in public. If they showed too great an interest in other men, especially strangers, the other women would berate them and their husbands would beat them.

The Man Who Became Black: The Ship-Totem Myth

The Makasans left an indelible impression on the aborigines. Groote Eylandt was the terminal of their trading voyages. They anchored at Jarapa, Wallaby Swamp Beach on Groote Eylandt, and at Winchelsea Island, then returned to their homes on the southeast trade winds. As is true of most Groote Eylandt myths, the basic story is brief and simple. I have combined several related episodes and added local color typical of the region to form this version. Old Bill of Angurugu on Groote Eylandt, who remembers the trepangers' visits, gave me much firsthand information.

PAGE 206　Groote Eylandt is about thirty miles from the coast of Arnhem Land, in the Gulf of Carpentaria. Bickerton Island lies between Groote Eylandt and the mainland.

PAGE 207　Medicine men often practiced white magic to help people. They usually carried a medicine bag or pouch with magic substances.

PAGE 208　The aborigines believe that a person's sweat carries some of his spiritual power. Thus a father will take sweat from his armpit and rub it on his son to give him some of his own strength.

PAGE 209　According to Old Bill, the Makasans wore white shirts and shorts. They often brought a "clever man" or magician with them who had his own cabin on the ship and doubled as a priest. The Makasans traded with the Dutch and Chinese. They were familiar with firearms and gunpowder.

PART VI: THE COMING OF DEATH: FUNERAL MYTHS

Many of the aboriginal bark paintings and carved figures were used in the funeral ceremonies. Every tribe and clan has designs which are used for this purpose. The ceremonies may be carried on at intervals for months and the myths will be sung and danced repeatedly during this time. The five myths I have given are representative of the much larger number that exists.

How Death Came: The Purukapali Myth

I have secured much information about the *pukamani* ceremonies from the aboriginal men at Snake Bay on Melville Island, especially Mani-luki (Harry Carpenter), Aurangnamirri, and Wombiaudimirra (Black Joe); and from John

Morris, Darwin. Dr. Maria M. Brandl, Darwin, has checked some data. John
Morris has provided me with translations of the Purukupali legend made from the Tiwi as told by Kardo Kerinaiua, Bismark Kerinaiua, and Nugget Illortamini. Published sources are Mountford (49), Goodale (26), and Hart and Pilling (27: 88–93).

The forked fighting stick, called *miluanta,* is still used. It is painted with the PAGE 219 owner's totemic designs to give him strength and courage.

The Killer Snake: The Gurramuringu Myth

This myth is the property of Malangi, one of the greatest of current aboriginal painters. The story is sung as part of the funeral rites shortly after an Urgigandjar clansman dies. A bark painting by Malangi that depicts part of this myth is reproduced on the Australian one-dollar bill.
   I secured the information for this version of the myth from Malangi, Alan Fidock, and James A. Davidson.

The poisonous brown king snake, *Demansia textilis,* is also called the mulga PAGE 225 snake. It often grows to more than six feet in length.

How Mutjinga Lived Again: The Crab and Crow Myth

Although Mutjinga had been divested of most of her powers, she was still important to the clan and their ceremonies. They did not want her to die.

A discussion of Mutjinga's death and its consequences is found in Stanner (65: PAGE 226 42–43). He cites the Murinbata men as saying that Mutjinga's act was wrong only in that her victims were children; if she had waited until they were grown and ready to become fully initiated, swallowing them would have been all right.

The newly dead were not usually buried in Murinbata society. The prescribed PAGE 226 funeral proceeding began by isolating the body on a platform out in the open. Women's bodies were left there to rot; men's bodies underwent a series of ceremonies and were eventually cremated. Stanner (65: 118–125) details the funeral ritual conducted after the death of a mature man.

The Morning Star: The Barnumbir Myth

This is one of the most popular of aboriginal myths; however, it is told with many variations. I have based this version on information from many sources in Arnhem Land. These include Gakupa, who has the right to the myth on Elcho Island and makes the beautiful and distinctive morning star totemic figures; Bininjuwi, an outstanding painter at Milingimbi, and Madaman at Yirrkala. James A. Davidson and Alan Fidock have also been helpful.
   Published sources include Chaseling (12: 148–149); Mountford (48: 325–332); Warner (69: 524–528); and Wells (72: 16–18).

The Happy Spirit: The Murayana Myth

The Murayana spirit appears in the funeral rites, known as *Djalambu,* of the *jiridja* moiety. During the ceremony, Murayana gathers honey that the people may eat after the rites are completed. When the ceremony is over, Murayana blows a cheerful tune on the drone pipe. The *Gubabingu* people believe Murayana was the first one to blow the *didjeridu.*

The sources from which I constructed the Murayana myth include versions provided by the artists, especially Djikalulu and Wululu. A primary source was Warner (69: 524–530).

The Artists and Their Affiliations

Data on the artists whose work is cited is summarized below. Information is sparse and some specifics are uncertain; however, I have given names, birth and death dates, and social groupings where available.

In northeastern and central Arṅhem Land a primary social group is the clan, or *mala*. All of its members claim to be descended from the same Dreamtime creator spirit. Since they are related through this common paternity, to marry one another would be incestuous, so the clans are exogamous.

Another important grouping is made up of people who speak the same language or tongue. This is the *mada*, or linguistic group. People of different but related clans may speak the same tongue, so overlap occurs. The *mada* are also exogamous.

The *mada* and *mala* belong to the same moiety. Both own common totemic sites and water holes. Each *mala*, or clan, owns territory within the larger territory of a linguistic unit. Since a man must marry a woman from a different language group, each family speaks at least two dialects. This may be one reason for the aboriginal facility with languages.

Since the Tiwi were isolated for thousands of years, they spoke the same language and regarded themselves as the only people in the world. The term *Tiwi* means literally *"the* people." Social divisions were based on territory and some fourteen subtribes have been identified, each with its own "country." Descent is matrilineal—traced through the mother. I have been able to identify only the tribal affiliation of Tiwi artists.

The Groote Eylandt aborigines are divided into some twelve patrilineal clans, each of which has its own totems, songs, and myths. The clans fall into two moieties, known as Moiety 1 and Moiety 2.

Norman B. Tindale (personal communication, 1975) tells me the Groote Eylandt moieties are *Uwak* and *Iritja,* corresponding to *Dua* and *Jiridja* of Northeast Arnhem Land. These moiety terms are very widespread, he states, and have their roots in the south as *waak* or crow and *iritja* or eagle. My earlier information from Worsley and Judith Stokes provided only a separation into Moieties 1 and 2. However, Kneepad (Jabarrgwa) of Moiety 1 told me he was quickly recognized and welcomed by his moiety counterparts when he visited Yirrkala.

In the Port Keats region, five tribes have been identified and these are divided into about fifteen clans. Each tribe speaks a different dialect, but there is some overlap.

There are historical records of ten or more different tribes in the western region, but some have died out. Today, the Gunwinggu tribespeople are still numerous. They divide into several groups, based on matrilineal descent. The most important groupings are the two moieties, which subdivide into semimoieties, each of which has a distinctive symbol: stone, water, fire, or sun. With the help of Peter J. Carroll, I have been able to identify the semimoiety affiliations of many of the artists.

CENTRAL REGION

ARTIST'S NAME	LINGUISTIC GROUP (L) TRIBE (T)	CLAN	MOIETY
Bandarawui	Duwal (L)	Liagalawumiri	*dua*
Bininjuwi	Duwal (L)	Djambarbingu	*dua*
Burunday (b. 1914)	Duwal (L)	Djambarbingu	*dua*
Dardanga (b. 1915)	Duwal (L)	Liagalawumiri	*dua*
Dawudi (b. 1921, d. 1970) Daudaingalil	Duwal (L)	Liagalawumiri	*dua*
Djadjiwui	Duwal (L)	Djambarbingu	*dua*
Djawa (b. 1905)	Duwala (L)	Gubabingu	*jiridja*
Djikalulu	Duwala (L)	Gubabingu	*jiridja*
Djunmal	Duwal (L)	Liagalawumiri	*dua*
Libundja (b. 1912, d. 1968)	Duwala (L)	Gubabingu	*jiridja*
Mahkarolla	Dangu (L)	Wonguri	*jiridja*
Malangi	Djinang (T)	Urgiganjdjar	*dua*
Mutpu	Duwal (L)	Djambarbingu	*dua*
Nanganaralil	Duwal (L)	Djambarbingu	*dua*
Wululu	Duwal (L)	Gubabingu	*jiridja*
Yuwati	Duwal (L)	Gubabingu	*jiridja*

WESTERN REGION

ARTIST'S NAME	TRIBE	MOIETY	SEMIMOIETY	SYMBOL
Anchor Barrbuwa (b. 1924)	Gunwinggu	Nangarradjgu	Jarrijarninj	sun
Balirlbalirl (Old Bob)	Gunwinggu	Namadgu	Jarrikarnkurrk	stone
Bardjaray	Gunwinggu			
Ginilgini	Gunwinggu			
Manggudja (b. 1929)	Gunwinggu	Namadgu	Jarrikarnkurrk	stone
Mijaumijau (b. 1897)	Gunwinggu	Namadgu	Jarrikarnkurrk	stone
Nabadbara (b. 1895)	Iwaidja			
Nagurridjilmi	Gunwinggu	Namadgu	Jarrikarnkurrk	stone
Nameradji (b. 1926)	Dangbon			
Namirrki (Spider, b. 1924)	Dangbon	Nangarradjgu	Jarrijarninj	sun
Nguleingulei (b. 1920)	Gunwinggu	Namadgu	Jarrikarnkurrk	stone
Nonganyari (b. 1900)	Gunwinggu			
Yirrawala (b. 1903)	Gunwinggu	Nangarradjgu	Jarrijarninj	sun
Jambalula (b. 1908)	Maung			

PORT KEATS REGION

ARTIST'S NAME	TRIBE	TOTEM
Christopher Parumba		
Djinu Tjeemaree	Murinbata	Tortoise
Indji Tharwul (b. 1900)	Murinbata	Sugar Bag
Madigan	Maringar	Crocodile, Barramundi
Majindi	Maringar	Lala Berry
Rock Ngumbe	Murinbata	Sugar Bag
Simon Ngumbe	Murinbata	

MELVILLE AND BATHURST ISLANDS

ARTIST'S NAME	TRIBE
Ali (Oruputuwae)	Tiwi
Aurangnamirri (Young Brook, d. 1973)	Tiwi
Djulabiyanna	Tiwi
Mandarbarni	Tiwi
Mani-luki (Harry Carpenter)	Tiwi
Uringi (Harry Womba)	Tiwi
Wombiaudimirra (Black Joe, b. 1910, d. 1973)	Tiwi

GROOTE EYLANDT

ARTIST'S NAME	TRIBE	CLAN	MOIETY
Abadjera	Ingura	Wanungwadarrbalangwa	
Bakunda	Ingura		
Bunaya (d. 1972)	Ingura	Wanindiljangwa	Moiety 2
Jabarrgwa (Kneepad)	Ingura	Wanungwadarrbalangwa	Moiety 1
Mandaga	Ingura		
Mangangina (b. 1919)	Ingura	Wurramara	Moiety 2
Mini-Mini	Ingura	Wanungamulangwa	Moiety 2

NORTHEASTERN REGION

ARTIST'S NAME	LINGUISTIC GROUP (L) TRIBE (T)	CLAN	MOIETY
Bangul	Dangu (L)	Riradjingu	*dua*
Biragidji (b. 1898)	Daii (T)	Dalwongu	*jirijda*
Gakupa (Elcho Island)			
Gungujuma (b. 1916, d. 1970)	Duwal (L)	Djambarbingu	*dua*
Jama (b. 1920)	Duwala (L)	Gumaidj	*jiridja*
Lardjanga (b. 1932)	Dangu (L)	Ngeimil	*dua*
Madaman (b. 1920, d. 1970)	Dangu (L)	Riradjingu	*dua*
Mawulan (b. 1908, d. 1967)	Dangu (L)	Riradjingu	*dua*
Midinari (b. 1929)	Dangu (L)	Galpu	*dua*
Munggeraui (b. 1907)	Duwala (L)	Gumaidj	*jirijda*
Nanjin (b. 1918, d. 1969)	Duwala (L)	Manggalilji	*jiridja*
Naridjin (b. 1922)	Duwala (L)	Manggalilji	*jiridja*
Wandjuk (b. 1927)	Dangu (L)	Riradjingu	*dua*
Yirrillil			

Notes on the Photographs

I have tried to provide information that will help explain the meaning of the designs on the barks and carvings, and also to give some insight into the characteristics and style of the artist. Most of the works have been exhibited in museums and art galleries. The following abbreviations are used to designate these showings:

Qantas: Tokyo, Auckland, San Francisco, Montreal, Teheran, Qantas Travelling Exhibit of the Scougall Collection, *Australian Aboriginal Art,* 1961–1963. Catalog: Dr. Stuart Scougall.

Jones: Sydney, David Jones' Art Gallery, *Art of Arnhem Land,* 1963.

Lowie: Berkeley, R. H. Lowie Museum of Anthropology, University of California, *Australian Aboriginal Art, The Louis A. Allen Collection,* January 17–August 25, 1969. Catalog: "Australian Aboriginal Art." Text: Albert B. Elsasser and Vivian Paul.

UCSB: Santa Barbara, The Art Galleries, University of California at Santa Barbara, *Australian Aboriginal Art,* January 6–February 1, 1970. Catalog: "Australian Aboriginal Art." Foreword: James A. Davidson; text: Louis A. Allen.

Field: Chicago, Field Museum of Natural History, *Australian Aboriginal Art,* March 3–September 19, 1972. Catalog: "Australian Aboriginal Art: Arnhem Land." Introduction: Phillip H. Lewis; foreword and text: Louis A. Allen.

de Young: San Francisco, M. H. de Young Memorial Museum, California Palace of the Legion of Honor, *Australian Aboriginal Art from the Louis A. Allen*

Collection, September 14, 1973–March 24, 1974. Brochure: text by Louis A. Allen.

NOTES ON
THE PHOTOGRAPHS
263

NOTES ON THE COLOR PHOTOGRAPHS
Following Page 144

The Time of the Dream, by Malangi. During the Dreamtime period, the plants and creatures of the earth were created by the totemic spirits which have since made their homes in the water holes sacred to each of the clans. Here, Malangi portrays the water hole of his people on the Glyde River. Two water lilies are shown with fish swimming among their leaves. In the center is a pronged hollow log in which the bones of the departed are finally placed. The two "eyes" are holes cut in the log so the spirit may look out. At the left is Gurramuringu, a great hunter and ancestral hero of Malangi's people. At the right is the diver bird. Malangi, among the most famous of Arnhem Land artists, has one of his paintings on the Australian one-dollar bill. A gifted and prolific painter, Malangi has several wives and a growing family. He paints quickly and easily, generally confining himself to the Gurramuringu myth or subjects related to the sacred water hole of his clan. An intense and very serious person, he moves with great confidence and speaks in a calm, deliberate manner.

The Barramundi Fish Totem, by Yirrawala. This example of work found in the Oenpelli area is a masterfully executed bark by one of the foremost Gunwinggu painters. The artist has here employed several conventions of western region style. He shows the single figure of the barramundi against a solid red ground. The figure, which has a characteristic rounded quality, is outlined in white and partially filled in with crosshatching. However, the traditional X-ray technique is also used, so that the spine and digestive tract of the fish are visible. It is interesting to compare this work with treatment of the same subject in the Groote Eylandt style. Exhibited: Lowie, UCSB, Field, de Young.

Mimi and Kangaroo, by Yirrawala. This beautifully executed bark by a master painter shows several conventions of aboriginal art. Although the restrictions of the bark forced the painter to position the man almost touching the kangaroo, the figure is shown small in proportion to the animal to indicate that the hunter is actually quite far off. His feathered waist, knee, and arm bands are streaming to show he is running. The backline of the kangaroo is straightened so it will follow the edge of the bark and its feet and tail are contrived just to fit the available space. The internal organs are shown in X-ray design, a characteristic of western region cave art and bark painting. Exhibited: Lowie, UCSB, Field, de Young. (See Holmes, *Yirawala, Artist and Man,* 1972, pp. 72–73.)

The Djanggawul Brother, by Madaman. This exceptional carved and painted wood figure shows the Djanggawul brother as he came ashore with his sisters. The white dots on his face represent sea foam. Painted on the front of the figure is the sacred dilly bag which hung around the brother's neck. Exhibited: de Young. (See Berndt, ed., Australian Aboriginal Art, 1964, pl. 68.)

The Laindjung Story, by Biragidji. At the bottom, Laindjung, the Dreamtime ancestor, rests in the depths of the sacred water hole after pulling out the spears of his enemies, who had ambushed him. At the top he emerges from the water with the sacred designs he painted on his body and that he later taught the tribesmen. His friends who helped him—Garkman the frog and Minala, the long-necked freshwater tortoise—are also shown. Exhibited: Lowie, UCSB, Field (p. 18, cat.), de Young.

The Water-Walkers, by Midinari. The birds that live at the Mirarmina water hole, home of the great snake, Julunggul, have such large feet they are able to walk on the leaves of the water lilies, so they appear to be walking on the surface of the water. The great snake feeds on these birds. The crosshatching in the background represents the water and water weeds of the lagoon. Exhibited: Lowie (p. 6, cat.), Field.

Serpent and Eggs, by Dawudi. Julunggul is shown curled around his eggs—the oval shapes in the center—at the bottom of the sacred water hole at Mirarmina. The dots in the background represent the bottom of the pool. The totemic caterpillars are shown as oval shapes with lines at both sides. This design was "owned" by Dawudi and others could paint it only by permission. Exhibited: Jones, Lowie, UCSB, Field, de Young. (See Berndt, ed., Australian Aboriginal Art, Sydney: Ure Smith, 1964, pl. 55.)

The Mother Protector, by Nagurridjilmi. Ngalyod is shown encircling the young orphan boy she protected when the people ignored him. The sure touch, economical style, and sensitivity of the interpretation reflect the special genius of the aboriginal artist.

The Constellation of Scorpio, by Lardjanga. This is one of the rare astronomical paintings of the aborigines. It shows the stars that make up our constellation of Scorpio. The three large stars in the constellation are at the right, and this theme of three is repeated twice again: first in the three spirit beings who are shown in human form around the fire, with one of them playing the *didjeridu;* secondly in the two ibis and the opossum that can be seen at the top and lower right center of the painting. The crocodile at the bottom consists of all the stars in the tail of the constellation. Exhibited: Lowie, UCSB, Field (p. 26, cat.), de Young.

A very open and pleasant person, Lardjanga shows strong Makasan influence in his appearance. He works with vigor but is a careful and demanding craftsman. Lardjanga is also one of the outstanding wood carvers.

The Creator Ancestor, Laindjung, by Munggeraui. This carving, by one of the outstanding artists of Arnhem Land, shows Laindjung at a time when he was caught in a great fire which burned and blackened his face. The diamond design on the front of the figure is the special property of the artist and represents fire, flames, sparks, and smoke. The figure wears a headband of jungle string, whitened with clay. Human hair is fastened to the head with blood. The string of red parakeet feathers, terminating in a white tuft of sea-gull feathers, represents Laindjung's beard, and is affixed to the figure with beeswax. These white feather tufts are the property of the *jiridja* moiety. The feathered strings on the arms are for dancing. Exhibited: de Young.

Laindjung, by Mahkarolla. This carved and painted wooden representation of Laindjung was made by one of the most famous of the aboriginal leaders whose story is told in W. Lloyd Warner's classic *A Black Civilization.* The white paint on the face of the figure represents the foam, and the white dots on his chin the drops of water that clung to his body as Laindjung came up through the surf. Exhibited: Lowie, Field.

Banaidja, by Libundja. This outstanding figure of Banaidja, son of Laindjung, was carved near Milingimbi, in the central region, and shows a distinct difference from the northeastern style. The Vandyke beard is typical of the central region. On his chest and arms, Banaidja has cicatrices; on his front is painted a water bird and Minala, the tortoise, who befriended him in the pool when he was speared. Exhibited: Jones, Lowie, Field (p. 4, cat.), de Young.

The Younger Sister, by Dawudi. This carved figure also bears a caterpillar design on her body. Lack of sidestrokes on the oval shapes indicates they are immature caterpillars, and thus identifies this figure as that of the younger Wagilag sister. Her pendulous breasts show that she has already borne a child. The black lines with dots and diagonal red lines indicate the thunder, lightning, and rain which fell when Julunggul, the great snake, rose from his water hole and swallowed the sisters. Exhibited: Lowie, Field, de Young. (See Berndt, ed., 1964, *Australian Aboriginal Art,* Sydney: Ure Smith, 1964, p. 93.)

The Wind Makers, by Abadjera. The rectangle with three spines emerging from each end is the northwest-wind totem; it represents the bloodwood tree, and the spines indicate the wind rushing from it when the tree is cut. On both sides are tribesmen chanting the Barra song during the ceremony to encourage the wind to blow freely. Exhibited: Lowie, Field.

The Fire Spirit, by Naridjin. The diamond design in the background indicates fire, flames, and smoke. The black diamonds with white dotted lines symbolize the fire beginning; the diamonds with solid white crosshatching represent the fire at its height; and the black diamonds, the glowing embers. Two birds that flew from the fire are shown at the left. Exhibited: Lowie, Field, de Young.

Following Page 176

The Thunder Man's Wife, by Lardjanga. This rare bark shows the wife of Djambuwal, who is seldom painted. Above her head stretches the rainbow that forms when Djambuwal throws his great spear. In her hands are the double-headed clubs which she strikes together to create thunder. She is urinating to cause the waterspouts. The bars on her chest and stomach are cicatrices; the background design is "owned" by the *Dangu* linguistic group, and is seen on many of Lardjanga's paintings. The design is distorted here to represent the turbulence of the storm clouds. The deft handling of the figure and the warm humor that pervades it characterize the best of northeastern-region art. Exhibited: Lowie, Field, de Young.

Tortoises Mating, by Libundja. Two tortoises are shown mating in the water. The crosshatching at the sides indicates the soft mud by the edge of the pool. A gathering storm is indicated by the triangles at top and bottom, and on the tortoises' backs: The black triangles are thunder; the red, lightning; and the white, rain. The snake, repeated on each side, lives in the Sky World and sends the rain. Exhibited: Lowie, UCSB, Field (p. 30. cat.), de Young.

Prau, by Biragidji. This painting shows the main mast of the *prau* with the large rectangular sail raised and the smaller foremast and mizzen mast. The sweep rudder is pictured at the stern and the anchor at the bow. It was in *prau* similar to this that the Makasans attacked Djambuwal. Exhibited: Lowie (p. 16, cat.), UCSB, Field (p. 42, cat.), de Young.

The Shark, by Mini-Mini. This artist is one of the outstanding painters of Groote Eylandt. His work appears in the collections of a number of museums and art galleries. Mini-mini belongs to the Wanungamulangwa clan, Ingura tribe, which has the shark, bailer shell, and porpoise as its totems. Exhibited: Lowie, Field, de Young. (See Kupka, *Dawn of Art,* 1965, page 69a.)

The Water Carrier, by Naridjin. Napilingu is shown with her water carrier on her head. Beside her are two yam sticks, which she used to pry the bark for the water container from the tree. At the top is the tortoise whose shell gave Napilingu the idea for making the water container. Exhibited: Lowie, Field, de Young.

Two Funeral Skulls, by Yirrillil. These extremely rare carved skulls were used in the funeral rites to provide a place for the spirit of the dead person to stay between the time of death and the final rites, when his spirit departs and goes to the Island of the Dead. The heads are placed beside the body. After the ceremony, they are carried on a cord about the neck of the wife or other near relative, or are placed in a tree. This provides a temporary home for the spirit if it returns, so it will not wander about, bringing harm to people. Exhibited: Lowie (p. 12, cat.), UCSB (p. 20, cat.).

The Night Bird, by Naridjin. The night bird, Guwarg, perches on the totemic tree as he looks for the opossum, Marngu. Naridjin is the "owner" and the only one permitted to carve this totem; others may do so only with his permission. Exhibited: Lowie, Field (p. 20, cat.), de Young.

Bones and Skulls, by Djadjiwui. After an aborigine dies, and appropriate ceremonies have been completed, the body is placed on a burial platform, where it decomposes. During this period, the spirit of the dead person stays nearby. After about three months, the bones are cleaned, rubbed with red ocher, and placed in a temporary bone coffin, which has the totemic symbols of the deceased painted on the outside. The skull, or a wooden facsimile of it, is placed in a string bag, and both the bark coffin and skull are carried about for some months by the wife or a near female relative. The bones are then placed in a log coffin for final burial. This painting shows the skulls and bones after they have been painted with the totemic symbols of the deceased.

The Adulteress, by Aurangnamirri. This carved figure was by one of the out-standing Tiwi artists, known also by the English name of Young Brook. Bima is shown after her son Djinini was born, as indicated by her pendulous breasts. The heart carved on the base is a modern touch, for the Tiwi did not use this symbol. Exhibited: Lowie, Field.

Purukapali and His Dead Son, by Mandarbarni. Purukapali is shown holding his dead son in his arms, wrapped in a paperbark shroud, before he walked backward into the sea and drowned. The son is the oblong figure in Puruka-pali's crossed hands. Mandarbarni was one of the great old carvers of the Tiwi. Exhibited: Lowie (p. 13, cat.), UCSB (p. 19, cat.), Field (p. 38, cat.), de Young.

The Evil Tree Spirit, by Malangi. In the center of the painting is the black shape of the evil tree spirit which turned itself into a tree growing beside the water hole. One of the fish living in the pool is shown, together with a tree of wild fruit. The poisonous snake which killed the hunter is shown in the grass, in-dicated by the diagonal lines.

The Rainbow Snake, by Indji Tharwul. This exceptional bark shows Kun-manggur in his snake form. The circles represent the water holes; the white dots, the eggs in the water holes from which the first people came.

Kangaroo and Snake, by Malangi. This dramatic painting shows the kangaroo killed by Gurramuringu while hunting. In the lower left corner is the snake that attacked and killed the hunter. On the right is a tree that grew by the water hole, with the seed pods that the aborigines use as food. The kangaroo is portrayed in the old X-ray style, showing the heart, lungs, backbone, and stomach. This bark shows Malangi's easy mastery of the traditional idiom and his ability to convert it into an arresting composition while still retaining the authentic conventions. Exhibited: Field, de Young.

The Leaf from the Sea, by Libundja. A yam leaf floats in from the sea, alerting Yalngura to the existence of an island where lissome young women wait. In one hand is the bag in which Yalngura brought food for the journey; in the other is a club he carried for protection. To the left is the morning-star totem, commemorating Barnumbir, who guides spirits of the dead to Bralgu, the Island of the Dead. The totem is shown upside down; the white tuft of feathers on the end represents the morning star; the two cords ending in white feather tufts indicate the strings on which the two old sisters let out the star from their basket in the dark of early morning and with which they draw it back as the sun rises. Exhibited: Qantas, Lowie, Field, de Young.

Murayana, The Cheerful Spirit, by Libundja. Murayana's happy smile and cheerful laughter are infectious and help people forget their sorrow following mortuary ceremonies. Human hair is used to make the hair and beard of the figure. The design, which was the property of Libundja, represents the honey-comb; the red dots are bees and the white dots indicate the honeycomb and bee food. Exhibited: Lowie, UCSB, Field (p. 36, cat.), de Young.

PART I: ART AND MYTHS OF THE ABORIGINES
The People and Their Myths

PAGE 10   *Makasan Ship Captain*, by Mani-luki. The captain of the *prau* wears a sleeveless jacket for the formality of going ashore to initiate trading. Although the Makasans generally shaved, this figure is shown with a beard because the respected Tiwi "old men" grew full beards. Mani-luki, known by the English name of Harry Carpenter, is of the Tiwi tribe, Melville Island. A careful and deliberate craftsman, he specializes in carving the cast of characters in the Purukapali myth. Now old, he does very little sculpture and lives with his wife at Snake Bay. Exhibited: Lowie, Field, de Young.

PAGE 11   *Malay Parang*, by Mawulan. The Malay traders from Makasar introduced steel to the aborigines; the large knives, or *parang*, were a favored article of trade for trepang. Only an old man would remember the knives, as the Makasans ceased their visits in 1907 when legislation closed the northern shores to outsiders. Mawulan is one of the most famous of the aboriginal painters. His work, while invariably faithful to the traditional designs, has a distinctive elegance and economy of line.

PAGE 12   *Vengeance at Buckingham Bay*, by Djawa. This painting commemorates a tragic episode during the early days when settlers gave a gift of sweet biscuits made from flour mixed with arsenic to a group of aborigines at Buckingham Bay. The men attacked and killed several of the murderers. The painting shows the leader of the vengeance party with hatchet in hand. The diamond design on the figure, with circles at the intersections, represents a honeycomb and indicates that the man is of the *jiridja* moiety. A great leader of the central-region clans, Djawa is also an outstanding artist. His quick and incisive mind and commanding personality are immediately noticeable. In any group the men sort themselves out to surround him; when a judgment is to be made, all speak their piece and then fall silent for Djawa to state his conclusions. Exhibited: Qantas, Lowie, UCSB, Field, de Young.

PAGE 13   *The Angel of the Lord*, by Mahkarolla. The missionaries had a powerful impact on the aborigines. This interpretation of an angel with wings and a halo on his head was painted by Mahkarolla, a head man of the central region who befriended the anthropologist Lloyd Warner during his study of the Murngin. This bark was collected by Dr. Stuart Scougall in the late 1950s. It was identified with the help of Djawa at Milingimbi and Waidjung at Yirrkala.

PAGE 15   *Moses Striking the Rock*, by unknown artist. This painting, by an unknown artist from Groote Eylandt, shows Moses striking the rock. It is indicative of the strong positive influence Christian missionaries have had on aboriginal development. Moses' dress and hairdo are probably from a Sunday school text. The background is done in the traditional Groote Eylandt style.

PAGE 17   *The Clap-Stick Man*, by Madaman. Known as *bilma*, clap sticks are used in pairs. The clap-stick man holds the big one loosely, then strikes it with the small one to find the point of resonance. Sticks painted with totemic patterns are used only on sacred ground. Since constant use wears off the design, they are repainted periodically to renew the *mana,* or power. This painting shows Gongbirima, the clap-stick man who, together with Dulanganda, the *didjeridu* or drone-pipe player, taught the *Riradjingu* people the songs and dances for one of the most important ceremonies: that of Barnumbir, the morning star. Madaman, a great artist who died in 1970, was a brother of Mawulan. Exhibited: This is one panel from the full bark shown at Qantas and Lowie.

The Crow Man, by Midinari. The aborigines believe they are descended from Dreamtime spirits who had the form of birds, animals, or other creatures. This is the crow spirit who became a man and whose descendants revere the crow totem today. Exhibited: UCSB. PAGE 19

Mimi Spirit, cave painting. Today, as in the Dreamtime, long, thin spirits live among the rocks of the Arnhem Land plateau. Here one is shown running with its netted dilly bag on its back. A more recent painting of a fish overlays part of the legs. PAGE 20

The Tortoise Man, by Biragidji. This very unusual painting shows the tortoise, Minala, assuming his human form. The transformation is not quite finished: the lower half of his body is human, while the top half is still tortoise, complete with flippers. Biragidji, one of the great old painters, learned his craft before the time of the white man. He paints slowly, but with confident skill. His work ranks with that of the best of the aboriginal painters. Biragidji remembers the Makasans coming to Arnhem Land in his youth. He puffs frequently on a long Makasan pipe made from the hollow stem of the *lungin* bush, with a crab's claw for a bowl. Exhibited: Lowie (p. 7, cat.), UCSB. PAGE 22

Magpie Goose Totemic Figure, by Bininjuwi. This *rangga,* or totemic figure, is used to encourage the magpie geese to proliferate and be plentiful for hunting. Bininjuwi, one of the best of the aboriginal carvers, is also an excellent painter. He has the right to paint a number of the traditional designs, so his work is more varied than most. PAGE 23

Trip to Sydney, by Mawulan. One of the outstanding leaders and artists of the Yirrkala area, who died in 1967, Mawulan here showed his impression of his first visit to Sydney by airplane. The white dots are the city lights seen from the air, the dark oblongs the buildings and open spaces. The figures were his representation of the people hurrying to and fro. "*Balanda* [the white man] have many devil," said Mawulan. PAGE 25

Mawulan went through a conflict between his tribal traditions and the new beliefs brought by the Christian missionaries. He made his reconciliations neatly, keeping his own beliefs, but also outwardly accepting the new faith, so that he had something of the best of both worlds. He owned several of the important designs, including the Milky Way and the goanna totem. Exhibited: Qantas, Lowie, UCSB, Field (p. 42, cat.), de Young.

Regions and Art Styles

Central Region

Stingray Totem, by Mutpu. This shows the characteristic central region style. The figure is relatively bold and has a sense of vigor and movement as com- PAGE 27 pared to a similar figure from the northeast region that follows. There is considerable detail: the scales are shown, as well as the teeth in the open mouth. The tail is bent to fit the limits of the bark. The horseshoe shape is the fat that the aborigines consider a delicacy. Made to guide the men who paint these totemic designs on the abdomens of the dancers, this bark painting is used in the circumcision ceremony of the *Djambarbingu* people. The totem is known as *garma*, to signify that uninitiated boys and women can attend the ceremony, as opposed to *rangga*, which can be seen only by the initiated men. Exhibited: Lowie, Field (p. 8, cat.), de Young.

Northeastern Region

PAGE 28   *Stingray Totem*, by Biragidji. Typical of the northeastern region style, this bark by the old master painter Biragidji shows the detailed background, the angular composition and the stylized, more formal and static approach that differentiates it from the central region work. The fish is shown resting on a sandbank; the lines indicate the ripples it sets in motion in the shallow water. The stingray is Biragidji's mother's totem and he inherited the right to paint it from her. Exhibited: Lowie, Field (p. 10, cat.), de Young.

Groote Eylandt Region

PAGE 29   *The Barramundi Fish*, by Kneepad. This Groote Eylandt bark shows the characteristic black background, single bold figure, and short dashed lines used to fill the outline. The painting tells of the barramundi fish, Ukulpaindee, who came out of the sea in the Dreamtime and traveled across the land, leaving in his wake the streams that exist today. Water holes were formed where he urinated. Kneepad is the English name for Jabarrgwa, an old master painter, whose principal totem is Barra, the northwest wind. Exhibited: Lowie, Field (p. 10, cat.), de Young.

Port Keats Region

PAGE 30   *The Creator Snake, Kunmanggur*, by Indji Tharwul. The snake theme here contrasts with that of the Tiwi. The Port Keats artists have learned to paint relatively recently. Their barks usually have a plain background of brown or red and strong figures or designs representing prominent geographic features or the myths of the region. Indji is one of the best of the Port Keats artists. A steady and consistent worker, he prefers to delineate boldly executed figures on a rich red background. Exhibited: Jones, Lowie, Field, de Young. (See Kupka, *Dawn of Art*, 1965, back cover.)

The Artists and Their Work

PAGE 33   *The Master Painter, Marwai*, by Yirrawala. In the Dreamtime, Marwai traveled around the country of the Gunwinggu tribe, painting the designs now found in caves along the Liverpool River and near Oenpelli. He taught the men to paint as they do today. The two small dilly bags suspended about his neck by a cord contain the earth colors he used as pigments. Yirrawala is one of the greatest of the western region artists. His primary totem is the sun. He has traveled extensively, accompanying exhibits of his work both in Australia and abroad, and has had the rare honor of being made a Member of the Order of the British Empire for his artistic contributions. Exhibited: Lowie, UCSB, Field (p. 6, cat.), de Young.

Conception, by Mangangina. Paintings are made for magical purposes. Since PAGE 34 love-making and fertility of women are primary concerns, magic paintings are used to encourage both. This painting is used in a ceremony held at the totemic place of the snake, as indicated by the bottom figure. The two men, one with a spear and spear-thrower, the other with a clap stick, are dancing and singing, in an attempt to woo the woman shown in the center. Near her is a large representation of the vagina, which is intended to encourage her to have intercourse with the men. Mangangina's principal totem is the snake. Exhibited: Lowie, Field, de Young.

The Sea Gull Dance, by Bangul. This very rare painting is by one of the few PAGE 35 aboriginal women artists, Bangul, daughter of Mawulan, a strong leader and outstanding artist. The painting tells of Dreamtime people who turned themselves into the sea gulls we know today. They made a totemic figure of the sea gull from sacred fiber string and feathers, then danced and sang magic incantations around it until they became birds and flew away. The three black rays extending from the bottom of the sea-gull figure indicate the paths along which the aborigines danced. Exhibited: Qantas, Lowie, UCSB, Field, de Young.

The Yellow Ocher Site, by Jama. The locations in the northeastern region where PAGE 36 the yellow ocher used in painting was found were especially venerated because the earth colors were believed to have great *mana,* or power. The ochers could be dug only by initiated "old men," who crawled to the site on all fours. This painting shows the man, Wirrilli, who discovered the ocher site in the Dreamtime by chancing upon a burrow dug by a goanna. Noting pieces of yellow ocher in the earth thrown out, Wirrilli enlarged the hole with his digging stick, and the men have returned there ever since for their yellow ocher. Wirrilli is shown standing beside the site with his digging stick. His footprints can be seen in the soft earth near the hole.

PART II: CREATION MYTHS
The Djanggawul Myth

The Sacred Fish, by Madaman. In their travels the Djanggawul created water PAGE 46 holes near their campsites. At the water hole of Gundalmirri, they caused fish, known as *wurrakui,* to appear. As part of the mortuary ceremonies, the clansmen of the deceased catch one of these fish and eat it. The dead fish stands for the dead man. In this painting the circles around the root of the tail of the fish represent the water hole. The fish is painted in the X-ray style, showing the heart and lungs. The men are painted in the same way, identifying them with the fish and the dead man. The background design is "owned" by the *Riradjingu dua* clanspeople. Exhibited: This is a panel from a larger bark shown at Qantas, Lowie, UCSB, Field (p. 15, cat.), de Young.

The Sacred Fish, by Wandjuk. This provides an interesting contrast to the PAGE 47 painting of the same theme by Madaman. Wandjuk is the son of Mawulan, who is Madaman's brother. In this painting the sacred water hole, Gundalmirri, is indicated by the circle painted on the fish. The wavy lines represent the water running into the water hole. Wandjuk is not allowed to paint the X-ray design, for Madaman has sole rights to it. Exhibited: Lowie, Field (p. 16, cat.), de Young. (See Berndt, ed., *Australian Aboriginal Art,* 1964, pl. 67.)

PAGE 48   *The Promised Land,* by Wandjuk. The Djanggawul brother looks from a hilltop on the island of Bralgu toward the mainland, to which his wife, Walu, the Sun Woman, has banished him for committing incest with his sisters. In the background are the digging sticks he will take. The half-circle below him represents Walu, who will light the path of the Djanggawul with her rays. This is part of a unique series of "book barks" by the master painter, Wandjuk, a son of the great Mawulan. It was collected by Dr. Stuart Scougall about 1959. The bark is "signed" on the back with the handprint of the artist, which Wandjuk formed by spraying a mouthful of white ocher paint over his hand outstretched on the bark. At his best, Wandjuk is a clever and exacting artist. He adds his personal embellishments to many of the authentic patterns he paints. Sometimes he will add a sly touch, such as showing a white man's hat on one of the minor figures. Exhibited: *The Promised Land* is a panel from a painting shown at Qantas, Lowie, UCSB, Field, de Young. The next two by Wandjuk are from the same series.

PAGE 49   *The Canoe Voyage,* by Wandjuk. The two Djanggawul sisters and their brother travel to the mainland in their canoe. The brother is resting in the canoe bottom while his two sisters paddle. The aborigines learned to make canoes from the Makasan traders, who carried them aboard their *prau.*

PAGE 50   *The Lizard Design,* by Lardjanga. When the Djanggawul landed on the mainland, the first creature they saw was a goanna, or monitor lizard, walking along the crest of a sand dune. His feet caused small parallel streams of sand to run down the face of the dune; his tail also left a mark on the crest. The Djanggawul were so fascinated by the patterns of the lines of sand that they decreed that whenever the clans of the *dua* moiety painted the lizard, who was their totemic animal, they must also paint the patterns of the parallel lines. The diagonal lines in the painting are the sand rolling downhill. The horizontal lines mark the tail of the lizard. The circle in the center represents a water hole the Djanggawul made. The footprints of the bush turkey, which was the second living creature they saw, are shown in the two bands that run the length of the bark. Exhibited: Lowie (p. 4, cat.), Field, de Young.

PAGE 51   *Lizards and Birds,* by Lardjanga. When the Djanggawul came to the eastern side of Arnhem Bay after they had landed, they sat down to rest and started to sing. Seeing two sacred goannas searching vainly for water, they sank their digging sticks into the ground and made three water holes. In the painting the water can be seen running between the holes, which are repeated for emphasis. The bush turkey is shown in the center panel. The crosshatching on both sides of the bird tracks represents a special kind of water grass that grows in the pools. The goanna and birds are shown in pairs because the Djanggawul saw both males and females and told them to proliferate to feed the people. Exhibited: Lowie, Field, de Young.

PAGE 53   *The Unknown,* by Wandjuk. This is another of the "book barks" that show, in sequence, episodes from the Djanggawul myth. In this painting the Djanggawul brother is shown carrying his two spear-throwers, which are enlarged to indicate their importance, as he faces the unknown land he and his sisters are about to explore. The background, which is a sacred design of the *Riradjingu*-speaking clans, represents the trail of the lizard in the sand, as the Djanggawul saw it when they first landed.

The Sister Gives Birth, by Wandjuk. One of the sisters is shown in the birth PAGE 54
position as she is about to bear a child, who will become a progenitor of the
dua moiety people. She grasps two yam sticks for support in her labor.

Children in the Grass, by Djunmal. After the Djanggawul sisters gave birth, PAGE 56
they placed their babies in the grass. The girls, shown in the top two rows,
were nestled in soft grass and half-covered with the woven *ngainmara* mat; but,
as shown in the lower row, the boys were left exposed. Thus the boys are now
hairy and rough; the girls soft and smooth. Exhibited: One of two panels from
a bark shown at Qantas, Lowie, UCSB, Field (p. 15, cat.).

The Good Man: The Laindjung Myth

Laindjung. See color list.

The Laindjung Story. See color list.

Banaidja. See color list.

The Sisters and the Snake: The Wagilag Myth

Note on the Artists: Dawudi and Burunggur, his tribal brother, both had the
right to paint the Wagilag myth. Dawudi and Burunggur were classified as
brothers because their fathers were half-brothers. Dardanga, another of
Burunggur's brothers, also had the right to paint the Wagilag myth. Dawudi
died in 1970; Burunggur in 1973; and since then, Dardanga has had the primary right to paint the myth.

Burunggur's wife outlived him but had cataracts and couldn't see well.
One morning, in the dark before dawn, she was awakened by a great clatter in
her storeroom. She went to investigate and found that a huge python had
knocked down some tins of food. Her screams brought a neighboring man on
the run, armed with an ax. He pushed the old woman aside to attack the python, but as soon as she made out his intention, she threw herself upon him
with further screams. She believed the snake was the Great Rainbow Snake
and that Burunggur's spirit had returned in it, so she didn't want it harmed.

The Sacred Pool, by Dawudi. This masterful bark shows most of the Wagilag PAGE 68
sisters' story. At the bottom, the half-circle with diagonal stripes is the Mirarmina water hole. Two trees rise from it, together with Julunggul, who can be
seen as he emerges to swallow the sisters and their babies. At the lower right
are the two sisters as they approach the water hole; their footsteps are visible to the right of Julunggul. The two trees are pandanus, which grew beside
the water hole and provided poles for the sisters' lean-to. The singing stick is
immediately above the trees. The band with diagonal stripes at the very bottom represents the menstrual blood that tainted the water hole. At the far
left, the large triangular shape symbolizes the depression formed by Julunggul
when he crashed to the ground after admitting he had swallowed the sisters.
The black circle is Julunggul's anus. At the upper right, above the snake's coil,
the spears and spear-thrower the sisters carried are shown. Next to them are
more footprints and oval shapes with projecting lines, representing caterpillars, which are a clan totem. In the upper center is the *ubar*-log drum; standing

on it is the bandicoot that jumped out of the fire. The three long rectangles with rounded ends have a secret meaning which may not be disclosed. This theme is the noted classic of aboriginal bark painting; Dawudi is recognized as one of its greatest exponents. Exhibited: Lowie (p. 4, cat.), UCSB (p. 14, cat.), de Young.

PAGE 69   *The Wagilag Sister,* by Dawudi. This rare carved wood figure shows the elder Wagilag sister. Her identity is revealed by the type of caterpillars painted on her body. The white sidestrokes on the oval shapes denote the mature caterpillar; therefore, this is the elder Wagilag sister. Exhibited: Lowie, UCSB, Field, de Young.

The Younger Sister. See color list.

PAGE 70   *The Yam Sticks,* by Dawudi. These are the digging sticks known as *dhuna,* which are used in the Wagilag ceremony. They represent the sticks carried by the sisters to dig roots and bulbs in their journey across Arnhem Land. The Wagilag caterpillar totems can be seen on the sticks. Exhibited: Field (p. 14, cat.), de Young.

PAGE 71   *The Rainbow Serpent,* by Midinari. This is the rainbow the sisters saw as they approached the water hole at Mirarmina. In the center is the Great Rainbow Snake, Julunggul. He is really a freshwater python and hibernates in the water hole until the arrival of the northwest monsoons, emerging as the wet season sets in. At each end of the rainbow the water of the pool is shown. This design is "owned" by Midinari. Exhibited: Jones, Lowie (p. 6, cat.), UCSB (p. 13, cat.), Field (p. 12, cat.), de Young.

PAGE 71   *The Forked Stick,* by Dawudi. This is one of the *rangga,* or totemic objects, that is used when the Wagilag story is sung and mimed. The sisters thrust a forked stick such as this into the ground to support a pole for the shelter they built on the banks of the sacred water hole, Mirarmina. The crosshatching on the stick represents the water that flooded the country when Julunggul sang his power song and brought the rain. Exhibited: Field, Lowie.

PAGE 72   *Rain and Water,* by Midinari. This is another rendition of the Wagilag story. At the top is the singing stick the sisters threw into the air. The dots represent the rain that fell; the parallel lines, the creeks that were swollen by the rain; and the crosshatching, the run-off into the pool. At the bottom, the square black shape is the sacred water hole at Mirarmina. Down the center are two billabongs, or lagoons, connected by waterways, into which runs the rainwater, represented by the crosshatching. The caterpillar symbol is shown: The ovals with sidestrokes are the adult caterpillars; those without are the young. Midinari "owns" the right to paint the Wagilag myth in the northeast region, in the same manner that Dawudi and his successors have similar rights in the central region. Exhibited: de Young.

PAGE 73   *The Great Serpent,* by Midinari. Julunggul is shown in his water hole. A distinctive design that belongs to the *Galpu* linguistic group is painted on the body of the snake. Beside him are the water birds that live in the lagoon. Exhibited: Field.

The Coming of the Sisters, by Dardanga. This is a painting of the Wagilag myth PAGE 74 by an artist who "owned" rights secondary to Dawudi, the primary owner. In the lower center the great snake is shown with his head in a bark shelter. He has swallowed the babies and is now about to take the two sisters. The triangular shape in the middle represents the depression in the ground that Julunggul caused when he fell. The black circle is the anus of the snake. At the bottom right is the singing stick which the sisters threw into the air to stop the rains. Above them is the yam stick and the spear that they carried. At the left is the bandicoot that ran out of the fire, the yams, and some of the other food they tried to cook. Exhibited: Lowie, Field, de Young.

The Great Python, by Dawudi. Fashioned from a flat piece of bark, this repre- PAGE 74 sentation of the snake is used in the ceremony. The design represents the intestinal tract of the snake, signifying the swallowing of the Wagilag sisters. Exhibited: Lowie, Field.

The Didjeridu, by Midinari. Used in the circumcision ceremony, this *rangga* PAGE 75 symbolizes the *didjeridu* played by the great snake, Julunggul. When the old men blow it during the dance, it represents the snake's voice. During the ceremony, initiates are covered with sheets of paperbark and they pretend to sleep, as the Wagilag sisters did in their shelter. The *didjeridu* is then carried around the sleeping boys to represent Julunggul encircling the sisters. On the bottom part of the *didjeridu* is the form of the Rainbow Snake which can be easily identified as the design "owned" by Midinari. Above this is one of the fish found in the sacred water hole. The mouthpiece is made from beeswax. Exhibited: Lowie, UCSB, Field (p. 14, cat.), de Young.

The Snake Woman: The Ngalyod Myth

The First Mother, Waramurungundji, by Nguleingulei. The Great Rainbow PAGE 77 Snake of the Gunwinggu people turned into the first woman. Here she is seen as she travels through the country, carrying her digging stick and net bag on her back. A smaller bag is seen at her elbow. The figure is similar to those found in the cave paintings. The artist, Nguleingulei, who lives on the Liverpool River escarpment, is one of the few who has the right to paint the First Mother. (See Berndt and Berndt, *Man, Land and Myth in North Australia,* p. 158b.)

The Spirit Ancestor, by Jambalula. Wuragog, the husband of Wara- PAGE 78 murungundji, wanted to have intercourse with her so frequently that she finally turned back into her snake form. However, he persisted, and the first children were born. The painting shows the act of intercourse; the wallabies at the bottom are the personal totems of the artist. Exhibited: Lowie, Field, de Young.

The Mother Protector. See color list.

The Death of the Father: The Kunmanggur Myth

The Sacred Mountain, by Indji Tharwul. This shows the deep pool atop the PAGE 82 sacred mountain, Wagura, that was the home of Kunmanggur in his snake form. The concentric circles indicate the pool; the dotted lines, the mountain-side falling away from it.

The Old Woman: The Mudungkala Myth

PART III: MYTHS OF NATURAL FORCES

The Constellation of Scorpio. See color list.

How the Milky Way Was Created: The Catfish and Crow Myth

yet interacting figures has an allegorical quality that establishes the mastery of the artist. Exhibited: Lowie, UCSB, Field, de Young. (See *Field Museum of Natural History Bulletin,* January 1972, vol. 43, no. 1, cover.)

The Milky Way, by Mawulan. This painting shows the broad swath of stars of the Milky Way that were believed by aborigines to have once been the bones of the catfish that was thrown into the sky. The black lines indicate a river flowing through the Milky Way. One of the fish that lives in the river is shown. Exhibited: Lowie, UCSB, Field (p. 26, cat.), de Young.

PAGE 103

The Wind Tree: The Barra Myth

The Wind Tree, by Abadjera. The bloodwood tree that contains the northwest wind is pictured several times to show its importance. Each year, the aborigines who belong to the Barra totem conduct a ceremony in which they cut into the trunk so that the northwest wind, which has been held within the tree throughout the dry season, can be released. The triangles on both ends show the cuts. Exhibited: de Young.

PAGE 106

The Wind Makers. See color list.

The Coming of Fire: The Goorda Myth

The Fire Spirit. See color list.

Goorda Comes, by Munggeraui. Goorda runs across the grass, bringing fire with him. The diamonds represent fire and smoke. Exhibited: Lowie, Field, de Young.

PAGE 110

The Spider Man, by Munggeraui. As the fire raged, a man named Lualua, shown here as he turned himself into a spider, crawled into a hole in the rocks and was saved. Exhibited: Lowie, Field, de Young.

PAGE 111

The Spider Hides, by Munggeraui. The spider, Garwuli, hides from the fire in a deep cleft in the rocks. Exhibited: Lowie, Field, de Young.

PAGE 112

The Circumcision Boys, by Munggeraui. The fire brought by Goorda burns the boys who are waiting to be circumcised. The diamond design represents the flames; the crosshatched background indicates the flame and smoke that poured into the bark hut where the boys were huddled. Exhibited: Lowie, Field, de Young.

PAGE 113

The Circumcision Boys Burn, by Munggeraui. The fire, brought by Goorda, burns the circumcision boys to death. Exhibited: Lowie, Field, de Young.

PAGE 113

The Thunder Man: The Djambuwal Myth

The Thunder Man, by Lardjanga. The Thunder Man stands ready to hurl his spear, Larrapan, which will appear in the sky as a rainbow. He is urinating, and this causes the waterspouts which are prevalent in the early months of the northwest monsoon. Below is the codfish which Djambuwal spears. Exhibited: Lowie, Field.

PAGE 114

PAGE 115   *Master of the Storms,* by Lardjanga. Since Biragidji, who was the primary owner, was alive at the time, Lardjanga had to secure permission to paint this bark. In the background, Lardjanga shows his own clan design, rather than that of Biragidji; he has distorted the lines to show the turbulence of the storm clouds. Djambuwal holds his spear, Larrapan. The barbed symbols hanging from his arms represent flashes of lightning; around his waist can be seen the double-headed clubs he strikes together to create thunder. He is urinating to cause the waterspouts which are prevalent during the early months of the northwest monsoon. Exhibited: Field.

The Thunder Man's Wife. See color list.

The Lightning Man: The Namarragon Myth

PAGE 118   *The Lightning Man,* by Nameradji. The Lightning Man is shown holding the lightning symbol, which extends from his toes around his head. On his elbows, knees, and thighs are stone axes. Bold, yet simple, this figure is distinguished by an essential dramatic quality. (See Kupka, *Dawn of Art,* 1964, p. 57.)

PAGE 119   *The Lightning Woman,* by Anchor Barlbuwa. The aboriginals paint the wives of their totemic heroes very infrequently. This shows the wife of the Lightning Man with the lightning symbol extending from her knees to her head. Her breasts and female organs are clearly visible. Exhibited: Lowie, UCSB, Field de Young.

PART IV: MYTHS OF MEN AND WOMEN
The Lost Love: The Balada Myth

PAGE 128   *The Fight,* by Balirlbalirl. This bark is particularly interesting because it is in the traditional, symbolic style sometimes found in the cave paintings. At the left, the large bean-shaped figure represents the hill on which the Great Tree grew. The oval on the concave surface is the cave; the horizontal line represents the branches of the tree growing out of the rock. A small peanut-shaped figure in front of the cave is the woman; the larger one standing in front of her is the man. The attackers, represented by the two oblong shapes at the right, are throwing their spears, which pierce both the man and the woman. Balirlbalirl, known as Old Bob, was one of the best of the traditional painters of the Gunwinggu tribe in western Arnhem Land. Exhibited: Lowie, Field.

PAGE 129   *The Burial,* by Balirlbalirl. After being killed, Balada and Waiula were wrapped in paperbark and carried by their clanspeople for burial into the high country that Balada loved so well. The outer line indicates the hills. Top center is the clearing in which they were killed. At the left, the two joined oblongs represent the two groups of people near the Great Tree as they started to sing and dance the mortuary ceremonies. The snakelike line shows the path they took as they began their ascent into the hills. Stopping where the two oblongs are shown again, the mourners conducted a further ceremony, then climbed up the escarpment and higher into the hills, as shown by the long curving line. Finally they reached the place where the bodies were to be buried. Each group held a separate ceremony, as shown by the two oblongs in the upper right. The Xs with the black dot in the center represent the bodies of Balada and Waiula, while the large, irregularly shaped object in the center indicates that their bodies were finally wrapped in paperbark and left to rest on the rock. Exhibited: de Young.

The First Wife: The Dolphin Myth

The Bailer Shellfish, by Bunaya. The single figure boldly presented on a black background is common in Groote Eylandt work. The outline is filled with dashed lines. Bunaya was from the Wanindiljangwa clan, Moiety 2, which has the southeast wind and the shark as totems. Exhibited: Field.
PAGE 131

The Shark. See color list.

The Tortoise Totem, by Djikalulu. This carved wooden totem is used in ceremonies to represent the tortoise. The aborigines believe that the long neck is associated with the penis, and they frequently use the totem in circumcision ceremonies. Exhibited: Lowie, de Young.
PAGE 135

Tortoises in the Water, Bininjuwi. This shows two tortoises in the water. The smaller circular shapes are bits of food and shellfish on which the tortoises feed.
PAGE 136

The Faithful Wife: The Tortoise Myth

The Tortoise Totem, by Yuwati. Carved from wood and painted with earth colors, this is used in the circumcision ceremony.
PAGE 137

Tortoise in the Grass, by Libundja. Minala the tortoise moves through the grass toward the river. The wavy lines on each side indicate movement of the grass; the white dots represent the ground. On the tortoise's back is a design "owned" by the Gubabingu people. It represents a hollow tree in longitudinal section, inside which is the hive of the wild honeybee. The diamond shapes are the cells, and the various colors represent eggs, wax, honey, and bee food. This design is painted on human skulls, bull-roarers, weapons, bark sheets, totems, and the body. Libundja, one of the great master painters of Arnhem Land, died in 1968. His work has a delicacy and balance rarely equaled in aboriginal work. Exhibited: Lowie.
PAGE 138

The Tortoises, by Daudaingalil. Two tortoises are shown in the movements preparatory to copulation. The parallel lines around the water represent the grass that grows there, and the bands of crosshatching indicate mud at the edge of the water. Exhibited: Field.
PAGE 138

Tortoises Mating, by Bininjuwi. Two tortoises are mating in the mud by the riverbank. The zigzag lines represent their tracks as they pass through the grass, and the crosshatched lines are the soft mud in which they rest. Exhibited: Field.
PAGE 139

The Tempted One: The Mimi Myth

Mimi Hunter and Kangaroo, by Nguleingulei. This outstanding bark shows the Mimi hunter poising the spear in its spear-thrower as he prepares to launch it at the kangaroo. A dilly bag hangs around his neck. The Mimi's small size compared to that of his prey indicates that he is some distance away from the animal, although the limitations of the bark have forced the painter to show them touching. The rendition of the kangaroo, which is exceptional, employs the X-ray style, showing the backbone, lungs, viscera, and other internal organs. Exhibited: Lowie, UCSB (front cover, cat.), Field (p. 4, cat.), de Young. (See Berndt, ed., Australian Aboriginal Art, 1964, pl. 22.)

The Greeters, by Manggudja. Three Mimi women are shown dancing in greeting. Two of them have lengths of banyan string around their thumbs, with which they make cat's-cradle figures as they dance. Manggudja paints in the authentic tradition; his work is direct and forceful and conveys his deep feeling for the myths of his people.

Mimi Women Wait, by Namirrki. Two Mimi women wait to make love to Djala, the hunter. The figures are portrayed in X-ray fashion that shows ankle, knee, pelvic, elbow, and shoulder bones. The practice of simply outlining the subject against a plain background, and making visible various internal organs, is very similar to the style found in cave paintings that are believed to date back as much as ten thousand years. Older bark paintings, such as this one, were all done with a red color which was made from blood mixed with red ocher. Namirrki is called Spider in English. Exhibited: Lowie, UCSB, Field, de Young.

The Man-Eater: The Mutjinga Myth, I

The Goanna Runs, by Madigan. This bark shows Mutjinga, disguised as a goanna, as she runs toward a hidden pit, luring men to their deaths. The painting is executed in a representational manner not common in the Port Keats area. The rhythmic curves of the goanna's body and tail create an impression of vigor and movement in this skillfully rendered shape.

The Snake Woman, Kukpi, by Madigan. Kukpi is shown in her snake form, entwined among the water holes of the artist's home country. The black circles are the sacred water holes from which the spirit children come to be born in human form. The oval shape of the bark, which is unique to the Port Keats region, is derived from the oval stone *tjurunga,* which serve as sacred totems.

The Snake Woman, Kukpi, by Rock Ngumbe. The woman Kukpi gloats after sending one of her male visitors down the trail to a hidden cliff and death. Rock Ngumbe is a Murinbata artist who here departs from the traditional nonrepresentational style of the Port Keats area. His Snake Woman is rather dragonlike; her sinuous, snarling form giving dramatic life to the painting. The artist balances his stark composition by adding the tree, which is carefully distorted to fit the bark format. The forked-stick motif of this tree is repeated in Kukpi's headdress and in the pattern of her teeth.

When I visited Port Keats, I found that the men had forgotten most of the ancient myths. Only after I had won their confidence did some of the old men recount the tales of Kunmanggur and Kukpi. Soon they did so with great zest, as if delighted to find a listener interested in their tribal lore.

The Singing Woman: The Kukpi Myth

The Bull-Roarer, by unknown artist. Cut in an oval shape, the *tjurunga,* or bull-roarer is whirled around the head on a cord to make the roaring sound said to be the voice of Kukpi, the Snake Woman. Exhibited: de Young.

The Unloved One: The *Ubar*-Drum Myth

The Ubar *Ceremony,* by Nonganyari. The story of the *ubar*-drum myth is recounted in the *ubar* ceremony, as illustrated in this painting. The hollow log is shown in the center with Gula and her mother on either side and Yirrawadbad in the form of the snake below. At the right is the bandicoot that hid in the log. During the *ubar* ceremony, the hollow-log drum is beaten by old men concealed in a shelter made of leafy branches. The drum is said to be the voice of the First Mother. Exhibited: Lowie, Field (p. 20, cat.), de Young. (See Berndt and Berndt, *Man, Land and Myth in North Australia,* 1970, p. 158.)

The Man-Killer: The Wilintji Myth

The Dancers, by Yirrawala. Two men are shown as they try to outdo Wilintji in dancing. One holds a dilly bag in his left hand; both brandish dancing sticks. Exhibited: Lowie, Field.

The Man-Killer, by Nabadbara. Wilintji is shown as she dances the men to exhaustion and death. In the habit of aboriginal women, she holds a loop of banyan string between her thumbs with which she makes cat's-cradle figures as she dances. Nabadbara was one of the old traditional artists of the Gunwinggu tribe. Exhibited: Lowie, Field, de Young.

The Quarreling Women, by Mijaumijau. The two wives of Malamu are shown quarreling, while he stands to one side in exasperation. Between the two women is a bark container for carrying honey. The painter, born in 1897, is one of the best known of the Gunwinggu artists. His figures generally follow the cave-painting style, with bold white outlines, a good sense of movement, and a strong feeling for the drama of the mythical stories.

The Wife-Killer: The Malamu Myth

The Wife-Killer, by Anchor Barlbuwa. This is another symbolic painting which can be explained only by the artist. The two rounded projections are stones that represent the breasts of the wives whom Malamu killed because of their quarreling; the two longer projecting stones represent Malamu's penis. The crosshatched rectangle on which they rest is the mountain.

The Fishermen, by Madaman. The two friends, Munjurr and Nurru, paddle out beyond the breakers to catch fish. Their canoe is hollowed out of a large tree in the style taught to the aborigines by the Makasans.

PART V: MYTHS OF EVERYDAY LIFE
The Heroic Fisherman: The Munjurr Myth

PAGE 174   *The Humpbacked Whale*, by Gungujuma. The aborigines believe that the whale, called *dianmeri*, has two mouths in its tail with which it grasps canoes and overturns them. The curved lines at the head indicate the water parting as the whale swims. Gungujuma, who died in 1970, was an old man who learned to paint before the white men came. Exhibited: Field.

The Spirit Messenger: The Opossum-Tree Myth

PAGE 177   *Night Birds and Opossums*, by Nanjin. The more times a design is repeated, the more *mana*, or power, it has. For this reason, Nanjin often repeated the bird and opossum motif as many as the ten times seen in this painting. The artist was born in 1918 and died in 1969.

PAGE 178   *Possum and Night Bird*, by Naridjin. The messenger bird, Guwarg, is shown at the top of the tree, while the opossum, Marngu, climbs up to talk with him. The repeated figure of Marngu indicates that he is ascending; the parallel horizontal lines on both sides, with regular white dashes, represent the marks left by his claws. The cicadas are also shown. Naridjin, a prolific and expert painter, born in 1922, was Nanjin's brother. He has a larger repertoire of designs and myths than most of the other artists. Well versed in tribal traditions, Naridjin has two stories for every bark painting: the inside and the outside versions. He relates the inside story only to those who have his full confidence. Small but significant details, which only Naridjin can point out, differentiate the inside style from the outside.

     Naridjin has a ready smile and a good sense of humor. On my last visit I found him ensconced beneath the stripped body of an old automobile. He had set it up on a log tripod so it provided welcome shade from the sun. Seated beneath, on a blanket, he proceeded with his painting, effectively shielded from children, dogs, and all but the most persistent visitors.

The Night Bird. See color list.

PAGE 179   *The Opossum*, by Naridjin. Hearing Guwarg calling, Marngu awakens at nightfall and responds. This figure is rarely carved. Exhibited: Lowie, Field (p. 18, cat.), de Young.

PAGE 181   *First-Year Body Design*, by Yirrawala. The painting is made for the guidance of the men who paint the bodies of young men of the *dua* moiety in preparation for the first year of age-grading rites. The boys participate in rites that introduce them to the sacred and secret knowledge known only to the initiated men. (See Berndt, ed., Australian Aboriginal Art, 1964, pl. 29; Holmes, *Yirrawala, Artist and Man*, 1972, pp. 60–61.)

PAGE 181   *Second-Year Body Design*, by Yirrawala. This is the design for the second year of the age-grading rites, which usually occurs at seventeen or eighteen years. Food and behavioral sanctions apply at each stage.

Keeper of the Secrets: The Luma Luma Myth

The Whale Who Became a Man, by Ginilgini. This painting shows Luma Luma as he changed from whale to human form.

The Jealous Leader, by Bardjaray. Luma Luma is shown in human form. In his right hand is the dilly bag in which he carried his sacred totems; at his left are his *woomera,* or spear-thrower, and two sacred totemic boards used in the ceremony he taught the tribesmen.

The Barramundi, by Mijaumijau. Luma Luma first painted this design of his friend, the barramundi fish, on his own body, and then taught it to the Gunwinggu, who paint it on their bodies for the Luma Luma ceremony today. The crisscross markings shown on the belly of the fish, known as *rarrk,* were first made by Luma Luma on himself and are now cut as cicatrices on the bodies of the tribesmen during their initiation ceremonies. Exhibited: Lowie (p. 10, cat.), UCSB, Field de Young.

Luma Luma as a Whale, by Nguleingulei. Luma Luma is shown swimming down the sun path toward the open sea, accompanied by his friend, the barramundi fish. Nguleingulei is an outstanding artist who paints in the traditional style.

The Greedy Boy: The Djert Myth

The Fishermen, by Munggeraui. Three fishermen go out in their canoe. Tindale (67b, pp. 103–12) states that the Malays brought hollowed log canoes, but sewn bark canoes were known as far south as Victoria and were not inspired by Malay contacts.

The Bitter Fruit: The *Lala* Myth

The Berry Picker, by Majindi. This unusual bark is done in the pictorial style found only rarely at Port Keats. It shows a man with his dilly bag in his right hand, filled with *lala.* He is taking the berries to a water hole, where he will soak them to take out the bad taste, preparatory to roasting them for food. Majindi "sings" *lala;* that is, *lala* is his totem. Exhibited: Lowie, Field, de Young.

When the Rains Came: The Napilingu Myth

The Bearer of Water, by Nanjin. Napilingu is shown with the paperbark water container on her head. At each side are the yam sticks, greatly enlarged to show their importance, with which she pried the bark from the tree. The background design is "owned" by the *Duwala* linguistic group, and Nanjin has the right to paint it. Exhibited: Field, de Young.

Bark Water Container, by Naridjin. This container represents the bark vessels used by the aboriginal women ever since they were taught how to make them by Napilingu. The background design can be painted only by artists of the *Duwala* linguistic group. The yam stick is also shown. Exhibited: Lowie, Field, de Young.

The Spear-Maker *and* The Crocodile Man:
The Jirukupai Myth, I and II

PAGE 197   *The Crocodile Dance,* by Ali. The crocodile dance is a feature of the mortuary
ceremonies of the Tiwi people. The rectangles represent the skin of the crocodile and commemorate Jirukupai, who was speared by his enemies and turned
into a crocodile. The diagonal lines stand for carpet snakes which live near the
river.

PAGE 198   *Male and Female Spears,* by Wombiaudimirra. These ceremonial spears are
used to commemorate the feats of the first spear-maker, Jirukupai. The top
spear, with barbs on one side, is used by men only. The barbs represent the
tail of a crocodile; the painted designs are symbols for the crocodile, carpet
snake, and fish. The bottom spear, with barbs on both sides, is a female spear,
but may be used by both men and women. It is also employed as an assassi-
nation weapon by the men, who creep up at night on a man who has run off
with another's wife and spear him. Wombiaudimirra, one of the outstanding
Tiwi painters, was commonly known as Black Joe. He was born in 1910 and
lived on Melville Island. We had become well acquainted during my early
visits. Following the *pukamani* ceremonies he often saved for me the ornate
barbed spears, of which he was the acknowledged master. During my visit in
1973, as we drove past the sawmill in the settlement truck, one of the men
pointed to a staff from which a white cloth hung. "Your friend," he said simply. Black Joe had collapsed and died of a heart attack at the spot marked by
the staff. His spirit, recognizing the white cloth, would stay close by until the
pukamani ceremony could be held. The last of the spears Black Joe had saved
for me were broken and placed on his grave.

PAGE 202   *The First Crocodile,* by Uringi. Speared by his enemies, Jirukupai escaped by
leaping into the river. There, he became the first crocodile. The wounds on his
back healed to become the crocodile's knobs, while the single barbed spear he
carried became the characteristic tail of the crocodile.

The Bold Woman: The Spider Myth

PAGE 204   *The Soul-Catcher Spider Web,* by Ali. Spiders have a special totemic significance to many of the aboriginal tribes. This bark shows the great soul-catcher
spider web which the Tiwi of Melville Island paint for their mortuary ceremonies. They believe that, just as the spider web catches insects, so the painted
representation will catch the souls of the departed so they will not stray before
final burial and bring harm to the living. Ali, one of the great headmen of the
Tiwi, was a famous dancer as well as artist and leader.

PAGE 205   *The Spider,* by Djinu Tjeemaree. This bark painting shows the totemic design
of the sacred spider, with the body, legs, and biting jaws clearly visible. At
each side is depicted the great snake, the primary totemic ancestor of the
Murinbata tribe. Djinu Tjeemaree is now too old to paint, but in his time
was one of the best artists in the region. Exhibited: Field (p. 10, cat.), de
Young.

The Man Who Became Black: The Ship-Totem Myth

The Medicine Man, Mungada, by Mandaga. The aborigines believe that Mungada helps them in time of trouble; for example, he heals the sick by sucking from their bodies foreign objects such as pieces of bone, wood, and stone that are the cause of illness. The object in his right hand is a bag in which he keeps the charms that are necessary for his work. The triangular lines and oblongs at the lower left represent Mungada's home country.

Malay Prau, by Bukunda. The sailing vessel is shown in cross-section. The tripod mast that supported the great rectangular sail is clearly seen, as are the high bow and stern, and the double steering paddles. The six oblongs represent sections of the hold, in which cargo is stored and the crew have their living quarters.

PART VI: THE COMING OF DEATH: FUNERAL MYTHS

Pukamani Grave Pole and Baskets. These poles were erected during the mortu- ary rites for a man named Mungatopi when he was buried beside the sea on Karslake Peninsula, Melville Island. Food for the dancers is brought in the bark baskets. At the conclusion of the ceremony, the baskets are split and placed on the prongs of the poles, to show that all is finished.

Pukamani Grave Pole, Melville Island. This marks the recent burial of a Tiwi clansman at Snake Bay on Melville Island.

Burying the Dead, by Madaman. The bones are placed in a hollow log for final burial. At this stage, songs and chants encourage the spirit to leave the place of death and go to its final home on Bralgu, the Island of the Dead. Several fires are shown, for the smoke and flame of the fires is believed to discourage the spirit from returning.

How Death Came: The Purukapali Myth

Bones and Skulls. See color list.

Preparing the Bones, by Madaman. Following the death rituals, the body is left to decompose. Burial ceremonies are then conducted in which the bones are cleaned, painted with ocher, and placed in a hollow log for burial. This painting shows the bones in the left corner as they have been pulled apart and placed on a sheet of paperbark. In the typical aboriginal style, the next sequence is then shown on the same painting, with two men now cleaning the bones, painting them with red ocher and laying them out for burial. The object at the upper right corner of the bones, that looks like a searchlight with rays, is a fire. Men are shown dancing and singing in the funeral ceremonies. At the upper left, a seated man keeps time with clap sticks, while the *didjeridu* player beside him places the end of his drone pipe in a large conch shell to increase resonance. Exhibited: Qantas, Lowie, UCSB, Field, de Young.

Purukapali and His Dead Son. See color list.

PAGE 218   *The Entreaty of Tjapara,* by Maniluki. The Moon Man holds out his arms, asking Purukapali to give him his dead son for three days to bring him back to life. The large circles painted on the head represent the full moon. The carving is by one of the Tiwi master artists, known also by the English name of Harry Carpenter. Exhibited: Field (p. 38, cat.).

PAGE 219   *The Grief of Bima,* by Djulabiyanna. This masterful carving by one of the old men of the Tiwi shows Bima in her desolation and grief after she allowed her son to die. Djulabiyanna, one of the finest of the Tiwi carvers, was a ceremonial leader of the Tik'lawilla horde. This figure, one of the last he made, was carved in 1965 when he was past eighty years old. Exhibited: Jones, Lowie, Field (p. 38, cat.), de Young.

The Killer Snake: The Gurramuringu Myth

PAGE 221   *Wife of the Mighty Hunter,* by Malangi. The wife of Gurramuringu is portrayed with pendulous breasts to indicate that she has borne and nursed children. On the side of this figure also appears wild fruit that grows beside the water hole. Exhibited: Lowie, UCSB (p. 9 cat.), Field (p. 36, cat.), de Young.

The Evil Tree Spirit. See color list.

Kangaroo and Snake. See color list.

PAGE 224   *The Hunter Rests,* by Malangi. Gurramuringu, the hunter, is seen as he approaches the tree in which the evil tree spirit lurks, and as he sits down to prepare his meal. In accordance with aboriginal convention, movement is shown by the two figures of the hunter: one, as he approaches the tree; the second, as he settles down. The kangaroo, goanna, and emu he caught are shown. In the bottom panel is his dog, which was hunting with him and hid in the grass after Gurramuringu was bitten by the snake. Berries and fruit can be seen hanging from the tree. Exhibited: de Young.

PAGE 225   *Death of the Great Hunter,* by Malangi. Gurramuringu's painted corpse is shown in the center of this painting as it was laid out after he was killed. The snake can be seen just to the right, surrounded by water lilies, trees, fruits, and berries that grow near the water hole. The funeral ceremonies will be held as soon as the clanspeople can be summoned. This passage of a short time is indicated by the three smaller figures who are singing the funeral songs. Above to the left, four still smaller figures are shown performing the final funeral rites which will take place about twelve months after death, when the flesh has decomposed and the bones can be prepared for burial. The four figures are reduced further in size, to indicate another passage of time, in keeping with the convention of aboriginal artists. Exhibited: Field.

Gurramuringu, The Mighty Hunter, by Malangi. This carved figure represents PAGE 225 Gurramuringu, the great hunter. One day, after a successful hunt, he was camped under a tree, cooking his meal, when a huge snake emerged from the grass and killed him. His spirit became the guardian spirit of the Urgiganjdjar people: whenever a member of the clan dies, the story of the great hunter's life, and the manner of his death, are sung. On the side of this carved Gurramuringu figure is shown the wild fruit that grows near the water hole; painted on his back is the snake that gave him the fatal bite. Malangi is one of the most famous of Arnhem Land artists. Exhibited: Lowie, UCSB (p. 9, cat.), Field (p. 34, cat.), de Young.

How Mutjinga Lived Again: The Crab and Crow Myth

The Mutjinga Myth, by Nanjin. This painting illustrates a myth of the *Manggalilji* people, similar to that of the Murinbata. Here, the crow is seen pecking at the crab. Exhibited: Field, de Young. PAGE 227

The Morning Star: The Barnumbir Myth

The Morning-Star Totem, by Bininjuwi. This bark painting is used in the morning-star, or Barnumbir, ceremony. The morning-star totem is shown in the center. Its streamers are made of parakeet feathers and represent starlight. The aborigines believe that when a person dies his spirit follows the morning star to its final destination, thus arriving at the Island of the Dead. Barnumbir's journey symbolizes the spirit leaving the body. Sacred yams, represented by the dumbell shapes, are carried for food. A spirit called Banumbu (not Barnumbir) guides the spirit of the dead person on its trip. Here the Banumbu figure is shown twice to indicate his importance. He eats nectar gathered and fed him by butterflies, who can be seen as they go about their work. Exhibited: Lowie, Field (p. 38, cat.), de Young. PAGE 230

The Barnumbir Totem, by Gakupa. This is an exceptionally good morning-star totem. The tuft of white feathers at the top is the morning star herself, while the branching tufts represent the rays of the sun. Gakupa, a master of feather *rangga,* comes from Elcho Island in the northeastern region. Exhibited: Field (p. 38, cat.), de Young. PAGE 231

Bark Coffin—Morning-Star Ceremony, by Djadjiwui. The body of the deceased is placed on a burial platform where it remains for about three months. The bones are then cleaned and placed in a temporary bark coffin that has the totemic emblems painted on the outside. The totem on this coffin is that of Barnumbir, the morning star. The skulls with crosshatching represent the deceased, whose spirit follows the morning star to the Island of the Dead. The skull is usually carried in a dilly bag, accompanying the bark coffin containing the bones, which is borne from camp to camp by a near female relative of the deceased. Exhibited: Lowie (p. 11, cat.), UCSB, Field (p. 33, cat.), de Young. PAGE 232

The Happy Spirit: The Murayana Myth

 Bibliography

1. Basedow, H. *The Australian Aboriginal.* Adelaide, Preece, 1925.
2. Berndt, Ronald M. *Djanggawul.* London: Routledge & Kegan, 1952.
3. ———. *Kunapipi.* Melbourne: F. W. Cheshire, 1951.
4. ———. "Some Methodological Considerations in the Study of Australian Aboriginal Art." *Oceania,* vol. 29, pp. 26–42 (Sept. 1958).
5. Berndt, Ronald M. and Catherine H. *Arnhem Land, Its History and People.* Melbourne: F. W. Cheshire, 1954.
6. ———. *Man, Land and Myth in North Australia.* Sydney: Ure Smith, 1970.
7. ———. "Sacred Figures of Ancestral Beings of Arnhem Land," *Oceania,* vol. 18, pp. 302–326 (1948).
8. ———. *Sexual Behavior in Western Arnhem Land.* New York: Viking Fund, 1951.
9. ———. *The World of the First Australians.* Sydney: Ure Smith, 1964.
10. Campbell, Joseph. *The Masks of God: Primitive Mythology.* New York: Viking Press, 1959.
11. ———. *Myths to Live By.* New York: Viking Press, 1972.
12. Chaseling, Wilbur S. *Yulengor.* London: Epworth Press, 1957.
13. Cole, Keith. *Oenpelli Pioneer.* Parkville, Victoria: Church Missionary Society Historical Publications, 1972.
14. Davidson, D. S. "The Family Hunting Territory in Australia." *American Anthropologist,* N.S. 30, pp. 614–631 (1928).
15. ———. "Northwestern Australia and the Question of Influences from the East Indies." *Journal of the American Oriental Society,* vol. 56 (1938).
16. Durkheim, Emile. *The Elementary Forms of Religious Life.* 1915. Translated from the French. New York: Free Press, 1965.
17. Elkin, A. P. *The Australian Aborigines.* 3d ed., rev. Sydney: Halstead Press, 1954.

18. ———. "Marriage and Descent in East Arnhem Land." *Oceania*, vol. 3, no. 4.
19. Elkin, A. P., and R. M. and C. H. Berndt. "Social Organization of Arnhem Land." *Oceania*, vol. 22, pp. 253–301, no. 1.
20. Falkenberg, Johannes. *Kin and Totem*. Oslo: Oslo University Press, 1962.
21. Frazer, Sir James George. *Totemism*. Edinburgh: A. & C. Black, 1887.
22. ———. *Totemism and Exogamy*. London: Macmillan & Co., 1910.
23. ———. *Totemism: A Supplement to Totemism and Exogamy*. London: Macmillan & Co., 1937.
24. Gale, Fay, ed. *Woman's Role in Aboriginal Society*. Canberra: Australian Institute of Aboriginal Studies, 1970.
25. Goldenweiser, Alexander A. "Totemism, An Analytical Study." *Journal of American Folk-Lore*, vol. 23.
26. Goodale, Jane C. *Tiwi Wives*. Seattle: University of Washington Press, 1971.
26a. Groger-Wurm, Helen M. *Australian Aboriginal Bark Paintings and Their Mythological Interpretation: Vol. 1 Eastern Arnhem Land*. Canberra: Australian Institute of Aboriginal Studies, 1973. Restricted sale and circulation.
27. Hart, C. W. M. and Arnold R. Pilling. *The Tiwi of North Australia*. New York: Holt, Rinehart & Winston, 1960.
28. Hiatt, L. R. *Kinship and Conflict*. Canberra: Australian National University, 1965.
29. ———. "Local Organization Among the Australian Aborigines." *Oceania*, vol. 32, pp. 267–282, no. 4.
30. ———. "Social Control in Central Arnhem Land." *South Pacific*, vol. 10, no. 7 (1959).
31. Holmes, Sandra. *Yirawala, Artist and Man*. Melbourne: Jacaranda Press, 1972.
32. Kaberry, P. M. *Aboriginal Woman, Sacred and Profane*. London: George Rutledge & Sons, 1939.
33. Kellett, E. E. *The Story of Myths*. New York: Harcourt Brace & Co., 1927.
34. Kluckhohn, C. "Myths and Rituals, A General Theory." *Harvard Theological Review*, vol. 35 (1942).
35. Kroeber, A. C. "Totem and Taboo: An Ethnologic Psychoanalysis." *American Anthropologist* (1920).
36. Kupka, Karel. *Dawn of Art*. New York: Viking Press, 1965.
37. Lang, Andrew. *The Secret of the Totem*. London: Longmans Green & Company, 1905.
38. Leach, Edmond, ed. *The Structural Study of Myths and Totems*. London: Tavistock Publishing Co., 1967.
39. Levi-Strauss, Claude. *The Savage Mind*. Chicago: University of Chicago Press, 1966.
40. ———. *Totemism*. Boston: Beacon Press, 1963.
41. ———. *Totemism Today*. Paris: Presses Universitaires de France, 1965.
42. Lowie, R. H. *Primitive Religion*. New York: Boni & Liveright, 1924.
43. McCarthy, Frederick D. "The Prehistoric Cultures of Australia." *Oceania*, vol. 19 (June 1949).
44. MacKnight, C. C. *The Farthest Coast*. Melbourne: Melbourne University Press, 1969.
45. Mead, Margaret. *Culture and Commitment*. New York: Doubleday & Co., 1970.

46. Meggitt, M. J. "Social Organization: Morphology and Typology." In *Australian Aboriginal Studies,* edited by Helen Shiels. London: Oxford University Press, 1963.

47. Morris, John. *History of Bathurst and Melville Islands.* Unpublished manuscript, 1970.

48. Mountford, Charles P. *Art, Myth and Symbolism: Records of the American-Australian Scientific Expedition to Arnhem Land.* Melbourne: Melbourne University Press, 1956.

49. ———. *The Tiwi: Their Art, Myth and Ceremony.* London: Phoenix House, 1958.

50. Mountford, Charles P., with Ainslie Roberts. *Dawn of Time.* New York: Taplinger Publishing Company, 1972.

51. ———. *The Dreamtime.* Adelaide: Rigby Limited, 1965.

52. Murray, Henry A., ed. *Myth and Mythmaking.* Boston: Beacon Press, 1960.

53. Osborne, C. R. *The Tiwi Language.* Canberra: Australian Institute of Aboriginal Studies, 1974.

54. Pye, John. *The Port Keats Story.* Port Keats: Port Keats Mission, 1972.

55. Radcliffe-Brown, A. R. *The Social Organization of Australian Tribes.* Oceania Monographs no. 1., Sydney.

56. Radin, Paul. *Primitive Religion, Its Nature and Origin.* New York: Viking Press, 1937.

57. Robinson, Roland. *Aboriginal Myths and Legends.* Melbourne: Sun Books, 1966.

58. ———. *The Feathered Serpent.* Sydney: Edwards & Shaw, 1956.

59. Roheim, Geza. *Australian Totemism.* London: Allen & Unwin, 1925.

60. ———. *The Eternal Ones of the Dream.* New York: International Universities Press, 1945.

61. Rose, Frederick G. G. *Classification of Kin, Age Structure and Marriage Amongst the Groote Eylandt Aborigines.* London: Pergamon Press, 1960.

62. Seligman, C. G. and Brenda. *The Veddas.* Cambridge: Cambridge University Press, 1911.

63. Spencer, Baldwin. *Native Tribes of the Northern Territory of Australia.* London: Macmillan & Co., 1914.

64. Spencer, Baldwin, and F. J. Gillen. *The Northern Tribes of Central Australia.* London: Macmillan & Co., 1899.

65. Stanner, W. E. H. *On Aboriginal Religion.* Oceania Monograph no. 11, 1966. (Reprint of an article which appeared in *Oceania* from December 1959 to September 1963.)

66. Stokes, Judith. *Groote Eylandt Family Stories, Parts 1 & 2.* Angurugu: Church Missionary Society, 1971.

67. Strehlow, T. G. H. *Aranda Traditions.* Melbourne: Melbourne University Press, 1947.

67a. Tindale, Norman B., *Aboriginal Tribes of Australia,* Berkeley, University of California Press, 1974.

67b. ———. *Natives of Groote Eylandt and of the West Coast of the Gulf of Carpentaria,* Parts 1 and 2, Records of the South Australian Museum, Vol. III, Nos. 1 and 2, 1925–6.

68. Turner, David H. *Tradition and Transformation.* Canberra: Australian Institute of Aboriginal Studies, 1974.

69. Warner, W. Lloyd. *A Black Civilization.* New York: Harper & Brothers, 1937.

70. Watts, A. W. *Myth and Ritual in Christianity*. New York: Vanguard Press, 1954.
71. Webb, T. T. "Tribal Organization in East Arnhem Land," *Oceania*, vol. 3, pp. 406–411 (1933).
72. Wells, Ann E. *This Their Dreaming*. St. Lucia: University of Queensland Press, 1971.
73. Worsley, P. M. "Totemism in a Changing Society." *American Anthropologist*, vol. 57, pp. 851–861 (1955).

Index

Numbers in boldface refer to illustrations.